CITIZENSHIP IN TRANSFORMATION IN CANADA

Edited by Yvonne M. Hébert

In recent years, changes in concepts of citizenship have brought about a reconsideration of political and educational policies in Canada. In *Citizenship in Transformation,* leading thinkers and practitioners from a number of fields argue persuasively that, since conceptions of democratic citizenship are changing, operational definitions of citizenship education should be reassessed.

Focusing on four themes – conceptual foundations, institutional policies, social and cultural realities, and education – the contributors address two critical questions: What constitutes a "good" citizen in today's liberal democracy? And, what social and educational policies are needed to sustain the lives of these citizens, while not impinging on liberal democratic principles? Bringing together a variety of theoretical and practical perspectives, this book will have broad implications for social and educational policies and institutions in Canada.

YVONNE M. HÉBERT is Professor in the Faculty of Education at the University of Calgary

Edited by Yvonne M. Hébert

Citizenship in Transformation in Canada

UNIVERSITY OF TORONTO PRESS
Toronto Buffalo London

ISBN 0-8020-0850-X (cloth)
ISBN 0-8020-7835-4 (paper)

Printed on acid-free paper

National Library of Canada Cataloguing in Publication Data

Main entry under title:

Citizenship in transformation in Canada / edited by Yvonne M.
Hébert

Includes bibliographical references.
ISBN 0-8020-0850-X (bound).   ISBN 0-8020-7835-4 (pbk.)

1. Citizenship – Study and teaching – Canada.   2. Citizenship –
Canada.   3. Citizenship – Study and teaching.   I. Hébert Yvonne M.,
1942–

JL187.H42 2002   323.6′07′071   C2002-902595-8

Financial assistance for the preparation of the manuscript from the
Multiculturalism Programme, Department of Canadian Heritage,
is gratefully acknowledged.

University of Toronto Press acknowledges the financial assistance
to its publishing program of the Canada Council for the Arts and the
Ontario Arts Council.

University of Toronto Press acknowledges the financial support for
its publishing activities of the Government of Canada through the
Book Publishing Industry Development Program (BPIDP).

Contents

CITIZENSHIP IN TRANSFORMATION IN CANADA

The Citizenship Debates:
Conceptual, Policy, Experiential,
and Educational Issues

YVONNE M. HÉBERT and LORI WILKINSON

Citizenship is in transformation, its meaning is expanding, and interest in the subject is exploding. Citizenship has moved from being closed to being open, from exclusion to inclusion. Once having had a unitary, stable meaning, citizenship is now diffuse, multiple, and ever-shifting. Originally defined clearly by geographical borders and a common history, citizenship is increasingly in question. Frontiers have become permeable in the midst of massive social changes, including international trade agreements and ententes as well as global migration. These transformations are occurring in open, pluralist, and democratic societies, including Canada, and we are preoccupied with their significance. Crucially concordant with social change, the transformation of citizenship is important, for it concerns who we are, how we live together, and what kind of people our children are to become.

Citizenship is a complex part of collective identity. This concept refers to the relationship between the individual and the state, and between individuals within a state. Situated critically within a pluralist democratic country with two official languages and a policy of multiculturalism, Canadian citizenship exists today within multi-layered belongings and complex understandings. Within the Canadian state, which is both multinational and polyethnic, First Nations peoples and Francophones hold collective rights as peoples in place prior to Confederation. Many other groups – that is, polyethnic groups, who, for the most part, have chosen to settle in the country – have representational status. Within this rich context, notions of citizenship, identity, and civic education are hotly contested. Models of citizenship hold special interest, while participation and common values are seen as the means of assuring a cohesive future.

Much of the citizenship debate is concern with four dimensions of citizenship: (1) the conceptual foundations of citizenship and identity; (2) policies and institutional goals; (3) citizenship set within the realities of Canadian society; and (4) citizenship education. The contentious debate engages many disciplinary perspectives, including philosophical, political, literacy, educational, historical, and sociological. Debating citizenship has given rise to an increase in academic and policy writings, government reports, public exchanges, and an electronic newsletter,[1] all to explore the topic, examine options, and propose action plans.

In this introductory essay, we deal with each of the four major dimensions in turn. We situate the complex chapters within the citizenship debate, while paying particular attention to education for citizenship. Together, the contributors to this book present and acknowledge current complex realities. We support the view that there are various interpretations and multiple identifications that are compatible with democratic citizenship rather than a single, undifferentiated notion of citizenship, a perspective that we term "multiple citizenship." Today, identity is plural, each person belonging to many groups and defining him/herself in these multiple belongings without necessarily placing the levels and forms of belonging in hierarchical order. We no longer live in a society that can be defined and understood in terms of one group, one territory, one language, one religion, one economy.

As we shall see, these realities create exciting challenges to the process of attempting to determine what would be essential in the education of citizens, and no easy solutions are readily available, since the debate has not come to a close. In this collection of essays we address multi-faceted issues and advocacy positions which are at the forefront of contemporary political, social, and educational thought and that are of particular concern to policy makers and practitioners.

Conceptual Foundations of Citizenship and Identity

Models of Citizenship

Models of social order seek ways for humans to live together in peaceful ways with limited resources. Citizenship models of Canadian society must be able to include individuals and groups of people across the country in such a way that their diversity contributes to the creation and sustenance of a cohesive democratic state. This means that Aboriginal First Nations as well as Québécois and Francophones in a minority context must be included, since they hold collective rights according to treaties, the British North America Act of 1867, and the Constitution Act of 1982. Ethnocultural, religious, and other groups must also be represented in a significant way, and in doing so, the social cohesion of the country must be assured. Thus, respecting differences while finding and fostering commonalities are the main challenges that face any proposed models of Canadian citizenship.

We discuss here a few of the possible models in terms of relevant characteristics: consent, descent, pluralism, and national identity. For easy reference here and in the rest of the book, additional details for several influential models of citizenship mentioned are provided in a chart in the appendix in which citizenship models are analysed according to key concepts, locus of power, the role of government, the role of citizens, as well as the implications for educational and government policy.

Roots of the Consent/Descent Distinction
Evident in its earliest realizations as citizenship by birth or by choice, both of which are possible in Canada, this fundamental distinction of consent/descent[2] informed the Greek and Roman conceptions. It has been intertwined in most subsequent models and is often described in terms of either active participation or the enjoyment of rights. The *Athenian model* of the ideal participation of citizens limited citizenship to male property owners and to their male progeniture, excluding women, children, the poor, and slaves. Aristotle, for example, understood citizenship to be an active sharing in the constitution, not as a condition grounded in a territorially based idea of sovereignty. By comparison, the *Roman republican model* considered citizenship to be a legal status with cosmopolitan character. It was widely distributed throughout the empire, holding an assimilative strength in order to create loyalty among a rapidly growing population of great diversity. The notions of consent/descent, however, do not map neatly upon liberal and republican conceptions of citizenship which have influenced one another and intermingled in some models.

Models of citizenship based on *consent* – such as the Machiavellian model in Florence, the American republican model, Rousseau's vision, the Jacobin model of seventeenth-century France, as well as the French republican model – are woven around the key notion of *citizenship by choice.*[3] What consensual models have in common is that the citizen accepts subjugation to the state, understands his status as a voluntary allegiance, and has legal status with certain rights and responsibilities.

Models based on citizenship by *descent* have given rise to the notion of the "nation-state" and to the nationalist movement which has swept the world in the past century. For example, in the liberalism of John Stuart Mill[4] nationality is considered to be the basis of belonging to the state. He commits to the principles of utilitarianism and abandons the universality of natural rights as revolutionary cause. A people are considered to constitute a "nation" as a cultural community of historical descent which provides the basis for popular allegiance, whereas an emphasis on individualism allows individual eccentricity and the exclusion of others. Sovereignty is lodged in the people who share a common background within a political community. The government has the authority to protect rights and to create institutions to reinforce them. The citizen is a member of a "nation-state" by his common sympathies, such as race, heritage, language, religion, geography, and national history. His loyalty and solidarity flow from the beneficial protections provided by the government. The citizen is actively engaged in monitoring the conduct of public affairs as well as in social and civic participation.

Nationalism, however, has a dark side and can be excessively bleak. State governments are paradoxically both the guardians of human rights as well as the sources of abuses of such rights in countries where citizens are denied active participation and responsibilities.[5] Setting the stage for the oppression of some peoples, an ethnicized nationality is fundamentally exclusive, since it defines political content according to ethnic and racial differences. Meditating upon the excesses of nation-states, especially totalitarian ones, Arendt proposes a model in which the people are sovereign and the power of the people balances the power of government.[6] Citizens have universal human rights, including natural rights, which are integral to each person as part of his humanity. According to Arendt's model, the development of political virtues – such as courage, love of glory, political spirit, or patriotism – would motivate political participation, non-violence, and free speech, so that free agents could act within the public domain created by themselves.

Relevance to Canadian Citizenship

Influenced by several models over time, this fundamental distinction, descent-consent, is relevant to citizenship in Canada today.[7] At the time of Confederation, the patriarchal and elistist Burkean philosophical model was in vogue, as were liberal democratic and republican conceptions, the latter evident especially in the views of Mackenzie and Papineau. In the afterwar period, the social democratic model of T.H. Marshall held sway. More recently, the communitarian conception and a revised model of liberalism allowing for multicultural citizenship have emerged in response to the pluralistic nature of our country and are very much part of the contemporary debate; for the liberal democracy that is, Canada suffers from problems of exclusion/inclusion.

Only within this century have women gained the federal vote (1918) and the status of "persons" (1929), have Canadians become citizens of their own country instead of British subjects (1947), and previously excluded groups, such as the poor, workers, and Aboriginals, made claims for an equal share and belonging without fault. In this volume, Veronica Strong-Boag deconstructs the patriarchal nature of citizenship and documents the efforts of excluded or subaltern groups, vis-à-vis certain political elites, to acquire full membership in Canadian society, to acquire the rights to participate in all social and political institutions, and to gain recognition as having done so. Her argument, that citizenship education has long ignored these issues, since it has been based on a history told from the vantage point of the winners, helps to define an important range of problems that must be addressed if we are to succeed in educating Canadians about who we are as a people.

Issues of cultural pluralism were not foreseen until after the Second World War, although a national system of education had been introduced to assure knowledge of civic, political, and social rights, including the right to work. Evolving beyond civic, political, and socio-economic rights,[8] cultural citizenship is the most recent dimension and deals with the relationship between cultural communities and the state, especially with respect to rights. What is essential here is the manner of taking into account the increasing diversity in our societies, an openness to other cultures, as well as the recognition of minorities, immigration patterns, and global mobility.[9]

Within competing models of citizenship, it is largely owing to the discourse and increasing political pressure of minorities and the marginalized since the post-war period, that citizenship in Canada and elsewhere in the western world has continued to be transformed. The historian Harold Troper documents in this volume the nature of multiple belongings emerging from successive waves of immigration which contributed to the expansion and creation of Canada as an industrial, pluralist country, first in the Canadian Prairies, then in the cities, notably Toronto. In so doing, he traces the development of federal policies in response to Canadian realities, leading to an expanded understanding of the notion of Canadian citizenship.

Pluralism and Contemporary Canadian Models of Citizenship
Although Canada is a liberal democracy, this model is seriously criticized, since it is unable to include many groups. Individuality is excessive
and lacks any sociocultural context. State neutrality is unable to cope
with a dominant ethos and with a tremendous range of pluralities.
Political participation is unable to protect individual equality by dealing
with inegalitarian and undemocratic institutions.[10] A renewed liberalism
in Canada includes calls for the preservation of the cultural context in
which each individual may exercise his/her capacity to choose, as proposed by Will Kymlicka.[11] Considering Canada to be multinational and
polyethnic in composition, Kymlicka argues for a model of multicultural
citizenship with distinct rights for national groups within the country,
distinguishing these rights from representational rights for polyethnic
groups.

Another contemporary approach proposed by Charles Taylor and
others, the communitarian model, holds particular appeal for the
Francophones and First Nations. This model allows a nation-to-nation
discourse with the federal government and strong claims for their categorical and collective rights to self-government and education.[12] The
vitality of these communities must be safeguarded because they are
crucial to the well-being of their citizens.[13] The source of power resides
in a democratic populism, which means that the role of the government
is to protect the nature of cultural communities and to recognize that
questions of collective identity are preliminary to the definition of citizenship. Principles of justice flow from shared interpretations defined in
specific and concrete contexts, whereas principles of profound diversity
legitimize different ways of belonging to a common political community.
Within this model, citizens have a civic sense of belonging that is understood in a specific cultural context which provides a distinct character to
the country and a substantial sense of belonging to Canada. The notion
of "shared collective goods" focuses upon the needs of peoples as expres-
sive cultural beings rather than as participants in a range of civic projects.

In the light of the distinction between consent-descent as fundamental
to citizenship, descent is the underlying concept for citizenship among
multinational and polyethnic groups, rather than consent. Unlike Canadian citizenship, which is attainable on a universal and procedural basis,
there are no established procedures for acquiring full membership in
either group other than by birth. In offering some first thoughts on First
Nations' citizenship taken as a sense of belonging, Marie Battiste and
Helen Semeganis in this volume explore a number of complex issues

associated with the ways in which citizenship has been understood in Canada, the influence these understandings have had upon schooling in general and citizenship education in particular, and what can be meant by citizenship in the context of today's pluralistic society.

Practical Considerations and Critiques of Communitarianism
Several different responses to First Nations citizenship in Canada fuel the citizenship debate and provide a test case for the communitarian model. Official policy until the late 1960s, the *assimilation* model reappears sporadically in reaction to advances in self-government. However, this model fails to right the historical wrongs and to address the equity issues central to the citizenship debate.[14] Based upon a desire for recognition of their unique contribution to the history and livelihood of Canada, the *"citizen plus" model* was proposed within the Hawthorn report in the mid-1960s and has been elaborated more recently by Alan Cairns.[15] Equal opportunity, equality before the law, and equality of outcomes are important but insufficient in this conception of citizenship. First Nations would be recognized as unique, on the one hand, and as maintaining the rights of Canadian citizenship, on the other.

Other models of Aboriginal self-government jurisdiction and authority for the Indian, Inuit, and Métis peoples of Canada have since emerged for three reasons: desire for fair treatment from the federal government; self-management of Aboriginal communities as more viable than that provided by current governments; and a prior and inextinguishable right to govern oneself.[16] At issue are the means of entrenching self-government and its content.

Rejecting existing political relations and mainstream institutions as a suitable framework for situating the citizenship of First Nations, the *treaty option* or *sovereignty model* recognizes Aboriginal and treaty rights and proposes the acquisition of treaty rights, as recognized by section 35 of the Constitution Act of 1982.[17] This model proposes restoration of an indigenous nationhood through control over local government by means of cultural sovereignty, and proposes an equal relationship with the federal government, that is, sovereignty-association within Canada without involving a separate state for Aboriginal peoples.[18] Since treaties are typically negotiated between international parties, however, it is currently beyond reach, since all parties to the necessary trilateral agreements – the federal government, the provincial governments, and the Aboriginal peoples – are within Canada. Moreover, international recognition as a people is not the same as recognition as a nation or as a nation-state. The trilateral negotiations between the federal government, the reluctant provinces, and the Aboriginal peoples for domestic treaties would be difficult, if not untenable. Each set of negotiations would bring unequal physical, human, and financial resources to the table, and the Aboriginals would be at a huge disadvantage in recurring negotiations, likely resulting in dissimilar authorities among Aboriginal governments and their land base.

Notwithstanding its shortcomings, two contemporary examples of this model recognize that treaty rights can be acquired in the present day. One is the Nisga'a treaty in British Columbia, signed in 1999, as a move by the federal government to recognize both rights of self-determination and of nationhood. In another example, the recommendations of the Royal Commission on Aboriginal Peoples as articulated in the summary volume, set the discourse within Canadian federalism, whereby an agreed-upon treaty process would be the only legitimate process for the establishment of a third order of governance, that is, the Aboriginal component of a multinational federation in Canada.[19]

Two other proposals offer alternatives for entrenching Aboriginal self-government. In the principled approach,[20] a general principle recognizing Aboriginal self-government would be entrenched in the Canadian constitution; but then the problem remains of assuring recognition in Canadian courts in a balanced fashion. A "first principle of interpretation" could "proscribe any impairment of an Aboriginal community's capacity to survive."[21] Even with such guidance, however, a court is likely to reflect the collective understanding of provincial and federal parties and to make decisions conservatively reflecting the history of the country. An alternative may be the establishment of Aboriginal advisory committees for Canadian courts when cases warrant, but this option, too, would be fraught with practical difficulties in resolving disputes and could lead to possible charges of bias rather than recognition of relevant knowledge and wisdom.

Drawing a lesson from the Indian tribal governments in the United States, the *domestic dependent nationhood* model also has been proposed for entrenchment in the Canadian constitution.[22] A recognizable concept, the model refers to a body of American laws for interpretation, although care would be needed in making applications in Canada, since our histories and issues are different. Entrenching this concept would recognize Aboriginal peoples' inherent right of self-government with jurisdiction over civil and criminal law matters on Aboriginal land. Sovereignty would be limited to that of a domestic nature, precluding international relations. State governments would retain civil and criminal jurisdiction over non-Aboriginal persons in Aboriginal territory if no Aboriginal person was involved and if no essential tribal interests were affected. Federal governments would retain authority over both tribal and state jurisdiction in Aboriginal territories. While this proposal begins to address the possible content of Aboriginal self-government, a note of caution must be sounded. Courts tend not to stray very far from constitutional norms; there would be no Canadian precedents upon which to draw for judicial decision making, and American jurisprudence has not always made use of a unique approach in its interpretations.

While respecting Canadian constitutional human rights like gender equality, self-governments may vary according to cultural norms. Yet how self-government for Aboriginal peoples is to be recognized formally has yet to be resolved. The practicalities of each of the five models reviewed illustrate well the theory and issues involved in the communitarian approach. They are partial models of citizenship, however, since none of the models proposed for Aboriginal self-government deals effectively with urban Natives, who constitute more than half of all Aboriginal people in Canada. Nor do they address the need for pan-Canadian cohesion of the state and of society as a community of citizens.[23]

In spite of its attractive and persuasive nature, the communitarian model of citizenship, developed to deal with Canadian specificities, continues to be subject to acute critiques. Romulo Magsino in this volume characterizes it as a conservative ideology likely to foster conformity and intolerance by its insistence on community values and the common good. This model also problematizes necessary accommodation in the light of changing societal cultures and demographics. It offers no shared viewpoint on the common good, values, rights, responsibilities, and societal arrangements. If the gaps between social categories, such as class, gender, age, ethnic membership, and so on, are accentuated to the point that the individual's moral independence lacks protection and if injustices lead to conflict and disorder, then there are additional concerns that the social order would flounder.[24]

Principled Agreement in Debate
The citizenship debate has yet to resolve which model is most appropriate for Canada as a multinational and polyethnic state. As each conceptual perspective is problematized, it becomes clear that no single citizenship model serves as an entirely adequate basis for the determination of citizenship rights, responsibilities, and constitutional arrange-

ments and for an appropriate civic education. Although issues of inclusion, productivity, and the nature of consent abound, we nonetheless note considerable agreement. Pluralism must be rightfully included within reasonable limits; some degree of common good must be achieved; and a civic culture that encourages participation and political virtues – with free, equal, and reciprocal relations – within a culture of deliberation is also required.[25] This principled agreement then allows researchers, policy makers, and practitioners to continue their quest for feasible policy and educational solutions, however complex these may be.

Collective Identity and Citizenship

Is collective identity preliminary to citizenship models or does it derive from social policy? Or is collective identity constructed in a tension between them? The communitarian view considers cultural identities as preliminary to citizenship and to models of society. Another view, however, considers identity to be primarily a question of situating frontiers.[26] By turning the question of the relationship between culture and the state around, as in a chicken-and-egg problem, this view takes into consideration international experiences as well as current research. Although the communitarian philosophy argues that identity politics become necessary in the face of the absence of recognition or mis-recognition,[27] much research on minorities maintains the complex view that collectivized identities – be these around religion, ethnicity, language, race, or other central value – are conditioned by the policies and categories of dominant societies. In the case of immigrants and refugees, collectivized identities are also conditioned by host societies as well as by the experiences in originating countries which compel people to leave.[28]

In this volume, Guy Bourgeault et al. consider important analyses of ethnicity which mitigate against the communitarian view of collective identity as predetermined. They argue that this view is problematized by the constant flux characterizing the majority of polyethnic communities. The social construction of ethnic identities and relations is now well accepted. Constructed primarily in separation, collective identity opposes "us–them" as one of its fundamental distinctions. Not only is this relationship unstable, moving, and porous, it is also subject to a complex dynamic of struggles and conflicts between groups and social actors. Thus, a model must take into consideration the shift of boundaries and cultural markers over time and allow for multiple belongings as a social norm.

In Canada, the experience of Québécois Francophones is so marked that, today, in the context of possible but somewhat ephemeral separation, the ideal of a Canadian citizenship characterized by a "Charter identity," that is, by a crucial adherence to a set of human rights, is set aside, since Québec did not sign the Canadian Charter of Rights and Freedoms of 1982. As a result, for Québécois nationalists, the ideal of "l'identité nationale québécoise" takes up all the discursive space accorded to a collective identity to a federal state, thus rejecting the possibility of any other identification with Canada as a whole, while nonetheless maintaining other multiple belongings. Therefore, identity is more a product than the source of political mobilization and activity.

Crucially defined by governments, collectivized identities are created most often in specific spaces as well as by "practices through which individuals and groups formulate and claim new rights or struggle to expand or maintain existing rights."[29] Within frontiers, the construction of collectivized identities and the conquest of recognition are both complementary and contradictory. Central to the process is the construction of the immigrant – adult or child – as an Other by dominant groups in host societies, with separation and distance being at the source of this identification,[30] a construction which sometimes is so distant as to block passage of political, cultural, or national frontiers. However, immigrant identities are inversely constructed by the affirmation of their own content. They are more than the constructed Other; for they have their own specific heritages and histories. In Toronto, for example, reactive claims for a legitimized identity are actualized by requests for access and participation in public spaces, by cultural practices and civic engagement in quest of a certain social and personal visibility. Yet these social actions are paradoxically the product of accelerating policies and processes on integration.[31] This results in the creation of intermediate spaces and places wherein immigrants may find support and necessary resources to live through the social and cultural shock experienced in host societies and in migration.

Collectivized identities are not entirely derived from sources of sociopolitical and cultural power. From constructivist and postmodernist perspectives, identity is framed as a more free-standing entity that establishes patterns of expectations, orders social processes, and drives social organization.[32] Understanding the individual as agent of his or her construction of self and moving beyond judicial and politico-ethical aspects of citizenship, Michel Pagé explores psycho-social aspects of citizenship in a pluralistic democracy.[33] Given the complexities of multiple identifications, of regulating a common life between citizens, of experiencing solidarity among citizens, and of obtaining services from institutions while being part of them, the posited unity of a common territory as a source of attachment is considered insufficient for constructing the social dimension of a common political identity. Students in educational institutions learn to have civil relations and dialogues with each other, to take pride in their school, and to treat each other as equals. From this perspective, civic education would give particular attention to the development of solidarity within common institutions and of a sense of impartial dialogue as part of educational aims.

One of the first requirements of pluralist democracies is the recognition of collectivized identities. Whether these collectivized identities are those of peoples with rights and histories prior to Confederation or whether they are produced with the integration of immigrants, it matters not. Today, Canadians of all ages are nurturing new expressions of urban citizenship, rooted in minority demographics, spatial settlements, and adversities. This requirement is especially relevant for Canada, as a country constituted largely by immigration since the colonial period; for the moral integrity of a state is based upon the treatment it affords its minorities.

Policies and Institutional Goals

Policy and institutional goals are marked by a range of conceptual possibilities and affect lived Canadian realities. We distinguish here between institutional goals relating to social cohesion, forms of multiculturalism policy, a glaring mismatch between some current policies, the impact of immigration and citizenship policy, and institutional responsibility for citizenship education in Canada.

Social Cohesion as Institutional Goal

The attention focused upon citizenship is situated instrumentally within the state's desire for viable social cohesion, which is a challenge in a pluralistic country like ours.[34] Very difficult to define, this convenient but nebulous concept, or quasi-concept,[35] includes many dimensions insufficiently explored and permits appeals to mutual confidence, social capital, and the perils of neoliberalism. Calls for social cohesion, however, also prescribe, often implicitly, remedies of compassion and a return to basic values, rather than assuring the redressing of social inequities and an institutional mediation of interests.[36] Constructed upon shared values, a common discourse, and a reduction of gaps in riches and revenues, social cohesion would mean that people generally have the impression of participating in a common enterprise, sharing challenges and equal opportunities, based upon a sense of trust, hope and reciprocity as members of the same collectivity.[37] This quasi-concept, however, can serve as only a partial response to the question of social order, necessitating a democratic dialectic, valuable in itself and in terms of institutional goals and policies. In this light, we review federal government policies, given the state's need to define itself, to implement versatile yet potent technologies of rule, and to manage individuals in such a way that citizens are free and equal yet acquiesce to participate in the desired social order.

Forms of Multiculturalism Policy

First articulated in Canada in 1971, multiculturalism as a social and civic paradigm has since been taken up as policy in many other countries, each in its own way. The policy lives in a plurality of guises which rest upon the specific developments of political, social, and cultural pluralism in each country.[38] What all the forms of multiculturalism policy have in common is their emergence as views of state authority and of society, in opposition to unitary conceptions of citizenship. Creating a dispersal of power among associations, groups, and interests in civil society, forms of political pluralism are understood differentially, either as a negative but necessary feature of democratic politics or as a beneficial feature of a healthy democracy in counterbalancing the centralization of the state.

Multiculturalism, however, does not displace various forms of pluralism but encapsulates them according to their own specificities. Known officially as an Act for the Preservation and Enhancement of Multiculturalism in Canada (1985), Canada's Multiculturalism Act promotes cultural and racial diversity as a fundamental characteristic of Canadian heritage and identity, acknowledging the freedom of all members of Canadian society to preserve, enhance, and share their cultural heritage, a heritage that provides an invaluable resource in the shaping of Canada's future in terms of equality, understanding, and harmony. Nonetheless, the Canadian policy, which provides political recognition of social and cultural pluralism as inherent to citizenship, is articulated differentially, and this reality has significant implications for access to social and state resources.

Policy Mismatch: Citizenship and Immigration

As articulated in its policies and laws on immigration and on citizenship, the federal government's views may be summarized as involving two competing interests, resulting in a policy mismatch.[39] The intention of the first policy is to attract new immigrants and to entice them into becoming citizens of Canada. Here, the government's role is to encourage newcomers to contribute to Canadian society through political and community participation, taking part in the labour force and economy, and becoming integrated into other spheres of Canadian life. Such discussions of immigration are contextualized in Canada's multicultural policy, embedded in law and in the Charter as the federal government urges immigrants to adapt to Canadian society while maintaining their cultural identities as long as these identities are not harmful to Canada or any individual.[40]

There is yet another view stemming from the federal government's position on citizenship: how newcomer citizenship affects other Canadian citizens. In a recent document providing an overview of government services, in part of the mission statement regarding immigration and citizenship it is stated that Canada must "derive maximum benefit from the global movement of people manage[ing] access to Canada and defining membership in Canadian society." Thus, it is not the interests of the immigrants which are of concern, but those of the Canadian population, seen as paramount in order to maintain a program that is both responsible and relevant to Canada's needs.[41]

The latter position on the citizenship of immigrants, the economic protectionist policy, can be described as liberal individualist.[42] In this view, citizenship is seen as singular, universal, and passive, because the individual is free and context free, that is, not defined by ethnic, socio-economic, religious or other collective identities. The contradictions between the two policy positions are glaring. The latter position denies the intentions of the Multiculturalism Policy (1971) and Act (1985), which were created to mitigate against unitary views of citizenship. Insufficient for the needs of a democratic pluralist society, the unitary policy position opposes much of the academic literature,[43] as reflected in the essays in this volume which are focused on various interpretations of citizenship and multiple ways of belonging.

Impact of Immigration and Citizenship Policies

The impact of immigration policy upon the shaping of Canada, particularly its urban contexts, is well presented by the historian Harold Troper in this volume. He traces the growth of Toronto, from an overwhelmingly Anglocentric city into a sprawling metropolis characterized by a patchwork of contiguous ethnic villages as an organic part of the mainstream. In previous eras, Canadian policy preferred agricultural immigration, in a descending order of racialized categories, but it worked by soaking up large numbers of people, especially during the opening of the West on the completion of the transcontinental railways. The immigrants did not stay down on the farm, however, and drifted into cities, precipitating industrial development and an enlarged job market as well as urban xenophobic sentiment. After the Second World War, a pent-up demand for consumer goods and the opening of an export market in Western Europe created an urgent need for urban labour; thus, additional immigration was needed and Canada's doors, closed in the 1930s and 1940s, reopened.

To cut loose from the xenophobic past, three federal policy initiatives – defining national community, promising equality of access and participation, and affirming the mosaic as a positive Canadian virtue – facilitated the creation of the new Canada, home to a wide diversity of peoples. The factors, background, and impact of these three policy developments lead today to the requirement that any form of citizenship education include and acknowledge the contributions of immigrants.

Responsibility for Citizenship Education Policy in Canada

The role of the government in citizenship education lies at the core of the issues flowing from citizenship education conceptions and from policy considerations; for the federal government as well as the provincial ministries of education and higher learning hold particular responsibility. Although the role of the federal government in granting citizenship is well known, its role in encouraging social and civic participation is less so. In this volume, Roberta Russell makes explicit the contribution of the former Department of the Secretary of State over a fifty-year period (the 1940s to the 1990s) in a well-informed, eclectic, and up-to-date exploration of the ways in which the idea of citizenship, and thus citizenship education, might be adapted to reflect more accurately the changing character of contemporary Canadian social and political life. Drawing on recent feminist literature, she raises some important questions about the sorts of values that might best inform our efforts to create a just and inclusive civil society.

The questioning of citizenship education has now reached educational decision makers, as the Council of Ministers of Education, Canada, turns to the possibilities of evaluation and research to inform decision makers and politicians. Various ministries of education, in coalitions or at the provincial level, look to their programs of studies as vehicles of response and of reconstruction of an active citizenry and engage in a programmatic process of renewal. Moreover, governmental officials and politicians reconsider their role in the maintenance of social cohesion and see civic education as a primary vehicle in attaining this societal goal. One of the national issues revolves around the notion that the quality of a school or educational system can be legitimately appraised by examining the behaviours or performances of students enrolled in them by means of a broad set of indicators.[44] Since the conceptual, social, and cultural dimensions of contemporary citizenship are contested, and since curricular programming and pedagogies offer multiple possibilities and perspectives regarding the social responsibilities and knowledge base considered necessary for citizenship, this is an extremely difficult and complex task. Even with agreement on numerous principles noted earlier in this chapter, great challenges are to be faced in deciding precisely which manifestations of a complexity of traits or qualities ought to be included in programs of study and what would count as evidence of citizenship values, knowledge, behaviour, skills, attitudes, and practices that could reasonably be expected of most students in Canada.

Canadian Realities

The unequal application of inconsistent citizenship policies in the Canadian context may well mean that Canadians do not live their citizenship equally, freely, and in solidarity. Given the daily practices of exclusion of those who are Othered, the dark side of nation reveals the serious inadequacies of Canada's multicultural policies and laws in a society that is marked by tangible currents of racism. In reaction to increasing diversity, there is considerable public pressure to reduce immigration, get rid of multiculturalism, string up feminist judges, and construct Canada as a unity rather than as complexity.

Given our colonialist and essentialist markers of identity into two primary inscriptions of "French" and "English," simplified as confrontational possessions, cultural typologies, and dominant ideologies, it is not surprising that Canada cannot escape its fragmented framework.[45] In view of the perceived need to create a nation that is unified and legitimated, one that does not question its deep cleavages and how they were constructed, those who are "different" are inscribed as inferior, negative, dark, and problematic, and pushed to opposite corners of the box that symbolizes Canada.[46] Imagining a political community and creating a just society out of such profound racialized crevices, fragmentation, and diffusion becomes difficult because of differences of class, race, gender, capital, and power.[47]

We examine here the impact of four aspects of these Canadian realities on the structure of the country, on individual lived experience, on access to economic resources, and on the acquisition of skills fundamental to citizenship. In doing so, we recognize that the mixity that characterizes Canada designates the realities of interwoven links between individuals and groups in the form of unions, musics, and cultures. The very words *mixity, diversity, pluralism, métissage, hybridity* signify violence – that of divisions, of wars, of emigrations, of outside norms, and of boundaries – as well as an ideal of going beyond frontiers, atomized cultures, and closed identities. Forms of exclusion, by definition, by principle, by whitewashing, by pacifying, and, paradoxically, by inclusion,[48] flow from the violence of mixity and are illustrated by several essays in this volume, thus documenting the difficulties of realizing an ideal citizenship.

Structural Impact

The call for an expanded model of citizenship, be it in the form of liberalism that makes room for cultural groups[49] or in the form of communitarianism which puts the politics of identity in the forefront of internal struggles for recognition,[50] is crucially situated upon an issue of balance. In Québec's affirmationist project,[51] for example, the historical argument for survival was lodged in a call for recognition on linguistic and cultural grounds. The contemporary argument is a matter of political recognition and empowerment, of economic profitability, and of participatory and distinctive integration in a Canada that is perceived as unitary and located in historical conditions. Critiques reject attempts to relocate Canadian-ness by inventing an artificial pan-Canadianism which negates the real constitutive realities or which petrifies them by having recourse to the fetish notion of multiculturalism.[52] In this spirit, Canada is seen as being bicephalous, that is, consisting of two countries, Québec (+ French) and Canada (+ English), reinforced by memories and symbolic dialogues. This dualistic view pleases the Québécois sovereignists who call for a strong form of separation, as well as the regionalists who claim that the Québec project is compatible with a greater recognition of the many regions of Canada.

There are not really two countries, one pitted against the other. Instead, there is a plurality of actors characterized by variable positions, conciliatory or divergent, in time and in conjuncture. Without balance, the danger is that the federated state could devolve into competitive regional micro-empires or interprovincial struggles, especially if powers accrued by one entity are seen by others as unfair advantages. The tradition of accommodation which has marked the Canadian political culture since 1867 has been significantly eroded in the last fifteen years,[53] and, as a result, restructuring the country, possibly in terms of an essentially legal constitutional arrangement, becomes a major challenge.

Since 1759 a basic issue has been the place of francophones within a larger political unit. Since the rise of the separatist movement, the constitutional and identity debate has been limited to francophones within Québec, thus setting aside francophones in other provinces and territories. They have consequently lived a process of parcelization, but with attention to pan-Canadian linkages to maintain a sense of connectedness as well as a larger sense of identity and awareness. From one perspective, reconstructing the future of Francophones requires a grand balancing act. The specificities of "region-nations" and minorities need to be assured and perpetuated in an international economic context. While common values of civic patriotism, individual democracy, and cultural equality are respected in a renewed version of liberalism, they must be implemented without rupturing ambitions, values, and ideals of modern emancipation at the heart of the Québécois project.[54] Yet in this search for balance between individual and collective interests and powers, between equality and autonomy, lie all the dangers and disadvantages of an ethnicized state, in the fact of being Québécois yet not strictly only that.

In this fractious context, two proposals are of interest to the education and interaction of citizens, for pluralism: individualism and economic dominance need to be limited in practical ways that provide people with principled means of living together peacefully. Proposing three principles – liberty, equality, and solidarity – Paul Bernard argues that these are key to the construction of a democratic society that is pluralistic, inclusive, and participatory.[55] In bipolar relationships, liberty-solidarity sustain pluralistic democracy; solidarity-equality sustain participatory democracy; and equality-liberty sustain inclusive democracy. Although these bipolar relationships may also be fragile, they nonetheless provide some key principles on which to develop a Canadian state in which multiple nations and polyphony of ethnic groups may live together peacefully. The application of these organizing principles would permit the achievement of a reasonable degree of social cohesion without the excesses of a society driven by the inequalities of a market economy and by exclusive individualism

According to a second proposal, Eamonn Callan considers that the prime virtue of citizenship for a free people is justice as reasonableness, centered around the notion of reciprocity.[56] A reasonable citizen proposes fair terms of cooperation with others, settles differences in mutually acceptable ways, and abides by agreed-upon terms of cooperation so long as others also are prepared to do so. Along with the principle of justice as reasonableness, accepting the burdens of judgment acknowledges that many others adhere to values at odds with our own without being any less reasonable than we are, and that "a pervasive virtue of public reasons ... inclines us to devise and interpret rules of coexistence so as to accommodate the scope of reasonable pluralism." Moreover, this principle requires us to care about what we can do only together, that is, to construct a non-divisive political morality; but even then our differences could pull against the commonality of justice, although patriotism is defined as an identification with a particular political community in "the rational pursuit of good and reasonable deference to the claims of others."[57]

Individual Impact

As the mixing of peoples intensifies in our society and around the entire planet, by virtue of global migration, economies, and accelerating communication, complex interactions across time and space become a daily necessity. From the ensuing unions are born children who belong to several groups. Thus, frontiers and customs are relativized, resistances and racism are reduced, and education transforms in a few years what took centuries to build in other places and times.[58] The very co-existence of multiple groups in a particular territory brings about significant interweaving, leading to an unforeseeable mixture which questions the totality of being, of institutions, of traditions, and of the state with its political and symbolic references.

Individuals who live this interactive mixing in Canada feel its impact in discriminatory experiences on a daily basis which affront a person's sense of dignity and self-worth, and they respond with a call for recognition. Deliberate omissions and commissions against individuals are documented in this volume by Celia Haig-Brown, who recalls the consequences of the deletion of significant material from her father's manuscript, without permission or even consultation: the essay then presented an innocent view of the past, devoid of any mention of racism, a topic which at the time passed silently and invisibly. In yet another example, she recalls the subjective and subjugating experiences of research carried out by individuals external to a particular group, for their own purposes, and she calls for democratic research under the control of the peoples involved.

Personal barbs are still vivid for Cecille DePass and Shazia Qureshi, who relate in this volume their sense of exclusion as symbolized by the words of the national anthem, "O Canada," and lay bare the paradoxes of the multi-layered forms of inclusion and exclusion underpin the notion of citizenship in Canada. In bringing to our attention a number of provocative examples of contradictions, paradoxes, and ironies, the authors' lived experiences of exclusion by definition and by principle poignantly and painfully question whose freedom is served in a democracy.

Many immigrants, Aboriginals, people of colour, francophones, men and women alike have made and continue to make significant contributions to Canada. Full citizenship requires centralization of heretofore marginalized individuals and peoples to create a more equitable society; any adequate view of democratic citizenship education needs to take into consideration the indispensable notions of inclusion, belonging, and recognition.

Economic Impact

One of the critical issues germane to a culturally pluralist society is the integration of minorities both as citizens and as workers. Participation in political, social, economic, and civil life does not necessarily follow upon the granting of formal membership. Moreover, being marginalized and continuous targets of racism does not guarantee integration and the full enjoyment of human rights to which all citizens are entitled. Moving beyond the rhetoric which marks much of the citizenship debate, Fernando Mata, in this volume, examines some cross-linkages between labour force integration, citizenship, and visible minority status in Canada on some recent demographic data. Of particular interest are those peoples included in the contested statistical designation of "visible minority" ("vizmin" in popular parlance). Describing visible minority members as non-Aboriginal, non-Caucasian in race, and non-white in colour,[59] this category includes Blacks, Chinese, Filipinos, South Asians, Japanese, Korean, and South East Asians in the census count, thus making possible analyses that distinguish their characteristics from those of non-visible minorities.

Generally, the results show that, regardless of citizenship status, groups with larger numbers among visible minorities occupied somewhat secondary positions in the occupational hierarchy. When compared with non-visible minority groups, the visible minority groups of similar citizenship status, demography, and/or human capital did not occupy commensurate positions in the Canadian labour force. This finding suggests that the granting of Canadian citizenship to new immigrant visible minorities appears to have no bearing on their patterns of integration into the labour market, possibly because of problems related to the recognition of their educational credentials or owing to racial discrimination on the part of employers. Thus, there is a risk of creating an underclass.

Given the rigours of the world economy, the requirements of pancontinental free trade, innovations in production, and the necessity of enhancing the workforce, the possibility of a visible minority underclass is serious in the context of global markets in which there are new exporters of natural resources. In the light of Canada's reduced productivity in the primary sector, a traditional source of strength,[60] Canadian governments look for indicators of employability and for training programs for the workforce to prepare more effectively for an uncertain future. Employability skills are usually classified in four areas – competencies in problem resolution, communication, critical thinking, and interaction – since personal attributes are considered remediable and a guarantee for employment. Speculating on human deficiencies,[61] however, serves only to assign culpability to the individual him/herself in the face of moral judgment, since employment is a function of social structure and global market forces beyond the control of the individual.[62]

Impact on Skills Acquisition for Citizenship

Skills fundamental to citizenship include the acquisition of literacy, which involves the mastery of the cultural codes and symbols of a society so as to foster informed, active, and engaged participation in full-fledged citizenship. The correlation between literacy and civic participation in one's locality and the limitations inherent in its absence may appear to be anomalous, but it strikes at the very heart of democratic life, as Paulo

Freire's highly influential literacy campaigns among the oppressed amply demonstrated in South America.[63] Yet do all Canadians have the opportunity and will to do so? In a study of adult literacy in Newfoundland and Labrador, where average rates of literacy fall below national standards, Linda Phillips and Stephen Norris in this volume examine the values which people in eight communities place on literacy, career advancement, political involvement, and education. The findings demonstrate that literacy is related to politicization, that is, to active citizenry, which then makes its own demands on educational institutions. The data show a tendency among participants not to seek out additional literacy education, not to demand quality literacy instruction, or not to make demands for their children's schooling. On the basis of a low value placed on literacy in relation to career advancement, the authors suggest that federal literacy policies are upside down and should value literacy in and of itself, rather than linked to career advancement, since there are limited possibilities in this part of Canada, where work is limited largely to the fishing, service, and hydrocarbons industries. The relationship between literacy and citizenship appears to be reciprocal. Citizens who actively value literacy and make demands on educational institutions attain the highest literacy levels and have much to contribute to society. Until literacy improvement is achieved in Newfoundland and Labrador, these citizens can hardly be said to be free, equal, and standing in solidarity with the rest of Canada.

The implications for citizenship education are profound, especially in the light of the high drop-out rate of about 30 per cent among Canadian youth. Optimism is uncertain, since forecasts for the year 2000 set the mark at an average of seventeen years of schooling to meet the demands of employers.[64] Dynamic and challenging, our review of Canadian citizens' realities, the mixture of violence and idealism and the implications for citizenship education, raises serious questions about policy and institutional goals. We move on to considerations of citizenship education in practice.

Citizenship Education in Practice

The transformation of citizenship gives way to a rethinking of education for citizenship which holds promise for a renewal in the near future. Flowing from contemporary research, thought, and advocacy on this important dimension of the citizenship debate, which is well represented in this volume, questioning the role of the school and of government in educating citizens critically offers different stances on issues of curriculum reform, pedagogy, evaluation, and educational research without neglecting the school's mandate and authority to prepare students for citizenship and the labour force. Our faith in the power of schooling, especially of the common school, as an instrument of social progress is less than could be hoped for. We are well aware of the limits of successive institutional solutions; moreover, educational arrangements must be more responsive to private preference and cultural diversity.[65]

Conceptions of Citizenship Education

One of the essential functions of the school is to contribute to the formation of citizens who believe and live their freedom, equally and in solidarity. This requirement flows not only from the needs of society but also from individual needs. On the one hand, a democratic society depends upon the informed and active engagement of all of its members. On the other hand, to be able to participate fully in social life, the individual must acquire the necessary competencies to play his/her role effectively as a citizen in a society characterized by global and local interdependencies and challenges.[66] In this light, historical and contemporary conceptions of citizenship education that inform programs of study and curricular reform take on great significance for policy and practice.

Historical and Contemporary Conceptions of Civic Education
Four historical periods of civic education may be distinguished in Canada, according to Ken Osborne,[67] who situates them with respect to their links to social, political, and global movements. The first period, from 1890 to the early 1920s, coincided more or less with compulsory education, which was focused upon the Canadianization of children as a vehicle of the nationalism with which a nation-state could be built. The second period stretches from the 1920s to the 1950s and, without abandoning its nationalist theme, accentuates the preparation for democratic life, often in a non-political sense; for American ideas of progressive education began to make their way in educational thought in Canada. Encompassing the 1960s to the 1980s, the third period is motived by the fear that Canadian students know little of their own country, a fear that surfaces even today. This period emphasizes the importance of what is termed an increasing knowledge and a pan-Canadian understanding of what is Canadian, represented, for example, by the "Canadian Studies"

movement. Also characteristic of this era is a distancing from assimilative approaches of citizenship typical of yesteryear, replaced by an acceptance and promotion of multiculturalism. Finally, the fourth period, which dates from the beginning of the 1990s, represents a step back from, if not even the abandonment of, citizenship as an educational goal in favour of a reassignment to schools of an economic agenda so as to prepare students for the competition and entrepreneurship supposedly necessary to our survival in a globalized economy.

Among the priorities of educational policy makers,[68] the posited links between schooling and the economic prosperity create a vulnerability to corporate critiques, broadcast on the public scene by the media and politicians alike, to the effect that schools do not succeed in preparing youth for an economic future. The basics are re-emphasized and redefined to include not only the three Rs (reading, arithmetic, and writing), but also computers, entrepreneurship, competitivity, teamwork, and so on. Reflecting the corporate and economic agenda, this educational tendency reveals that citizens have been reconceptualized as consumers, and students as clients, wherein exuberant individualism sets aside questions of community and social obligation, and whereby American values and presuppositions become increasingly the norm in Canada.

Focusing upon the period of schooling between the ends of the two World Wars, Rosa Bruno-Jofré in this volume exposes the prevalent model of Anglo-conformity and relates how it was constructed and lived. This dominant notion of citizenship in the 1920s sought to shape proper members of the national polity, a view which emphasized service to the community, duties, responsibilities, and social integration. By the 1930s the influence of progressive education was beginning to reshape discourses of democracy and civic education. By the end of the Second World War, a new international reality affected Canadians' self-perception, leading to a questioning of racist and ethnocentric ideas and of theories of cultural relativism that subsequently made possible the reconstruction of citizenship formation. Drawing on documentary and interview data, Bruno-Jofre examines the official discourses and explores oral testimonies and case examples, such as the Franco-Manitoban communities, where, typically, a minority reconfigures the school for its own purposes. In so doing, she shows that people develop a sense of being Canadian in their own terms in a contested process of resistance and negotiation.

According to a policy study, four contemporary conceptions of citizenship education are current in Canadian schooling. Evidence is provided by an analysis of a variety of educational documentation, such as programs of study, policy statements, background and discussion papers, and lists of approved resources, obtained from all jurisdictions except Québec and francophone New Brunswick.[69] Ranging on a continuum from elitism to activism, these conceptions identify common and distinctive characteristics in terms of knowledge, skills, and dispositions or values as principal components of citizenship education, with a clear tendency towards active conceptions of civism. Supported by other research on themes, similarities, and tendencies of programs of study across Canada[70] and for francophone programs and jurisdictions,[71] these four conceptions of citizenship education recall and nuance the dual distinction, drawn in an earlier section of this essay, between models of citizenship around the enjoyment of rights or active participation, thus echoing the tensions between descent and consent as the basis for state membership.

Citizenship Education Today: Curriculum Reform, Pedagogy, and Evaluation

The debate about curriculum reform necessary for a renewal of citizenship education often centres upon the appropriate disciplinary basis. In the anglophone tradition, social studies is seen as the appropriate school discipline for locating citizenship education and the debate focuses upon the selection of appropriate objectives and content as well as upon the preponderance of historical perspectives.[72] In the francophone tradition, the disciplinary debate is between history and geography, even in the face of agreement that the two are complementary.[73] Recalling that civic education was already present in schools, the Québec ministry of education retitled all history courses "Histoire et l'éducation à la citoyenneté," since history is considered to be the discipline most capable of preparing the citizen by providing appropriate intellectual equipment and enquiry-based discipline and approaches.[74] Within the francophone scholarly tradition in France and in Canada, however, geography, as the science of spatial organization of societies, also is seen as an appropriate disciplinary basis for citizenship education. From this perspective, citizenship is lived in public spaces and in politically defined territorial spaces, which, in turn, define collectivities and phenomena. Preparing citizens to witness cultural mixing and to share public spaces critically contextualizes thinking about problems of utilization of space and about similar social concerns.[75] Both history and geography have a strong potential for the formation of citizens, regardless of the disciplinary tradition.[76] Moving beyond the social sciences, the debate draws in the humanities as well as the entire school, whose mission is to prepare democracy.

Democracy is a reasonable act of faith, and the citizen is animated by values, is open to change, is militant, masters critical thought, is capable of perspective, receives alterity favourably, constructs his/her identity, chooses his/her belongings, and knows how to liberate him/herself from the constraints of memory.[77] The availability of active pedagogical approaches and teaching techniques makes possible a response which considers the student to be a person able to exercise his/her citizenship at school. Going beyond efforts at containment, such an education develops active participation among children and adolescents, within a democratic school, so as to form youth to the exercise of freedoms, rights, and responsibilities. It is in social practice, in learning by doing, that society's youth are to be formed, so that later an individual will know how to conduct him/herself freely, equally, and in solidarity in a diversity of life situations.[78] The preparation of adult immigrants for life as new Canadians similarly necessitates active approaches based on social participation.

Pedagogies which have a strong potential for this form of citizenship education include those based on active participation in and beyond schools which build links with communities and society. We first think of examples which are focused directly upon democratic education, like service pedagogies,[80] deliberative democratic education, the classroom as democracy,[81] and the democratization of campuses. Reflective pedagogical approaches which involve the development of a keen sense of individual and group awareness, fundamental to democratic education in a pluralist society, may also serve the objectives of lived social participatory forms of citizenship education.[82] Examples include critical theory and pedagogy,[83] reflective narrative, literary and literacy education,[84] and pedagogies of difference, social participation, and identity formation.[85]

A wide range of teaching techniques is also available, often in combination with more fully developed pedagogies. Included are problem solving, cooperative education,[86] local and community-based pedagogy, and cultural and intercultural approaches.[87] Moreover, the content of activitist, process pedagogies may focus upon legal education,[88] peace education, and social justice,[89] as well as the multiple perspectives of global or planetary education.[90] Fundamental to curricular and pedagogical approaches are four interwoven principles at the heart of a global integrative approach to democratic citizenship: the cohesion of human rights and of democratic responsibilities; the respect and accept-ance of diversity; the dialectic and participatory basis of the develop-ment of collective identity formation; and the development of cultural consciousness and competence towards social peace and for harmoni-ous living.[91]

In the light of this array of curricular and pedagogical possibilities, evaluating the outcomes of citizenship education is highly problematic. Evaluation has two general functions, selecting out students and assist-ing students to learn.[92] In the case of citizenship education, the function of evaluation would necessarily be to confirm student learning and to assist students in their learning process. Educational systems and teach-ing professionals face important issues when devising appropriate means of evaluation. Even in the acceptance of a constructivist approach and the relevance of evaluation for democratic education, challenges lie in the identification of citizen knowledge; of the skills that permit students to live democratically, especially in the face of rapid economic, social, and technological changes; and of the civic values and dispositions, attitudes, and behaviours, including a commitment to sustainable devel-opment, that could reasonably be expected of most students.

Decisions about choices of curricular objectives and content and of pedagogical approaches and teaching techniques, as well as about the means and methods of evaluation of learning, cannot be made by educa-tors alone, regardless of level, be it in ministries or departments of education, school districts, local schools, or the Council of Ministers of Education, Canada, although it is common for general frameworks to be developed by national and provincial decision makers and for teaching professionals to decide upon educational strategies and activities appro-priate to their particular classrooms. Given the complex array of possi-bilities for citizenship education for a democratic pluralist country, as argued by Haig-Brown in this volume, the voices of a multitude of stakeholders, including parents and interest groups, must be heard. Professionals, however, have an obligation to make public their reason-ing as well as to listen and to take seriously the responses of the public. Given the contestation of citizenship, the diversity of society, and the changes of educational objectives over time, as documented by Bruno-Jofre and Troper, both in this volume, a broad consensus on the details of citizenship education is not really possible. A good understanding of principles and approaches, however, developed in a reasonable delibera-tive process is essential to a rigorous egalitarian presentation of cultures in curricula and school practices as well as the accommodation of differences in order to ensure the relevance of schooling for minority groups and the validation of their lived experiences.

Citizenship Education: The School's Mandate and Authority

Citizenship education today is less restrictive, more ethical, more active, and more oriented to the planet than civic education was in the past. Even if civic education is as old as the notion of schooling, how can the school assure its mandate to form citizens for democratic living when it is a pre-democratic institution? How can a few courses on citizenship education suffice when we are faced with the need for comprehensiveness of today's education for democratic pluralist citizenship?

Although citizenship education has the potential to serve as the driving force generally lacking in education today, teaching professionals need solid theoretical foundations, new competencies, approved programs of study with clearly articulated guidelines that still leave room for professional responsibility and reflection, as well as an array of curriculum materials. Strong administrative support in partnership with parents and the surrounding community also is necessary, as is the privilege of initiating the necessary school transformation and of serving as models of democratic virtues.[94] In the school itself, consultation with students would be ongoing, with teachers and students alike engaging in negotiation on the organization of school life, interactions, and content. The democratization of the school would be drawn from their own realities, which would create more commitment to the democratic project as educational preparation for citizenship.

Since the school is a non-democratic institution, it retains responsibility for the proper functioning of the establishment, the overall organization of teaching and learning, as well as student discipline. The acceptance of the notion of "rule" is essential to both school and democratic life; for to live together means having rules to deal with common aspects in which individuals share as citizens in the use of public spaces, including schools.[95] Part of this mandate is the role attributed to the school in various models of citizenship that emphasize the citizen's need and right to work. The school is perceived to be an important agent in teaching students civic virtues, which include being effective in labour and leisure. Thus, schools are assigned a responsibility to prepare students for the world of work, and to that end a number of educational establishments offer work-study programs. Nonetheless, the school does not replicate the workplace, bureaucratic or otherwise, especially as it concerns the notion of authority,[96] and teachers may be concerned more about their effectiveness than about living democracy in a pedagogy of freedom.[97]

Citizenship Education Research for the Future

Citizenship and citizenship education receive a great deal of attention, as does citizenship education research, from governmental policy makers and politicians, educational practitioners, and researchers themselves. Recent research reports and coordinated action, especially by members of the Citizenship Education Research Network, discussed by Yvonne Hébert and Michel Pagé in the final chapter of this volume, are likely to serve influentially to define government policies, educational responsibilities, and approaches to action.[98] Bringing the findings of a systematic corpus of research on citizenship education to the attention of decision makers, teacher educators, and the public, towards the development of evidence-based policies and programs, is likely to occur well into the next century.

Conclusion

This introductory chapter we have raised questions and addressed ambiguities pertaining to the four dimensions which characterize the interminable citizenship debate which revolves significantly around conceptual foundations, policies, realities, and citizenship education in practice. Situated within these dimensions, the important contributions inherent in the advocacy, thought, and scholarship in this volume, taken together, offer interwoven, interdisciplinary, plural, and competing perspectives. Such an approach is typical of a debate, but there is also considerable convergence among the voices in this volume. The multiplicity of citizenship and agreement on principles relevant to citizenship education are commonly seen to be key to contributing to the enhancement of social cohesion in the face of upheaval as Canada becomes a complex, post-industrial state.

Situated within contestation and transformation, citizenship and citizenship education in a democratic pluralist society hold the hope for an idealized world, one in which peace, social justice, and harmonious living are daily reality but also reflect the violence of change and mixity, experienced both individually and collectively. Meeting the citizenship challenges involved in pluralist societies is likely to be difficult, yet exciting; for, given increasing interdependencies around the globe as well as shared risks and challenges of the future, we need to learn to know, to do, to live together, and to be.[99] Being impartial, reasonable, respectful, and deliberative in the face of different civic values, conceptions, and cultural practices is likely to be heady. Negotiating change among school staff and students towards a more democratic mode of learning and living civic community is likely to be rewarding. Learning to take one's turn, to be treated fairly and equally, to treat others in the same way, to experience solidarity among peers, be they colleagues, co-workers or students, is likely to be satisfying. Moving beyond rhetoric: the realization of the citizenship transformation has just begun.

Notes

1 Contributions to the citizenship debate are listed in several sources, the most comprehensive of which is the *Citizenship, Democracy and Ethnocultural Diversity Newsletter*, under the direction of Will Kymlicka since 1995, with back issues posted at: http://qsilver.queensu.ca/~philform/news.html.

2 See Klusmeyer, *Between Consent and Descent: Conceptions of Democratic Citizenship*.

3 Brinton, *The Jacobins: An Essay in the New History*.

4 Mill, *Utilitarianism, On Liberty, Considerations on Representative Government*, and *Autobiography*.

5 Examples of fifteen ongoing violations of human rights include the conflicts in Kosovo, Senegal, the Democratic Republic of the Congo, and Sudan; see « État des lieux pour quinze conflits », *Le Monde diplomatique*, 541 (avril 1999): 15.

6 Arendt, *Human Condition, Origins of Totalitarianism*, and *On Revolution*.

7 Ajzenstat and Smith, "Liberal-Republicanism"; Magsino, "From Eclectic Theory to Coherence," in this volume.

8 Marshall and Bottomore, *Citizenship and Social Class*.

9 Audigier, "Citoyenneté?"

10 As also noted by Bourgeault, Gagnon, McAndrew, and Pagé in this volume.

11 Kymlicka, *Multicultural Citizenship*; Walzer, *Spheres of Justice*.

12 Kallen, *Ethnicity and Human Rights*.

13 Taylor, *Reconciling the Solitudes*; Saul, *Reflections of a Siamese Twin*; Walzer, *Spheres of Justice*.

14 Barman, Hébert, and McCaskill, *Indian Education in Canada*, vols 1 and 2; Cairns, *Citizens Plus*, 49–71.

15 Cairns, *Citizens Plus.*
16 Russell, *A People's Dream,* 40–1.
17 Fleras and Elliot, *Unequal Relations.*
18 As critically analysed in Russell, *A People's Dream,* 40–57.
19 Canada, *People to People.*
20 Russell, *A People's Dream,* 58–87.
21 Ibid., 59; the "first principle of interpretation" was proposed by Pentney, "The Rights of Aboriginal Peoples."
22 Russell, *A People's Dream,* 65–87.
23 Cairns, *Citizens Plus,* 134–6.
24 Cope et al., *Immigration, Ethnic Conflicts and Social Cohesion*; Jenson, *Les contours de la cohésion sociale.*
25 See, for example, Magsino as well as Bourgeault, Gagnon, McAndrew, and Pagé in this volume; Callan, *Creating Citizens*; Sears, Clarke, and Hughes, "Learning Democracy in a Pluralist Society."
26 Lapeyronnie, « De l'altérité à la différence », 253.
27 Taylor, "Politics of Recognition."
28 Dewitte, *Immigration et intégration*; Driedger, *Multi-Ethnic Canada*; Hébert, "Collectivized Identity among Shi'a Imami Isma'ili Muslims of Calgary."
29 Siemiatycki and Isin, "Immigration, Diversity and Urban Citizenship."
30 Germain, « L'étranger et la ville ».
31 Siemiatycki and Isin, "Immigration, Diversity and Urban Citizenship."
32 Lorber, *Paradoxes of Gender.*
33 Pagé, « Citoyenneté et pluralisme des valeurs »; "Pluralistic Citizenship."
34 Cope et al., *Immigration, Ethnic Conflicts and Social Cohesion*; Canada, *Social Cohesion Research Workplan.*
35 As labelled by Paul Bernard in « La cohésion sociale ».
36 Jenson, *Les contours de la cohésion sociale.*
37 As defined by Judith Maxwell in *Social Dimensions of Economic Growth* and utilized in the federal *Social Cohesion Research Workplan.*
38 Multiculturalism is understood differently in various states; see, in this regard, Samad, "Plural Guises of Multiculturalism."
39 Wilkinson, "Government View on Immigration and Citizenship Issues."
40 Canada, *A Newcomer's Introduction to Canada,* 8.
41 Canada, *Outlook on Program Expenditures and Priorities,* 1.
42 Sigurdson, "First Peoples, New Peoples," 64.
43 Wilkinson, "Academic Views of Immigration and Citizenship."
44 The Council of Ministers of Education established the School Achievement Indicators Project in cooperation with Statistics Canada and completed national testing in mathematics in 1993, in language in 1994, and in science

in 1996. In addition to achievement, the other indicator areas are accessibility, student flows, citizenship, school/work transitions, and satisfaction. Partially in response to the contentious nature of the citizenship debates and of federal fiscal involvement in education, especially that of Human Resources Development, work on the citizenship area was set aside by a ministerial decision in 2000.

45 Bannerji, *The Dark Side of the Nation.*
46 Day, *Multiculturalism.*
47 Henry et al., *The Colour of Democracy: Racism in Canadian Society*; Calliste and Sefa Dei, *Anti-Racist Feminism.*
48 Bancroft et al., *Framework and Issues.*
49 Kymlicka, *Multicultural Citizenship.*
50 Taylor, "Politics of Recognition."
51 Létourneau, « L'affirmationnisme québécois ».
52 Ibid., 33.
53 Stevenson, "The Decline of Consociational Democracy in Canada."
54 Létourneau, « L'affirmationnisme québécois ».
55 Bernard, « La cohésion sociale ».
56 Although this is couched in Rawlsian terms in his 1997 book, *Creating Citizens*, Callan retracts this framework while maintaining his theory of deliberation in "Discrimination and Religious Schooling."
57 Callan, *Creating Citizens*, 175.
58 For a study of complexity in a Toronto high school, see Yon, *Elusive Culture*; for reflections on mixity in France, see Audinet, « Vous avez dit «métis»? ».
59 Government of Canada, Employment Equity Act, 1985.
60 Larochelle, Robichaud, et Tremblay, « Le développement de l'employabilité au Canada ».
61 For example, finding a meaning in life, clarifying one's interests and values, motivating oneself.
62 Larochelle, Robichaud, et Tremblay, « Le développement de l'employabilité ».
63 Possibly the most important educator of the decade, Paulo Freire's work in literacy and democratization is crucial; see his *Pedagogy of the Oppressed*; and his last book, published posthumously, *Pedagogy of Freedom.*
64 Government of Canada, *Programmes and Employment Services*, Vol. LM-158-08-93, 1993, 1.
65 Callan, *Creating Citizens.*
66 Ouellet Benoît, et al., *L'éducation à la citoyenneté dans une perspective mondiale.*
67 Osborne, "Education Is the Best National Insurance."
68 Ibid.

69 Sears and Hughes, "Citizenship Education and Current Educational Reform."

70 Masemann, "Current Status of Teaching about Citizenship."

71 Hébert, Buteau, et Delorme, *Rapports entre apprentissage, identité, communauté, citoyenneté.*

72 Sears, "Social Studies in Canada."

73 Laville et Dionne, *La construction des savoirs.*

74 Martineau et Laville, « L'histoire : voie royale vers la citoyenneté? ».

75 Laurin et Klein, *L'éducation géographique.*

76 Laville, "History Taught in Québec Is Not Really That Different."

77 Martineau et Laville, « L'histoire : voie royale vers la cityoyenneté? ».

78 Le Gal, *Coopérer pour développer la citoyenneté.*

79 Derwing and Munro, *Citizenship Instruction for Adult ESL Learners*; Derwing, "Instilling a Passive Voice"; Hébert, "Research-Based Focus on Literacy and Citizenship Education."

80 Sweeney, « La pédagogie du service », 69–71; Cameron and Varma, "Citizens for a New Century."

81 Orr and McKay, "Living Citizenship through Classroom Community."

82 Smits, "Citizenship Education in Postmodern Times."

83 See Magsino, "From Eclectic Theory to Coherence," in this volume.

84 Johnston, "Dilemmas of Identity and Ideology." Masny, "Meta-Knowledge, Critical Literacy and Minority Language Education."

85 Hébert et al., *Rapports entre apprentissage, identité, communauté, citoyenneté.*

86 Le Gal, *Coopérer pour développer la citoyenneté.*

87 Hébert et al., *Rapports entre apprentissage, identité, communauté, citoyenneté.*

88 Audigier, « Valeurs et enseignement de l'histoire et de la géographie ».

89 Masemann, "Current Status of Teaching about Citizenship."

90 Ouellet, Benoît, et al., *L'éducation à la citoyenneté dans une perspective mondiale*; Delors et al., *L'éducation.*

91 Proposed in Hébert, "Citizenship Education" and applied in Marzouk, Kabano et Coté, *Éducation à la citoyenneté à l'école.*

92 Philippe Perrenoud, *L'évaluation des élèves. De la fabrication de l'excellence à la régulation des apprentissages: Entre deux logiques* (Bruxelles: De Boeck Université, 1998).

93 Clermont Gauthier, « Culture de l'évaluation et professionalisation de l'enseignement ». *Vie pédagogique*, 109 (nov.-déc. 1998): 51–2.

94 Francoeur, « Former des bons citoyens ».

95 Audigier, « Citoyen, civique, citoyenneté ».

96 Clifton and Roberts, *Authority in Classrooms.*

97 Freire, *Pedagogy of Freedom.*

98 See, for example, some of the early work of the Citizenship Education Research Network: Gagnon et Pagé, *Cadre conceptuel d'analyse de la citoyenneté*, 2 vols, available in both French and English; Clarke, and Hughes, "Learning Democracy in a Pluralist Society"; Hébert, Buteau, et Delorme, *Rapports entre apprentissage, identité, communauté, citoyenneté*; as well as Wilkinson and Hébert, "Citizenship Values."

99 See also Delors, *L'éducation : Un trésor est caché dedans*.

Who Counts? Late Nineteenth- and Early Twentieth-Century Struggles about Gender, Race, and Class in Canada

VERONICA STRONG-BOAG

Citizenship education is, ultimately, about who counts and who has counted in the past, today, and in the future. It reveals, at one step removed, both the state of public debate on the meaning of "belonging" to Canada and the relative power of the various actors in that debate. It is not surprising that discussions about citizenship education at the start of the twenty-first century reflect the unsettled nature of relationships, constitutional and otherwise, among Canadians. Groups long disadvantaged as citizens – notably women, visible minorities including First Nations peoples, and workers – are reclaiming their place in Canadian history and their place at constitutional and other tables where the nation's future is determined. This is what Charles Taylor has called "'the politics of recognition' waged by minority or 'subaltern' groups."[1] Feminists and Aboriginal and working-class activists, among others, today point to the hegemonic state's persistent misrecognition of or total blindness to their interests. Whether the specific debate involves land claims, multiculturalism, childcare policy, free trade, citizenship education, recognition of the full humanity, or, more narrowly, the full citizenship of different groups of Canadians is at issue.

The failure of major Canadian institutions to embody in a meaningful way the reality of long-standing diversity has ensured their weakness as national symbols. As the political theorist Raymond Breton has pointed out, "When communities of people cannot recognize themselves in public institutions ... [they] feel that they are strangers in society, that the society is not *their* society."[2] A sense of alienation from what tradition has dictated as "normal" citizenship lies at the heart of the modern Canadian dilemma.[3] In general, until very recently citizenship education has done little to acknowledge the reality of misrecognition and alienation, or what Will Kymlicka has termed "differentiated citizenship."[4] Its traditional preoccupations have largely ignored the consistent shortcomings of claims for so-called universal citizenship. The experience of citizenship education for much of our history has given relatively few Canadians – notably those who are male, European in origin, middle class, heterosexual, able bodied, and so on – reason to feel full members of the nation state that came into being in 1867.[5] An unacknowledged politics of dominance reflects and contributes to the crisis in national legitimacy that we are confronting at the start of the twenty-first century.

The history of citizenship education, then, is the history of failure, of the ultimate failure of largely non-representative institutions to impose their homogeneous and homogenizing vision on diverse communities of citizens. Rejection of the false universalisms of long-standing citizenship theory, which are effectively based, as Iris Marion Young explains, on the privileging of White males,[6] requires us to discover bases of working and living together which do not require the subordination or misrecognition of some voices and the domination and celebration of others. This discovery usefully begins with a revisiting of the past. Whatever students might have concluded from civics texts or the Canadian history which was perceived to be "duller than ditch water," the meaning of citizenship, of belonging, has been hotly contested, passionately argued, and bitterly lost. Indeed, the vigour of our current debates is no greater than that in the decades after Confederation.

Early initiatives in citizenship education were elaborated, in fact, in the context of a fierce battle within a settler colony to determine the contours and meaning of community. The period from 1867 through to the First World War saw some of the very groups who today are seeking to enlarge notions of the public good challenging the country's political elites. Although their insights never entirely disappeared, feminists, First Nations activists, and organized workers emerged as the relative and indeed often the absolute losers in these early struggles to set a national agenda. Not coincidentally, women, Native peoples, and the working class have been largely absent from social studies and other texts in citizenship education which, like the early constitutional debates outlined by Alan Cairns, defined Canadians in terms that were deferential to governing elites.[7] What citizenship education could report, in other words, was one side of a story, a story of the nation from the vantage point of winners, a story with compromising parts left out.

In this chapter I revisit the turn-of-the century struggles of feminists, First Nations peoples, and organized workers.[8] In particular, I am interested in these groups' insistence on speaking for themselves, their claims to a distinctive and meaningful experience, and their belief that the inclusion of their perspective meant something significant for the construction of the young nation. While powerfully disadvantaged in discussions and battles about precisely who counted, and for what, in Canada, they were, nevertheless, self-conscious opponents of legislative and constitutional arrangements that relegated them to inferiority. Like their successors in our own time, turn-of-the-century feminists, Aboriginal leaders, and working-class activists demanded recognition as communities who had the right to expect that their experiences and needs would be embodied in Canadian institutions which were to emerge in the northern half of the continent. Such critics were not readily heard in a society that was simultaneously patriarchal, racist, and classist. Challenges to the dominant narrative that privileged the few against the many were routinely ignored, ridiculed, and punished, often severely. While the views of these groups were not always in accord – indeed at times they found themselves in sharp disagreement, in the process frequently demonstrating their own sexism, racism, or classism[9] – important similarities existed among the different subversive politics they pursued. The claims on Canada of feminists, and self-conscious Natives and workers, with their common preference for pluralism and collaboration rather than assimilation and subjugation, are critical parts of a too often untold story of Canadian citizenship.

Decades of Protest

The decades between Confederation and the First Great War were years of unrest and conflict involving different genders, races, classes, and other groups within the developing settler society. The problems associated with urbanization, immigration, and industrialization mobilized thousands in petitions, associations, strikes, lobbies, and even battles. National and local elites were challenged to defend new and old initiatives in everything from legislation to patronage and school curriculum. Conflicts could be polite, like lengthy discussions between women's groups and school boards about the introduction of domestic science classes; they could be brutal, like the fierce confrontations between capital and labour in the streets and on the picket line and between the prairie tribes and the Canadian military during the 1885 rebellions. As the persisting preoccupation of many Canadian texts with English-French divisions in these years has reiterated, there was little political consensus on many of the crucial issues facing Canadians. Divisions, however, went well beyond those between Anglophones and Francophones or among regions. Women denounced governments and laws that refused to take their interests into account. Native peoples protested the abrogation of their fundamental rights in the rush for western and northern resources. Workers argued that businessmen and industrialists were reaping unfair advantage from technological change and an immigration-fuelled labour market, in the process forcing them and their families into poverty. As the lines became drawn between dominant and oppressed groups in post-Confederation Canada, the political system became a recurring focus for agitation.

For much of Canada's early history, those with most to complain about were, however, least likely to be able to vote. In 1867 the franchise at all levels remained largely restricted to male property holders. Women anywhere generally had no vote until the 1880s, when most provinces gave propertied widows and spinsters the municipal franchise. Status Indians, legal wards of the state, could not vote anywhere. The province of British Columbia disenfranchised Chinese residents and Native Indians in 1874, the Japanese in 1895, and East Indians in 1907. For many years, property qualifications, though gradually lowered, generally kept most unskilled workers and farm labourers off electoral lists. Gender, property, and age restrictions ensured that in 1871 only 15 per cent of Québec's population could vote in provincial or federal elections, and only about 20 per cent had this right by the end of the century. Municipal property qualifications were often stricter still. In 1906 Winnipeg, with a population of over 100,000, registered only 7,784 voters.[10]

Early attempts to widen the basis of franchise to include less privileged White males reflected growing awareness that North America's political realities required more than an electorate limited to elite men. Moves to diversify representation, however, were limited. In 1869, Ottawa passed a bill permitting gradual enfranchisement of male Indians, which effectively required proof of full assimilation to European ways. Later provisions of the Indian Act automatically enfranchised Indians who qualified as doctors, lawyers, and ministers or priests: persons, in other words, who were likely to have embraced a good part of the immigrant imperial culture. The fact that only 102 Indians were enfranchised between 1867 and 1920 reveals the failure of such policies.[11] Franchise restrictions, with their privileging of White and middle-class males, have been conveniently ignored by most later commentators. Despite their significance for political relations, classroom texts in civics routinely failed to take up the questions raised by the very different voting histories of various groups of Canadians.[12] In the process, of course, power and oppression have been rendered invisible and protest has been trivialized or irrationalized. Reformers appear on history's stage as random, somehow inexplicable, even semi-comic phenomena, rather than legitimate responses to sexism, racism, or classism.

Indeed, it can be argued that what is amazing in the face of constant assaults on their credibility and self-esteem, not to mention direct punitive action of all sorts, is that disadvantaged groups and non-hegemonic voices over the course of Canadian history have developed a wide range of strategies both to secure political rights and to influence the political system in general.[13] Feminists, for example, emerged by the mid-nineteenth century as some of the severest and most wide-ranging critics of British North American society and politics. The costs of male privilege were catalogued in detail. Legal, economic, and political disabilities were identified as leaving many women in poverty, as victims of violence, and with little hope of independence or respect.[14] Their plight was mobilizing reformers well before Confederation.[15] The situation of many of the nation's children, especially those who were poor, disabled, or otherwise in distress, likewise encouraged female activism beginning early in the nineteenth century. Moved to remedy abuses by a combination of religious sentiments, desires for social leadership, and the need to feel useful, middle-class women, in particular, championed themselves and, to varying degrees, other victims of prejudice and discrimination. Separate women's groups, such as the Woman's Christian Temperance Union and the Women's Institutes, as well as the appearance of fifty-one new communities of Catholic nuns in Québec between 1837 and 1899, reflected a powerful consciousness of distinctive gender interests and a desire not to have them subordinated to men's agendas.

Many women, Ontario's Emily Stowe and Clara Brett Martin, for example, fought to enter fields dominated by men, such as medicine and law. Like these two feminist pioneers, some women also struggled to reform their new professions, to make them more responsive to women's needs and aspirations. The post-Confederation expansion in female activism inspired the creation in 1893 of a dominion-wide federation, the National Council of Women of Canada. This assembly comprised a diverse groups concerned with issues from temperance to child welfare, rural isolation, working conditions, and suffrage. Women in every province wore themselves out trying to win reforms from reluctant policy makers and voters.[16] Rejecting the oppressive relations that were a matter of course in their society, feminists demanded full rights as citizens to remake the social and political order.

Despite the cautious maternalist politics which often typified the intervention of women's groups, even minor attempts to alter the balance of power at home and in the state roused fervent opposition. Anti-feminists and misogynists in general resisted any change to the advantageous status quo. Victorian notables such as Goldwin Smith, Andrew Macphail, Stephen Leacock, and Henri Bourassa broadcast their hostility to equal treatment in law, education, and politics in newspapers and halls across the country.[17] Proponents of equality took their courage, and sometimes their lives in their hands when they asked for entry into all-male professions, a fair deal in homesteading, better protection for victims of male violence, or full citizenship. While significant advances were made, notably in the campaign for enfranchisement, the struggle for justice in the public and private realms which began in the mid-nineteenth century was far from finished by the time of the Dominion's centennial in 1967. The 1970 *Report of the Royal Commission on the Status of Women* recorded a host of disabilities which still handicapped one sex.

Like feminist campaigns, Native protest was also a marked feature of Canadian life at the turn of the century. White settlers had been encroaching on Indian lands for many years, but after 1867 pressure increased, fuelled by, inter alia, rising levels of racial prejudice and mounting immigration. While the Aboriginal inhabitants of Canada and the Maritimes had long faced desperate conditions and a routine disregard for their rights and welfare, Canadian expansion into the Northwest and Pacific regions highlighted yet again the failure of governments of any political stripe to deal fairly with the land's original inhabitants. It is fair to say that leaders such as John A. Macdonald, Alexander Mackenzie, and Wilfrid Laurier, not to mention their provincial counterparts, made little or no effort to cooperate with Native peoples in designing the fundamental contours of the nation they were establishing. Instead, every move to expand the Canadian empire brought the federal government into new conflicts with First Nations peoples about territory and sovereignty, the same flashpoints which had already provoked strong protests from the Iroquois Confederacy, among other tribes, in the east.[18]

The transfer of the Northwest from the Hudson's Bay Company to Canada in 1869, with no consultation with either the Indian or EuroIndian[19] population, helped to incite the Red River Rebellion and the EuroIndian Provisional Government under Louis Riel. Although the

Manitoba Act of 1870, which created a postage-stamp-size province, supposedly provided a negotiated settlement, federal troops followed to guarantee EuroIndian and Indian acquiescence. In the next decade, Ottawa tried to avoid other such contests by negotiating treaties with First Nations peoples of the region. Promises of land and assistance in farming were readily compromised, however, by politicians who were eager to promote White settlement and were generally indifferent to the Indians' plight. Confined to a decreasing land base and facing the disappearance of their staple resource, the buffalo, starving Indians and EuroIndian peoples were not, however, readily pacified.[20] Resistance ranged from private acts – rustling and refusals to accept eviction from tribal lands – to collective defiance. Cree chiefs, Big Bear and Poundmaker in particular but others as well, played key roles in attempting to communicate distress to Ottawa and its officials and in rallying Natives. Reasoned appeals to White Canada, however, found little sympathy. It is not surprising that some Indian leaders, seeing the starvation and distress of their people, were increasingly disinclined to wait and hope for a better deal from Ottawa and its allies. In 1884 almost 2,000 Cree gathered outside Battleford, the capital of the North-West Territories to demand promised rations. In that same year Indian councils gathered around the prairies as the Cree demonstrated their growing cohesion and desperation.

They were not alone. When their grievances were similarly ignored by Ottawa, the Saskatchewan EuroIndians became increasingly receptive to armed solutions. In despair, they invited Louis Riel again to champion their cause; the stage was set for the disaster of Batoche, Riel's execution, and the ultimate collapse of EuroIndian hopes. Before it died, however, the second Riel rebellion roused Cree leaders and their followers, who seized territory and the opportunity to take revenge on White abusers. Even then, calmer voices tried to counsel moderation, but they could rarely prevail over long-standing anger and distress. For their part in the 1885 Rebellion, the Indians ultimately paid far more heavily than the EuroIndians. Eight Aboriginal leaders were executed, three were handed life sentences, and many others, including the moderates, Big Bear and Poundmaker, were given shorter prison terms – which for many ultimately meant a death sentence. Unlike Riel's hanging, which inflamed English-French passions, few White Canadians appeared to care about the fate of the western tribes; all were to be disregarded and discarded in Canada's settlement of the western frontier, itself an expression of the European imperialism of the day.

The major goal of subsequent federal Indian policy became the removal of Natives from their lands without provoking another revolt. Racist policies in everything from residential schools to restrictive homestead and enfranchisement regulations, however, were doomed by Aboriginal unwillingness either to assimilate or to disappear. In 1885 Indians east of Lake Superior were offered the vote if they gave up Indian status; few did, because they recognized, as one later commentator put it, that doing so meant "self-alienation."[21] Measures to curb Indian freedom and suppress traditional ceremonies, such as the Sun Dance and the Potlatch, were regularly defied. However resourceful and industrious Natives might be in seeking to combine long-standing and newer practices in efforts at individual and community survival, massive White resistance to equality, which ranged from theft of reserve lands to discriminatory wages, consigned the vast majority to marginal status and citizenship. While individual and collective protests were commonplace, Indian voices were heard at best only intermittently by the nation's governing elites.[22] Continuing Native determination to decide their own fate in any joint future through collective action was routinely suppressed by the federal Department of Indian Affairs well into the twentieth century.[23] It is hardly surprising that, as one later commentator has pointed out, "Canadian mythology [which] portrays a transition from ally to subject to ward to citizen" is commonly referred to as "the Big Lie" by First Nations peoples.[24]

Canada's gender and race politics in the years from Confederation to the First Great War were matched by the hostility shown to workers' rights. In recurring confrontations in the workplace and the political arena, Ottawa and its allies in the provincial capitals routinely defended the rights of capital against labour. The benefits of industry and resource development were assigned as a matter of course to White and middleclass males. Such men, in turn, were likely to explain their good fortune not by any acknowledgment of such privileges but by reference to their hard work, skill, and divine providence.[25] As they reaped the hard lessons of "economic progress," which too often entailed greater profits for the few and tough times for the many, wage workers across the country became increasingly self-conscious and active on their own behalf. When individual acts of rebellion proved insufficient, working people built on early cooperative traditions. Craft and eventually industrial unions emerged to present collective demands to employers, to provide mutual aid, and to lobby governments. Hostility from business and government combined with recurring depressions to make survival always difficult and uncertain. Technological change doomed some craftsmen, such as the coopers or barrel-makers, who finally could fight only a rearguard action against obsolescence; the more fortunate, such as the moulders and the typographers, struggled to continue the craft union movement into the twentieth century. Whether they survived for the short or the long term, unionists laboured to control the impact of mechanization and to win a fair return for energy and skills. The situation was especially desperate for those designated unskilled, whose payment for hard and dangerous toil could well be, as was true for many of the Chinese workers who built the transcontinental railway, death and disability.

Working women and men had no easy time of it in winning recognition for their right to organize on their own behalf. Not until the Trades Union Act of 1872 did prohibitions against unions as combinations in restraint of trade disappear. Even then, the law's provisions were so loaded in favour of capital that they legalized only those unions that assumed liability for the individual acts of their members. Despite determined resistance from government and employers, thousands of workers fought to be recognized as more than mere hands, capital's human instruments, but as human beings with a full range of needs. Demands for the nine-hour day in the 1870s, a work day that would allow time for leisure and family life, reflected this determination. In the ensuing decades, strikes became a common weapon in campaigns to improve living and labouring standards.

The Knights of Labour, a reform organization emphasizing cooperation and education that originated in 1869 in the United States, spread across Canada in the 1880s. Dedicated to organizing wage-earners regardless of race, skill, or gender, the Knights articulated an emerging class consciousness and an idealistic awareness of the value of labour in all its forms. Their appeal roused many ordinary Canadians who found little to inspire them in the nationalist rhetoric of politicians. Unlike the older craft unions, the Knights organized entire industries. By the late 1880s Canadian Knights, 16,000 in number, included locals of shoemakers, barbers, women tailors, and journalists. In the same decade, the growing contrast between rich and poor and between the power of the few and the poverty of the many also encouraged a rapid rise in the number of labour organizations in general, from 165 to 760. In the 1890s their story was sadder. Hounded by employer opposition and hard times, the Knights ultimately failed. Their dream of a coalition of brain and hand workers never completely disappeared, however, finding new expression in the progressive politics that increasingly captured workers' imaginations.[26]

For unionists, the beginning of the twentieth century belonged largely to craft-based groups like the Trades and Labour Congress of Canada. Organization of any kind, while nominally legal, nevertheless remained fiercely opposed by most employers and viewed with considerable suspicion by most governments. Strikes against bad wages and conditions routinely called out local police and militia, who used clubs and horses to defend the established order by breaking up gatherings and pickets. The radicalism of the western labour movement as it evolved with the Western Federation of Miners and Industrial Workers of the World spoke directly to these bitter confrontations. In the decades before the First World War, the working class, already fragmented by gender and race, was further divided by changing immigration and growing regionalism. Labour militancy and class conflict nevertheless continued, feeding the nascent socialist and labourite parties of the same period. These parties, together with organized labour, articulated visions of Canada which went substantially beyond those proposed by the country's soi-disant leaders.[27]

As this all too brief introduction to the politics of difference has indicated, late nineteenth- and early twentieth-century Canada was a land of divided allegiances and deep-seated divisions that went well beyond those between Ottawa and the provinces and English and French Canada. Many groups of Canadians organized and protested discrimination and disadvantage at the hands of elites. Feminists, Natives, and workers were among those who recognized that governments elected under the old rules were rarely fully committed to their interests. Their battles for recognition and change were frequent and costly. Gains, such as woman suffrage, better provisions in some treaties, and the legal recognition of unions, nonetheless were critical in broadening and humanizing notions of common citizenship in a highly polarized world that was at best reluctant to acknowledge the contribution of women, Natives, and workers.

While each of these three groups was distinctive in many ways and far from homogeneous within themselves, certain general assumptions about living together, or citizenship in a common state, often surfaced. In the first instance, all tended to argue that they best spoke for themselves. No other group, however well intentioned, ultimately could adequately represent their interests. Secondly, women, Natives, and workers were credited with distinctive experiences, including (but not only) oppression, which gave meaning and specificity to their identity and views. Outsiders' understanding of their situation was inherently limited by a lack of a common experiential base. Finally, these groups believed, or at least hoped, that appropriate recognition of their voices and opinions would mean a difference, not only to their lives and those of their communities, but to Canada itself. As we shall see in the brief review of these arguments which follows, the common emphasis was on collaboration and partnership, not on assimilation and conformity. Feminists and self-conscious Natives and workers wished to contribute their distinctiveness to the creation of new arrangements for living together, not to disappear in the shadow of the old.

No One Else Speaks for Us

Alienated from political elites by gender, race, or class, dissidents repeatedly insisted on their right to speak for themselves. Since the Confederation debates and the union itself were, like their earlier counterpart to the south, the products of the aspirations of White, middle-class males, the fledgling Dominion soon encountered problems of legitimacy. The conviction that they were not well served by existing authorities was implicit in decisions by marginalized groups to organize separately and in the creation of distinctive women's, Native, and workers' presses.[28] As feminist women became more experienced in running their own groups, they increasingly questioned men's ability to speak validly about the concerns of their sex. As one defender of women and their rights to education and employment bluntly expressed it in 1879, "Very plainly, woman herself alone can tell what her true sphere is."[29] Such opinions were not unusual among critics of the status quo. On the Prairies, in the course of negotiating treaties, Native speakers made it very clear to any who would listen that they alone were properly consulted on what their people needed. White traders, government officials, and missionaries might have uses, but Indians were the ultimate interpreters and champions of their position. In 1870 one chief of the Fort Pitt Crees explained collective resistance to others' deciding their fate: "We hear our lands were sold and we do not like it; we don't want to sell our lands; it is our property, and no one has the right to sell them."[30] Recognition that changes in White-Indian relations had occurred without their informed consent explained the determination of Aboriginal leaders to take their collective case as far as the Crown and eventually to the League of Nations and the United Nations.

As class conflict deepened in the 1880s, self-conscious workers also repudiated paternalistic political regimes, together with their producer ideology, which presumed their acquiescence in the decision making of others. Tories and Grits, long accustomed to the politics of deference, had greater difficulty finding reliable labour men who had a following and who would, in turn, accept elite leadership and definition of issues. The growth in the insistence that workers should best speak for workers fuelled the radical class politics of the age. In the 1880s Cape Breton's Provincial Workmen's Association acted on such conclusions by running its own candidates for the Nova Scotia House of Assembly. In 1903 the Trades and Labour Congress of Canada endorsed independent political action.[31] While Native peoples confronted still greater odds in finding an official platform for their representatives, women and workers began slowly to appear as candidates and, occasionally, as winners in elections at every level across the country.

As their experience of the politics of the new nation deepened, Canada's subaltern groups became extremely critical of outsiders presumptuous enough to claim to represent their interests. In speaking of the "New Citizenship," for example, Nellie McClung, perhaps the most famous of Canada's suffragists, rejected the pretensions of men, especially male professionals, who assumed they knew women's best interests. In noting that "Women have never yet lived in their own world. Man has assigned woman her sphere. Woman's sphere is anything a man does not wish to do himself ... Men have given a great deal of attention to women. They have told us exactly what we are like. They have declared us to be illogical, hysterical, impulsive, loving, patient, forgiving, malicious, vindictive, bitter, not any too honest, not very reliable,"[32] she was explaining why women best told their own stories. In her feminist classic, *In Times Like These* (1915), she urged women, especially those favoured by material prosperity, to speak up on behalf of others of their sex. Women and the nation itself would be immeasurably poorer if men continued to monopolize decision making.

Representatives of Canadian workers similarly urged their constituency to wake up to their self-interest. The argument was typically made by the Ontario labour newspaper, the *Industrial Banner*, when it explained, "the working classes must work out their own salvation ... if they have gained concessions in the past it was because they were in a position to demand them and able to enforce the demand."[33] Similar conclusions moved a union advocate of the nine-hour day in 1872, when he emphasized that "Working men must become a power in the land, and send to the legislature men who knew what ten hours of work was."[34] As such comments suggest, critics of governing elites rejected the long-standing politics of dominance that assumed their acquiescence to the authority of others. Hard experience in the post-Confederation decades gave subaltern groups good reason to insist on the importance of speaking for themselves and to oppose the usurpation of that power by others.

Our Experience Is Distinctive

Insistence on self-representation was fuelled by a belief in the distinctive-ness of much group experience. Like post-colonial critics of the period and later, feminists and Native and working-class activists attempted to rewrite and realign history "from the point of view of the victims of its destructive progress."[35] Central to women's, Natives,' and workers' un-derstanding of their lives was the value they placed on day-to-day contri-butions to the life of the larger human community. Surrounded by critics and commentators, from professionals to politicians, who rou-tinely portrayed them as lazy, useless, weak or degenerate, representa-tives of marginalized groups defended the substance of their experience and claimed significance and value for contributions which others dis-torted or dismissed. Housework, childcare, routines of hunting and gathering, physical toil, and specialized workplace knowledges typically were defended as meaningful and valuable. Feminists, for instance, pointed to women's maternal and domestic responsibilities as essential to family and Canadian well-being in general. In giving birth to and rearing children, by keeping families healthy and happy, women matched men's labour and contributions. Such work, whether decreed by nature or culture – and there was disagreement on this point in feminist ranks – gave women specialized talents and sensitivities and prepared them to play distinctive roles as national housekeepers and nurturers.

Like their feminist contemporaries, Native leaders interpreted the practices of their people as a source of strength and pride. As the Mohawk writer E. Pauline Johnson said in defence of her community, "put a pure-blooded Indian in the drawing room ... he will shine with the best of you."[36] Interpersonal relations, including those between women and men and children and adults, particular patterns of resource de-pendence and extraction, and the religious values of North America's Aboriginal groups were regularly highlighted as worthy of mention. Traditional rituals and ceremonies were defended. On the West Coast, Ottawa's banning of the Potlatch drew an explanation from Nootka

Chief Maquinna, in which he tried to make sense of the practice in terms that White Canadians could appreciate: "Once I was in Victoria, and I saw a very large house; they told me it was a bank and that the white men place their money there to take care, and that by-and-by they got it back, with interest. We are Indians, and we have no such bank; but when we [have] plenty of money or blankets, we give them away to other chiefs and people, and by-and- by they return them, with interest, and our heart feels good. Our Potlatch is our bank."[37] History also supplied proof, if more was needed, of the merits of Aboriginal life. Homage to heroes like the Mohawk Joseph Brant and the Seneca Red Jacket countered the negative stereotypes favoured by White authors of the period.[38]

Champions of Native inheritance were also prepared to take on the pretensions of their critics. European traditions which failed to match those of Aboriginal communities might well be publicly criticized. One example of the ability to take full measure of their opponents was the criticism, by members of the Six Nations Confederacy, of Canada's all-male suffrage. As Deskaheh, Chief of the Bear Clan of the Cayuga Nation, pointed out to European Canadians, "Our Mothers have always had a hand in government."[39] In this instance, as in others, White Canada had something to learn. The obvious lesson was the superiority of some new combination of practices and values that would affirm egalitarian rather than hierarchical relationships between immigrant and founding societies.

Canadian workers shared other critics' determination to defend the basic fabric of their lives. While under assault from middle-class commentators who were quick to condemn the practices of other classes in everything from child rearing to work habits, champions identified the shortcomings of working-class life as a direct product not so much of human failure but of capitalism's unequal distribution of power and resources.[40] They were also likely to emphasize that working-class men and women defied hardship in maintaining qualities of life and living that drew on deep reserves of character, endurance, and industry. Like other advocates of the oppressed in their times and ours, devoted champions sometimes romanticized or idealized victims in their efforts to counter the calumnies which the dominant society, in its sexist, racist, and classist manifestations, regularly uttered. Such defence of subordinated cultures was nonetheless deeply subversive in its questioning of elite standards, its offering of alternative lifestyles, and its vindication of women, Natives, and workers.

We Make a Difference to Canada

Outsiders appraising an evolving political system and structures with which they had substantial disagreement were, naturally enough, likely to suggest that their inclusion would change matters for the better. Turn-of-the-century critics proposed visions – albeit inchoate and often uncertain of alternative realities which offered them and people like them the "fair deal" they so largely found missing in Canada. They demanded hearings and inclusion because they believed that the world they shaped would be different from and preferable to that being constructed by the governing elites in their own interests. They did not want to melt into an indistinguishable mass of Canadians. Dissidents like Nellie McClung summed up the recurring demand for public, as well as private, roles in the creation of society. Women, as she reminded her readers, might be "cooks and housemaids and home makers and dressmakers and nurses, but they are something more, they are citizens."[41] The old, unjust ways of organizing society would have to go. In the words of the National Council of Women, women wished to apply "the Gold Rule to society, custom and law."[42] Once enfranchised and empowered as political agents, women would bring, feminists trusted, all their qualities of altruism, nurturance, and industry to bear on the public realm to everyone's ultimate advantage.

Hopes for the new world could be high. Dr Augusta Stowe-Gullen, a suffrage pioneer who remained on the front line of much progressive thinking, set forth feminism's aspirations at their most generous: "Equity knows no sex, no class, no color. Invidious distinctions held and perpetuated, whether between man and woman, or one class of society over another, are not in accordance with basic principles, and the country, race and civilization, which is unmindful of the true spirit of ethics – will ultimately sink into oblivion."[43] Here was a revolutionary banner of equality which not all feminists adopted. Such radical views were nevertheless integral to at least part of the feminist vision for the better nation that would come about through women's full participation.

High aspirations also characterized First Nations' speakers trying to challenge racism in these years. The new confederacy, basically an alliance between and among groups, that they hoped to see come into being would be greater because of contribution from Aboriginal peoples. The Mohawk writer E. Pauline Johnson put the case for inclusion very plainly in regard to the Sioux, her heroic hunters of the plains:

"King Edward of England has no better subjects; and I guess it is all the same to His Majesty whether a good subject dresses in buckskin or broadcloth."[44] One Iroquois veteran of the First World War and proponent of Indian unity, Frederick Ogilvie Loft, articulated the moral basis for a more inclusive politics in arguing that Natives "have the right to claim and demand more justice and fair play ... for we, too, have fought for the sacred rights of justice, freedom and liberty so dear to mankind, now matter what their colour or creed."[45] For such speakers, allegiance to the monarchy – indeed, to the empire – permitted a pluralism in a way that W.L. Morton argued in his classic text, *The Canadian Identity* (1961). Here was the basis for an inclusive politics.

Working-class activists also looked forward to the day when they could assume greater responsibilities in the management of their country. In fact, the time needed to prepare for responsible citizenship was a feature of the arguments presented during the campaigns for the nine-hour work day in the 1870s. Advocates argued "that the time thus gained is necessary to enable us to improve our education, in order to fulfil with credit to ourselves and advantage to the State, the various duties and responsibilities of Fathers and Citizens."[46] Repeated conflict with dominant elites made other representatives of labour less optimistic. Statements from the Knights of Labour, for example, smacked less of the older deferential politics. One speaker before the Hamilton Assembly in 1885 summed up a more revolutionary agenda: "It is the work of modern chivalry in the persons of the Knights of Labor to save the nation from the fate that threatens it, a fate which, if it comes to pass, will be brought about by the war of irreconcilable elements in society. It is the duty of modern chivalry to champion the oppressed, to wage war against tyranny, and to elevate the type of manhood. It is a nobler chivalry than that of the Knights-errant fold for it knows no race, no color, no creed, and it labors for the cause of humanity everywhere."[47] The values of bourgeois Canada were not, such speakers trusted, to determine the meaning of the future all were to share.

A further component of the politics of difference expounded by these and other anti-hegemonic groups was an allegiance to, or identification with, supra-national communities. Feminists and Native and working-class activists regularly looked outside Canada for support, inspiration, and instruction. Suffragists such as Emmeline Pankhurst and Susan B. Anthony, like their counterparts in the Native and working-class protest movements of the day, criss-crossed the country on a regular basis. Identification with similar groups elsewhere fed both anti-nationalism (in other words, a refusal to identify narrowly with Canada) and, more positively, internationalism. Thus, the three groups treated here contributed, at least potentially, greater "world-mindedness," based on cooperation and shared interests, as opposed to the oppression and inequality that characterized imperial relations, to any collaborative enterprise they joined.[48]

As such heady sentiments indicated, turn-of-the-century Canada was alive with advocates of progressive reforms: individuals and groups who proposed fairer ways of constructing a country. Feminists and Native and working-class activists challenged conventions that consigned them and those they represented to alienation, despair, and powerlessness. They insisted that progress did not require their silence, or assimilation, or agreement with the plans and schemes of the country's rulers. Indeed, if given an opportunity, they promised to make a fresh start, to build as Nellie McClung suggested the "Land of the Second Chance." To be sure, persecution and pragmatism, as well as their own gendered, racial, and class prejudices, meant that activists did not always live up to the ideals of a more inclusive citizenship. Such shortcomings, while real enough, should not blind us to the promise of a fully realized citizenship. Canadian democracy was the loser when women's, Native, and working-class movements went down to defeat.

Resistance to Canada's imperfect democracy from feminists, Natives, and workers has ebbed and flowed since Confederation, but it has never disappeared. Today's lack of consensus is nothing new. The continuing reality of their dialogues about power, about who we are as a people, is a central element in the history of Canadian citizenship. When it has attempted to manufacture consensus, or patriotism, through the propagation of elite myths about inclusiveness and the sharing of power, citizenship education has ignored a more fundamental reality. When it gives way to the temptation to tell the story from the vantage point of the winners, a tendency that, as in most accounts of our past, has been only too common, we are no closer to discovering an educational or any other agenda which can take Canadians into the next century. In its origins, citizenship education, as the vehicle of a dominant politics, chooses for the most part to ignore the claims on Canada of non-dominant groups. Fortunately, for some time there have been signs that this situation is changing. Citizenship education, like Canada itself, faces the challenge of incorporating non-dominant groups into a new politics. For both education and the country this process requires a collaborative politics of pluralism, of equality and difference, rather than a politics of assimilation or subordination to false universals. It is a message which feminists, Natives, and workers have tried to deliver for a long time, and this effort, too, needs to be acknowledged.

Notes

1 Taylor, "The Politics of Recognition," 25.
2 Raymond Breton, "Multiculturalism and Canadian Nation-Building," in Cairns and Williams, *Politics of Gender, Ethnicity and Language*, 31.
3 On the failure of citizenship in general in Canada, see the essays in Kaplan, *Belonging*.
4 On some of the problems in citizenship education, see Sears, "Social Studies as Citizenship Education in English Canada." See also Kymlicka, *Recent Work in Citizenship Theory*; and Kymlicka and Norman, *Citizenship in Diverse Societies*.
5 On the Eurocentric nature of citizenship education and the curriculum in general, see Tomkins, *Common Countenance*, especially chap. 7.
6 Young, "Polity and Group Difference."
7 Cairns, "Introduction. Whose Side Is the Past On?," unpublished manuscript, 5. On the shortcomings of Canadian history with regard to gender, race, and class, see Strong-Boag, "Presidential Address. Contested Space: the Politics of Canadian Memory," *Journal of the Canadian Historical Association* (1995).
8 This chapter has been produced with the support of the SSHRCC through its funding of the UBC-based research project, "The Construction of Canada: The Changing Meaning of 'Race' and Gender 1860s–1990s."
9 Critics have emphasized these shortcomings. See, for example, Bacchi, *Liberation Deferred?*
10 See Conrad, Finkel, with Strong-Boag, *History of the Canadian Peoples*, 26.
11 Johnston, "First Nations and Canadian Citizenship."
12 On some of the problems such different political histories raise, see Alan Cairns, "The Fragmentation of Canadian Citizenship," in Kaplan, *Belonging*.
13 On earlier non-voting strategies to effect political results, see Campbell, "Disfranchised but Not Quiescent."
14 See Dubinsky, *Improper Advances*, and Bradbury, *Working Families*.
15 See Prentice, et al., *Canadian Women*, chap. 7.
16 On this point, see Prentice et al., *Canadian Women*, sect. II.
17 On anti-feminism, see Strong-Boag, "Independent Women and Problematic Men."

18 On the failure to deal fairly with the Eastern and Central Canadian tribes, see Mary A. Druke, "Iroquois and Iroquoian in Canada," and Virginia Miller, "The Micmac: A Maritime Woodland Group," in Morrison and Wilson, *Native Peoples*.

19 EuroIndian, the counterpart to Eurasian, is used in this paper to designate groups and individuals who have been commonly referred to as "mixed race" or "mixed blood" in Canada, that is, the product of Indian and European unions.

20 On the desperation, see Carter, *Lost Harvest*.

21 Johnston, "First Nations and Canadian Citizenship," 361.

22 On the history of Canadian Aboriginal populations, see Dickason, *Canada's First Nations*.

23 See Titley, *A Narrow Vision*.

24 Johnston, "First Nations and Canadian Citizenship," 349.

25 See Bliss, *Living Profit*.

26 See Kealey and Palmer, *Dreaming of What Might Be*.

27 On working-class protest in general, see Palmer, *Working-Class Experience*.

28 See, for women, inter alia, *Le Coin de Feu, Le Journal de Françoise, Freyja*, and *The Champion*; for Natives, *The Indian, Our Forest Children, Canadian Indian, Petaubrun (Peep of Day), Pipe of Peace, Na-Na-Kwa:* or *Dawn on the Coast, Kamloops Wawa* (Petrone, *Native Literature*, 84–5); and for labour, the *Industrial Banner, Cotton's Weekly, Western Clarion, Canadian Labor Reformer*, and the *Palladium of Labor*.

29 "The Woman Question," *The Canadian Monthly and National Review II* (May 1879), in Cook and Mitchinson, *The Proper Sphere*, 56.

30 Abraham Wikaskokiseyin ("Sweetgrass") as cited in Dickason, *Canada's First Nations*, 298.

31 See McKay, "'By Wisdom, Wile or War,'" and Babcock, *Gompers in Canada*, chap. 11.

32 McClung, "The New Citizenship," quoted in Cook and Mitchinson, *The Proper Sphere*, 289.

33 *Industrial Banner* (London, Ont.), February 1897, in *The Working Man in the Nineteenth Century*, ed. M.S. Cross (Toronto: Oxford University Press, 1974), 309.

34 Quoted in Battye, "'Nine Hour Pioneers,'" 33.

35 Ashcroft, Griffiths, and Tiffin, *The Empire Writes Back*, 34.

36 Quoted in Keller, *Pauline*, 112.

37 Nootka Chief Maquinna as quoted in Petrone, *Native Literature*, 92.

38 See Monkman, *Native Heritage*.

39 Quoted in Petrone, *Native Literature*, 104.

40 See Newton, *The Feminist Challenge to the Canadian Left*, passim.
41 McClung, "The New Citizenship," in Cook and Mitchinson, *The Proper Sphere*, 292.
42 Quoted in Prentice et al., *Canadian Women*, 180.
43 Dr Stowe-Gullen, "Woman as Citizen," 1904, in Cook and Mitchinson, *The Proper Sphere*, 259.
44 Johnson, "A Night with North Eagle," in Van Steen, *Pauline Johnson*, 263.
45 Frederick O. Loft, 1919, quoted in Petrone, *Native Literature*, 101.
46 Quoted in Battye, "Nine Hour Pioneers," 29.
47 Quoted in Palmer, *Culture in Conflict*, 174.
48 On the internationalism of feminism, see Strong-Boag, "Peace-Making Women."

From Eclectic Theory to Coherence: Citizenship Virtues for Our Time

ROMULO F. MAGSINO

Citizenship as a Problematic Notion

Citizenship has received increased prominence in political discourse in the last fifteen years. The term itself has been defined in a variety of ways,[1] however, and whether an underlying conception is identifiable remains a problem.[2] In his historical examination of the notion of citizenship, R. Freeman Butts attempts to identify the essence of citizenship by highlighting two elements that have coalesced and come down to us as the received conception of citizenship. In his words: "(1) Citizenship was based upon membership in a political community regulated by man-made laws rather than upon membership in a family, a clan, or tribe ... and (2) ... citizenship meant that the laws were made, administered, and judged by free citizens who were both rulers and ruled, not merely subjects of a king or priest who made or revealed the laws. In the first case citizenship entailed rights and responsibilities conferred by law (achieved status) in contrast to roles and obligations conferred by inherited class, kinship, or sex (ascribed status). In the second case the free citizens were members of a democratic or republican political community in which the citizen class participated actively in the affairs of the state."[3] These elements appear to have been assumed as common components of citizenship in the writings of contemporary political theorists. In recent years, they are obvious in the works of writers such as Galston, who noted that the purpose of civic education is "the formation of individuals who can effectively conduct their lives within, and support, their political community," and that "If citizenship means anything, it means a package of benefits and burdens shared, and accepted, by all."[4] The two components are also implied in R. Beiner's view of citizenship as a "form of attachment to a political community," which implies "the capacity to give effect to this attachment through various kinds of competent social, legal, and political praxis."[5] Simply, the citizen is a bearer of rights and responsibilities in a political community in which he/she is a participant.

It is worth noting, however, that this conception is a preferred product following the sociopolitical and historical developments experienced in democratic countries. As J.G.A. Pocock points out,[6] the first notion of citizenship exercised by the ancient Greeks was articulated by Aristotle in his *Politics*. This notion was embedded in the belief that, as intelligent and purposive beings, humans naturally direct, and desire to direct, their actions towards some purpose. Naturally inclined to pursue their purposes and actions in a social environment, individuals developed their fullest potential as humans in the political arena. In his words, "Therefore the citizen rules and is ruled; citizens join each other in making decisions where each decider respects the authority of the others, and all join in obeying the decisions." The subsequent predominance of the Roman civilization eventually brought about a conception of the citizen as a legal being rather than a politically active being. It reflected the Roman orientation, in which taking and maintaining possession was viewed as the distinctive mark of the person who was, by nature, a proprietor or possessor of things. Thus, citizenship came to be associated with possession of things and the practice of jurisprudence. Hence, the Roman notion of the citizen referred to "someone free to act by law, free to ask and expect the law's protection, a citizen of such a legal community of such and such a legal standing in that community."[7]

Clearly, Butts combines the Greek and Roman conceptions in his assumed conception of citizenship. This conception undoubtedly commends itself in a democratic society like ours, in which the citizen generally is seen as a rights holder and participant in political processes. As Pocock observes,[8] the eclipse of the Greek conception, with its emphasis on political participation, and the ascendancy of the Roman conception redefined the citizen as a legal entity who was more a ruled subject than an involved political actor engaged with others in the active determination of decisions and actions for the polity as a whole. As long as the citizen was a member of the community and partook of certain protected rights to ensure his/her well-being and enjoyment of material possessions, it was immaterial whether he/she ruled or was ruled, was directly involved or merely represented, or was active or passive in the exercise of participatory political rights. Each of these two conceptions, one emphasizing active participation and the other the enjoyment of rights (particularly social and economic), predominated under a particular political regime. Historically the Roman conception has been exemplified in countries under the ideological sway of fascistic and/or totalitarian governments which professed to work for the well-being of the masses even as they denied the people their participation rights in political processes.

However, the predominance of one conception or the other does not depend on ideological considerations alone. Socio-economic forces in modern history, deriving from the increasing availability and influence of property, enlarged economies, and the growth in size, needs, and power of the state, have also engendered the prominence of the Roman conception. P. Riesenberg depicts the relationship between these forces and the consequent conception of citizenship they foster. He characterizes the first conception as moralistic, idealistic, spiritual, active, participatory, communitarian, and even heroic, and as particularly suited to a relatively small and intimate polis where politics was intense and one was not considered a citizen until he/she was seen to participate in it. He depicts the other, for him the dominant conception after the French Revolution, as the conception which presupposes a state constitution acceptable to all its people, which thrives in big industrialized states and expects not much more than financial support from the merchant or labourer as adequate evidence of commitment to community membership. At the same time, it protects individuals' rights to pursue their own goods. Riesenberg reveals his own preference as follows: "Subjectively, the difference between the first and the second citizenships may be perceived as one of stance. Under the first, in its most challenging and uplifting formulations, man always leaned into the action summoned by notions of virtue. The good citizen recognized the importance of his personal contribution to the public good and gave it his commitment. Under the second, man, now mass man and woman, leans backwards away. He or she, now enticed by private distractions, often fails to grasp the potentiality for moral growth in the activities prescribed for citizenship."[9] Riesenberg's description, obviously in favour of participatory citizenship, exhibits the concern widely expressed about the character of societal membership in contemporary society.[10] Yet, as the history of the transplantation of citizenship from the old world to North America illustrates, the second conception has prevailed, despite the strong initial influence of the first conception upheld by the republican political theorists in the American colonies.[11] Bellah et al. struck a responsive chord when they documented the problems associated with individualism particularly in relation to the sense of community in the United States.[12]

In Canada, concern is reflected in P. Resnick's query: "How much attention are citizens prepared to give to public affairs, to the well-being of the *res publica,* in a period when private pursuits and economic development seem to dominate?"[13] Earlier, J. Crispo had issued an insistent call for citizens' willingness to take up the challenge.[14] Having enumerated pressing national problems, he summons his fellow Canadian citizens to develop the will to meet them and develop a competitive yet compassionate society. This call takes on a particular sense of urgency because of a number of developments in the country. Cairns identifies some of these developments, as follows: (1) the weaning of Canada from Britain, which has given rise to basic questions of sovereignty, identity, and entitlements; (2) globalization, which has problematized the links and allegiances of individuals to their society or community; (3) the threatened break-up of Canada, which has confronted each one with the question, "to which sort of political community do I give my commitment?"; (4) continuing and increased need for immigration, which necessitates bridging the links between "old" and "new" immigrants and ensuring that clear citizenship expectations are understood by recent arrivals; (5) the attenuation of deference to authority and elites, which makes compliance to established order on the part of citizens problematic; and (6) the arrival of the Charter of Rights and Freedoms, which has given individuals and minority groups a strong yet ambiguous instrument needed to pursue their entitlements and visions of the good life.[15]

The renewed interest in citizenship, however, has not been accompanied by agreement on the rights and responsibilities of citizens and groups or by any easy resolution of the role of government and citizens in the sociopolitical life of the country. This problem has become acute in multicultural democracies marked by diversity in beliefs, values, lifestyles, as well as the traditions lived by individuals, groups, and regional configurations within society. Such differences have resulted in conflicting views not only about the citizen's rights and responsibilities, but also about the corresponding roles of government and its legitimate agencies. The Charter of Rights and Freedoms, which recognizes individual and group rights, opened the way for Canadians to test the limits of their constitutional entitlements not only in the political realm but also in the courts of law. The consequent fragmentation of constitutional discourse, which Cairns has chronicled with grave concern,[16] is symptomatic of the difficulty of determining the specific content of the citizen's rights and responsibilities and of circumscribing governmental powers and institutions in relation to them. Given this fragmentation, which pervades not only in the law but also in our political and cultural life, how are we to ascertain the citizen's entitlements and obligations and the roles that government and citizens ought to play in the political realm?

The Debate between Liberalism and Communitarianism

Currently, a number of theoretical perspectives are competing to provide answers to this question. Predominant thus far, the liberal perspective assumes not only the plurality but also the incommensurability of goods in life and society.[17] Given this assumption, liberalism places its faith in the individual to determine for him/herself goods to value and life projects to pursue. Consequently, liberalism emphasizes the individual's capacity to transcend group or collective identity, to break the shackles of fixed identity, and to redefine personal goals and purposes. From the liberal perspective, freedom takes the pole position in any system of values. The consequence for government is clear. Insofar as values, goods, and preferred lifestyles are plural and incommensurable and thus are to be determined by individual choice, government must take the stance of neutrality with respect to their adoption or non-adoption by individuals, groups, or society as a whole. The task of government is to secure an environment in which each individual, group, or society could pursue self-defined projects and aspirations. To ensure that individuals pursue their own goods, the task of the state is not only to remain neutral with respect to these goods, but also to ensure that individuals' pursuit of their goods is protected through the unhampered exercise of their civil, political, and democratic rights. As a result, according to Sandel's trenchant observation, liberalism has fostered the procedural republic committed to the priority of the right over the good.[18]

The communitarian perspective has arisen, at least in part, as a critical reaction to liberalism.[19] As Kenneth Osborne has pointed out, the communitarian finds that liberalism is founded on an unsatisfying conception of human nature, which divorces the "disembodied" individual from his/her social or cultural contexts; presents a restricted view of the good life; distorts the nature of political participation and citizenship; is unable to argue against inegalitarian and undemocratic institutions; and has failed to address adequately the problems that our liberally oriented society has faced.[20] In contrast to the liberal viewpoint, the communitarian perspective highly values the individual's community which serves as the ground or context for the development of the individual self.[21] This view emphasizes cultural or ethnic group, solidarity among those sharing a history or tradition, and the capacity of the group to confer identity upon those otherwise "atomized" by the tendencies of a liberal society. Appalled by the problems associated with liberal societal structures and institutions, the communitarian advocates participation in political life and emphasizes community membership and initiatives. It is only through community participation and collaborative efforts that the common good for society and its members is to be attained. Bellah et al. characterizes the common good this way: "Some of the ideas we have just found in Dewey and Lippmann are part of our definition: a widening of democratic participation and the accountability of institutions; an interdependent prosperity that counteracts predatory relations among individuals and groups and enables everyone to participate in the goods of society; a peaceful world, without which the search for a good society is surely illusory."[22]

Challenging and persistent, the communitarian critique has served as a stimulus for liberal theorists to refine and strengthen their position,[23] and to dispel the communitarian thrust. However, efforts in this direction may not be sufficient. Though willing to concede that refined versions of liberalism survive much of the communitarian critique, Beiner finds that liberals still are unable to dispute that liberalism, "as defined by the bourgeois civilization of the last few centuries, is not good enough, and that liberal community defeats the possibility of a sense of meaningful collective purpose." Indeed, as Beiner sees it, the distinctive communitarian insight "reveals not merely conceptual errors or oversights in liberal theory but, more concretely, deficiencies in the character-building capacities of liberal culture."[24]

Yet neither is communitarianism free of criticisms levelled against it. It has been described as a conservative ideology and as likely to foster conformity, even intolerance, because of its insistence on community values and the attainment of common good. A more disturbing criticism might well be that, if communitarianism grounds its values on commonalities held by the community which determines the good life worth living, how minority rights or emergent values and lifestyles can be accommodated to reflect change in society's culture and demographics becomes problematic. Moreover, it appears true that, as kindred spirits, communitarians do not offer common or similar viewpoints on the good and, in particular, common values, rights, responsibilities, and societal arrangements.[25] It is no surprise that Bellah et al. cannot but openly admit: "the reader may wish to know exactly what we mean by 'the good society' ... our ultimate answer is that there is no pattern of a good society that we or anyone else can simply discern and then expect people to conform to. It is central to our very notion of the good society that it is an open quest, actively involving all its members. As Dennis McCann has put it, the common good is the pursuit of the good in common."[26]

The debate between liberalism and communitarianism continues unabated in both political and legal theory.[27] The limitations of each theoretical perspective are problematic, however, and neither can serve as an adequate basis for the determination of citizenship rights, responsibilities, and appropriate institutional arrangements in society. Perhaps a serious consideration of two other competing perspectives might lead to justifiable conclusions on a viable theoretical perspective and its possible implications for citizenship education.

The Revival of Republicanism

The predominance of liberalism and communitarianism as competing contemporary theoretical perspectives has overshadowed other perspectives which have made major contributions to political discourse in Canada and in the United States. One such perspective is known as republicanism or civic humanism. Taken for dead, or at least dormant, for a long time, this perspective recently has undergone resurrection in the literature. Its historical emphasis on citizenship justifies a reexamination for its potential contribution to the resolution of citizenship issues currently confronting us.

In his justly famous volume, *The Machiavellian Moment*, J.G.A. Pocock has attempted to show that the English-speaking political tradition has been a bearer of the historical republican concepts and values, including those of Niccolò Machiavelli, Hugo Grotious, John Locke, and Edmund Burke. In Pocock's account, James Harrington is credited as the theorist who "brought about a synthesis of (Greek and Roman) civic humanist or republican thought with English political and social awareness, and of Machiavelli's theory of arms with the common-law understanding of freehold property."[28] In M. Zuckert's account, theorists such as Hooker, Grotious, and Locke are shown to have kept elements of the ancient tradition alive.[29] Thereafter, John Trenchard and Thomas Gordon (also known as "Cato") are credited with a synthesis of new republicanism that fused the Lockean political philosophy and the older Whig political thought. Thus, the prevailing political philosophy of liberalism in the United States, descended from John Locke, among others, was initially republican in orientation. Whereas the current version of liberalism is a new arrival, the earlier version is based on the republican political theory. Central to this theory, in M. Sandel's words, "is the idea that liberty depends on sharing in self-government ... sharing in self-rule involves ... deliberating with fellow citizens about the common good and helping to shape the destiny of the political community ... To share in self-rule therefore requires that citizens possess, or come to acquire, certain qualities of character, or civic virtues. But this means that republican politics cannot be neutral toward the values and ends its citizens espouse."[30]

In Canada the received wisdom concerning its political development has had no place for republican thought. It is described by J. Ajzenstat and P. Smith as follows: "The standard view argued that Lockean liberalism was the dominant influence in the nineteenth century, modified only by a strain of tory conservatism. The synthesis of liberalism, with its emphasis on equality, and tory notions of collectivity and the common good gave rise to socialism in its turn. In the late twentieth century the impact of the nineteenth century ideologies could still be seen. Predominantly liberal, subject to occasional fits of toryism, Canada was increasingly ready to welcome a socialist future." Noting that this "picture of Canada's origin now lies in pieces," Ajzenstat and Smith argue that the "formative influence in Canada's past was not solely liberalism, or the combination of liberalism and tory conservatism, but a lively opposition between liberalism and a civic republican philosophy with a progressive agenda." Citing the works of Pocock, they point out that republicanism emphasizes civic participation and the sense of community; as an ideology, it competes with liberalism by "valuing democracy and community in opposition to liberalism's emphasis on the individual and bias toward commerce and economic development."[31] For them, civic republican philosophy contains a powerful challenge to the Lockean liberalism enjoying much acceptance until today.

Indeed, as Smith demonstrates, the received wisdom has prevented historians from studying the republicanism of the revolutionary radicals, such as Mackenzie and Papineau, as a significant influence in Canadian political history.[32] Further, after examining political thought in Britain and Canada in the eighteenth and nineteenth centuries, Smith insists that a more faithful historical interpretation "calls into question the commonly accepted notion of the conservative-liberal anti-thesis ... as a means of understanding the formation of the Canadian political culture"[33] whereas L.-G. Harvey insists that pre-Confederation political discourse is better understood through a reading of republican philosophy in the United States and Britain.[34]

Since Pocock's *The Machiavellian Moment*, the place of the republican perspective in the development of American political theory and institutions has been highlighted in political and legal theory.[35] Republican theories tend to be united, as C. Sunstein points out, by four central commitments despite differences among them: republican conceptions (1) treat politics above all as deliberative, and deliberation is to cover ends as well as means; (2) place a high premium on political equality; (3) assume the possibility of mediating different approaches to politics, or different conceptions of the public good, through discussion and dialogue; and (4) put a high premium on citizenship and participation.[36] Thus, republicanism emphasizes the intrinsic value of political participation for the participants themselves. While republicanism is frequently interpreted as incorporating the view that political life is the highest form of living together, the republican does not have to claim this. It is sufficient for the republican to argue that, because political matters have wide-ranging impact on all other societal arrangements and institutions, political participation will have to be valued very highly, since in this conception it is assumed that every member of the body politic has an obligation to participate in the political life of society. Another feature of republicanism is its stress on the Aristotelian view that humans are political animals who fulfil themselves by becoming involved in public life to contribute towards the resolution of civic concerns and in search of the public good. It is no accident that, in this regard, republicanism seeks the development of public virtue, that is, the moral quality of being able to act selflessly for the common public good. By eschewing what it takes to be the erroneous dichotomy between the liberal's individual on one hand and the communitarian's society on the other, the republican perspective is grounded on the holistic view that human thought requires communal resources without compromising individual autonomy.[37]

Unfortunately, the republican perspective, notwithstanding the common elements among its different versions, has followed different strands in its historical development. Though writers such as Michelman and Sunstein have endeavoured to advance some version that, in their minds, could survive scrutiny,[38] the project of formulating a coherent version free from difficulties is not easy. As legal scholars' responses to Michelman and Sunstein indicate,[39] these republican writers would still need to show that their perspective is much more than a romanticized construction of the past; that its ideal of citizens' participation is possible in post-industrial society like ours; and that, despite its emphasis on participation and deliberation, it nonetheless has real potential to provide answers to substantive concerns.

Critical Theory as a Radical Alternative

Equally insistent on citizenship participation, critical theory developed in Germany between the two world wars and appeared in North America before the start of the Second World War. Engendered and nurtured within the Frankfurt School, it became influential through the leadership of Horkheimer, who assembled a group of theorists – including Max Adorno, Herbert Marcuse, Friedrich Pollock, Franz Neumann, Leo Lowenthal, Eric Fromm, and Walter Benjamin – who were committed to uniting philosophy and the social sciences to develop a tool for the betterment of humanity. Originally housed in the Institute for Social Research, to escape Nazi persecution the Frankfurt School had to stay in Geneva in 1933 and then, from 1934 to 1953, in the United States. Through their influence on American theorists, such as Paul Lazersfeld and Moses Finley, and the theory's continuing attractiveness in the person of Jurgen Habermas (among the second-generation critical theorists), this perspective remains a viable theoretical alternative not only in political thought but also in education.[40]

For Horkheimer, the project of critical theory was the recovery for human beings of the full capacities of humanity. To this end, it was necessary to engage in a critique that would locate "human capacities, and thus the possibilities for social transformation, in the restoration of truly human relationships in place of inhuman relationships in which people were just the mediations between things, commodities."[41] These inhuman relationships would be uncovered through an "immanent critique" which included a dialectical analysis of the contradictions internal to every epoch, social formation, situation, or text. In so doing, the critique would reveal not only the dehumanizing forces shaping the status quo but also the tensions between the existent realities and latent possibilities. For critical theorists, this critique needs reason as its guide for a transformative criticism. However, the critical theorists' reason contrasts with positivistic reason, which separates facts from values under the pretence of pseudo-neutrality. It acknowledges the value-laden interests surrounding the development of knowledge yet critically reflects on "both the historical development ... of such interests and the limitations they may present within certain historical and social contexts."[42] Thus, critical theorists openly take sides in the interest of a better world in which humans are emancipated from domination and slavery.

Tracing the ramifications of a given political theory for educational theory clearly has been most active in the case of critical theory. The literature narrating or espousing its educational counterpart, known as critical pedagogy, has mushroomed in about two decades. Actively advocated in education by H. Giroux, it has also been popularized by Michael Apple, Paolo Friere, and Peter McLaren.[43]

Giroux not only criticizes older approaches to citizenship education for succumbing to positivism, with its underlying technocratic rationality which focuses on questions of technique, organization, and administration.[44] He also condemns them for failing to pursue "the imperative of educating students to affirm moral principles that renounce social injustice and encourage students to become involved in the world in order to change it. What is missing from these approaches is any notion of a public philosophy that gives credence to an emancipatory form of citizenship that puts equality and human life at its center and equates democracy not with privileges but with democratic rights that ensure meaningful participation in the political, economic, and social spheres of society."[45] This public philosophy requires that the teacher, as a transformative intellectual, should make the "pedagogical more political and the political more pedagogical." Doing so involves transforming schooling as part of a fundamental social project to help students to overcome economic, political, and social injustices. Emancipating students for this purpose necessitates the use of forms of pedagogy that treat students as critical agents, present received knowledge as problematic, use critical and affirming dialogue, and argue the case for a better world. Teachers should "take seriously the need to give students an active voice in their learning experiences. It also means developing a critical vernacular that is attentive to problems experienced at the level of everyday life, particularly as they are related to pedagogical experiences connected to classroom practice."[46]

Reiterating his view that "central to a politics and pedagogy of critical citizenship is the need to reconstruct a visionary language and public philosophy that puts equality, liberty, and human life at the center," Giroux outlines important considerations for the development of a critical theory of citizenship education as follows:

> First, it is important to acknowledge that the notion of democracy cannot be grounded in some ahistorical, transcendent notion of truth or authority. Second, a radical language of citizenship and democracy entails a strengthening of the horizontal ties between citizen and citizen. [Third] A revitalized discourse of democracy should not be based exclusively on a language of critique ... the discourse of democracy also needs a language of possibility, one that combines a strategy of opposition with a strategy for constructing a new social order. [Fourth] the insistence on incorporating the utopian notion of "unrealized possibilities" in radical theory provides a foundation for analyzing and constituting critical theories of schooling and citizenship. Finally, educators need to define schools as public spheres where the dynamics of popular engagement and democratic politics can be cultivated as part of the struggle for a radical democratic state.[47]

Giroux's education for the critical or emancipated citizen, which is intended to develop individuals who will pursue the cause of social justice, well-being, and freedom through active examination of the presuppositions and the forces underlying the inequitable status quo, follows from critical theory's insistence on critical or communicative discourse. Unfortunately, its optimistic emphasis on such discourse has elicited the criticism levelled generally against critical theorists, including Habermas. Critical theory's emphasis on the process of discourse may not result in the hoped-for result of consensus on values that will not only unite a multicultural society but also serve as the common goals for society. Although communicative discourse approximating Habermas's ideal may promote dialogue and mutual understanding, it need not necessarily give rise to the adoption of binding decisions that will serve as basis for societal or governmental action on behalf of society as a whole. As Chambers concluded, following an analysis of the Meech Lake and Charlottetown constitutional debacles, taking of a "decision, that is, the prospect of closure, will always place a constraint on the discursive process. The closer and more final the point of closure is, the more participants will be motivated to act strategically rather than discursively ... A realistic model of deliberative democracy must concede that decision rules in large democracies will always place constraints on constraint-free dialogues."[48] If this is the case, the undiluted reliance on the deliberative process may be unduly optimistic.

Yet, as the Meech Lake and Charlottetown discussions revealed, understanding of each other's substantive positions based on substantive values and principles do not necessarily result in agreement. Certainly the competing parties in these discussions remained in entrenched polar opposition, perhaps more deeply than before. This would indicate that rational processes, such as Habermas's communicative discourse, do not guarantee societal consensus and may need additional conditions for success, such as mutual respect and reciprocity.[49]

Giroux may argue that his particular views are less subject to this problem because of the fundamental character of his value position. He is explicit and unhesitating in stating his commitment to the substantive principles of social justice, individual and societal well-being, and freedom. Unfortunately, this stance will not do. Like Giroux, critical theorists of the Habermasian persuasion are concerned with promoting these principles or goals in advocating dialogue. The moment one attempts to specify the particular policy implications of these principles, however, lack of agreement is bound to arise and become contentious. Moreover, without having outlined and successfully justified his set of fundamental principles, Giroux can be seen as having presupposed, rather than established them on the basis of critical discourse.

Citizenship for Our Time: A Common Starting Point

Our survey of prominent theoretical perspectives aiming to ground the notion of citizenship shows that none may claim to have unquestionably succeeded. It is important to note, however, that despite their problems and differences, the theoretical perspectives have brought about a renewed focus on citizenship as an important element in the life of society. Careful analysis would also show that they agree on a number of things.

Citizenship and Pluralism

If any perspective is to be a viable political theory at all, its notion of the public good will have to be formulated in the light of the changed demographic realities in society. Rather than remaining as a fairly homogeneous society predominantly populated by people of British and/or French extraction, North America has become culturally diverse. Thus, in Canada about one-third of the population is classified as non-British or non-French; in the United States the influx of non-British or European immigrants is such that, "by the year 2050, the White population is expected to decrease to 60 percent, with the Black community increasing slightly, Asians increasing tenfold, and Latinos almost tripling in number." By the last quarter of the next century, "those who are now referred to as "minority" are expected to be in the majority."[50] In Canada, the demographic reality, marked by cultural diversity, was certainly an important consideration in the adoption of multiculturalism as a national policy. In this country, it has been recognized that if national unity and the public good are to be attained, the entitlements of cultural minority groups will have to be accommodated in its laws and institutions. Thus, the federal 1988 Multiculturalism Act[51] and similar pieces of provincial legislation seek to implement three important fundamental principles, namely, equal participation, freedom of cultural retention, and mutual respect, appreciation and cultural sharing. While they clearly demonstrate the Canadian commitment to respect for the plural character of the body politic and thus to provide for the rights and well-being of minority communities, the continuing debate about multiculturalism in the United States indicates a refusal to face the changed reality in that country. Whether or not minority groups in the latter country will persevere in claiming their rights remains to be seen.

Citizenship and the Common Good

Clearly, communitarians, republicans, and critical theorists are concerned that citizenship should contribute towards the achievement of the common public good. Their attack against liberalism has not been without the desired result, in that liberal defenders themselves have repositioned or reinterpreted themselves on this issue. Thus, S. Macedo berates his fellow liberals for their misconception of liberal doctrines and categorically states as follows: "Even in its limited forms, liberalism cannot be really neutral among public values. It stands for the supreme worth of certain values: individual liberty and responsibility, tolerance of change and diversity, and respect for the rights of those who respect liberal values ... Besides a set of positive values, liberalism represents a set of political institutions ... All liberal governments provide certain public goods ... These are not 'neutral' goods, but nearly all liberals would agree that some range of these goods should be provided by a coercive state ... So liberals have positive political values and political institutions and practices designed to embody and sustain these values."[52]

This liberal characterization of the public good in society, which will help to promote the individual good, is admittedly vague about the full shape and features of the good society or the common good, or the good of the individual citizen, for that matter. Nonetheless, it is important to note that communitarians, republicans, and critical theorists have not presented visions of the common good or the good of the individual much richer in content than those Macedo offers. At least for now, it appears that there is consensus in all four theories that the cause of the common good needs to be furthered. It necessarily remains that our notion of the substantive common good or the good for the individual may have to remain fairly thin, its surrounding specifications remaining relatively fluid and context related. Therefore, societal members, that is, citizens, must learn to live with ambiguities and to respect perspectives of others in the serious pursuit of the good. There is much to be said in favour of Hutchinson's view that the common good should be conceived in an open-ended manner: "There is no fixed or final version of what amounts to the best way to live: the good life is to be found in the details of living, socially and privately, which must be reworked and renegotiated constantly. Whereas liberals put representative democracy in the service of private values and marxists imagine that direct democracy can bring an end to politics, citizens accept that the relation between public virtue and public values is open to revisable articulation ... For the democratic citizen, a good life consists in the public spirited engagement with others over the shape and substance of 'the good life.'"[53]

Civic Virtue as the Mark of Citizenship

In pursuing the common good, Hutchinson calls for a "revitalized practice of citizenship" and suggests a vision of citizenship which "allows people to inhabit the contested terrain between individual rights and communal rights by colonizing it in the name of democracy."[54] Largely sympathetic to critical theory, Hutchinson appears not too distant from reputed communitarians like Sandel. Also cognizant of the fact that our pluralistic society requires adaptability, he claims that participation in the determination of the public and individual good requires, no less, "citizens who can think and act as multiply-situated selves. The civic virtue distinctive to our time is the capacity to negotiate our way among the sometimes overlapping, sometimes conflicting obligations that claim us, and to live with the tension to which multiple loyalties give rise."[55] Both Hutchinson and Sandel are echoed in the Michelman's republican view: "Understandings of the social world that are contested and shaped in the daily encounters and transactions of civil society are of course conveyed to our representative arenas. They also, obviously, enter into determinations of policy that occur within nominally private settings but that can affect people's lives no less profoundly than government action ... They are arenas of citizenship in the comparably broad sense in which citizenship encompasses not just formal participation in affairs of state but respected and self-respecting presence – distinct and audible voice – in public and social life at large."[56]

Irrespective of their theoretical labels, current theorists place unmistakable emphasis on the determination of societal arrangements and intersecting interrelationships between individuals, groups, and institutions by citizens actively involved in different aspects of social life. How the notion of civic virtue marking the citizen in contemporary society translates into a program of citizenship education in schools remains a question. Ascertaining the activities, curricula, instructional strategies, and institutional arrangements that are required to cultivate the "virtuous citizen" must still be undertaken. Clearly, delineation of these educational elements will require the difficult but anterior task of establishing the basic values, virtues, understandings, and skills that a fully developed citizen must possess.

Towards an Eclectic Citizenship Education

Since no one theoretical perspective provides an unquestionably superior and adequate framework for citizenship, educators may approach the education of the citizen with an eclectic orientation. Doing so may not be problematic if our view is correct that, despite their differences, the prominent perspectives in political theory share certain viewpoints.

If civic virtue is the mark of the citizen, then it will have to be an important objective of educational systems. If it is to serve as an operational basis for meaningful curriculum development and determination of methodology, however, it needs to be unravelled in terms of more specific dispositions, capacities, and abilities. Undoubtedly, liberals, communitarians, republicans, and critical theorists have contributions to make towards the explication of the notion of civic virtue and the kind of education it requires. This is no easy task, particularly in a multicultural society marked by sometimes irreconcilable value differences. But the task is necessary. In the words of Hutchinson, "The pressing and persistent challenge would ... be how best to incorporate such values (of personal autonomy and individual entitlement) with the equally important virtues of social solidarity and the acknowledgement of difference. While citizenship emphasizes a sense of belonging and connection, it respects the fact that different groups of citizens can have different concerns and interests ... the fate of each of us is unavoidably tied to the fate of all of us and ... the self and the collectivity are not antagonistic entities, but complementary components of a political community."[57]

The Liberal Inventory of Virtues

In pursuing the need to develop the virtuous citizen, W. Galston, a liberal who is sensitive to communitarian and republican views, has courageously outlined a list of virtues. [58] A slightly revised version may be presented as follows:

I. Virtues for interpersonal relationships
- independence
- tolerance
- respect for individual excellences and accomplishments

II. Virtues needed to sustain the political process
- disposition to respect the rights of others
- capacity to evaluate the talents, character, and performance of public officials
- ability to moderate public desires in the face of public limits
- capacity to engage in public discourse
- capacity to test public policies against our deeper convictions
- (for leaders especially) ability to narrow the gap between wise policy and popular consent

III. Virtues needed to sustain the state
- willingness to fight on behalf of one's country
- settled disposition to obey the law
- developed capacity to understand, accept, and act on the core principles of one's society.

Towards a Fuller Inventory

The specific virtues listed under categories I and II, if taken as minimal traits of the citizen, are likely not to be disputed by theorists of different persuasions. The question is likely to be whether they exhaust the traits of the virtuous citizen, a question which we will take up shortly. Traits under category III may not be problematic for communitarians and republicans, but they will arouse concern in liberals and perhaps opposition from critical theorists. Liberals and critical theorists will see in this category blind allegiance or an unthinking obedience to the state or the law. Nonetheless, as a sophisticated liberal, Galston would clearly be in a position to qualify each of the traits under the category to gain the agreement of his fellow liberals and even radical critical theorists. Thus, the latter's concerns may be alleviated by a stipulation that willingness to fight for one's country is to be expected only where the citizen has critically examined, and consequently agreed to, the necessity and/or justness of his/her country's war or dispute. Similarly, obedience to the law may be expected only where citizens have reasonably evaluated the law and have found it justifiable. The third trait in this same category of virtues will prove commendable, provided that the developed capacity includes capacity to rationally and critically analyse and examine core principles in society. It is arguable that, unless we would rather be "red than dead," unless we do not mind breakdown in peace and order, and unless we prefer a life that is "brutish, nasty, and short," Galston's proposed virtues under category III may prove acceptable after all.

It may be doubted that Galston's proposed list is adequate enough to include all the important virtues of the citizen. Category I will remain objectionable unless it is qualified to make each specific trait non-problematic. Thus, independence will be seen as threatening by republicans and communitarians because, unless exercised responsibly, it could disadvantage those already disadvantaged and also bring harm to oneself or the rest of society. But there is no reason why its liberal proponents will have to deny the need for the qualification, unless they wish to assert the extreme libertarian position.

Mere tolerance is equally problematic. On one hand, as Beiner points out, an important issue to address is "whether the liberal philosophy of toleration makes available suitably rich theoretical resources to uncover the social and political sources of ethical deficiency." Further, as he sees it, "to be equally open to everything is to be left with nothing in terms of cultural and civilizational resources ... For all that one celebrates the openness and tolerance of the West, too much openness does not liberate – rather, it casts one into the shapeless abyss of nihilism."[59] Indeed, one might shudder to think of Macedo, who nonchalantly says, "Liberalism holds out the promise, or the threat, of making all the world like California"[60] where everything happens! Further, tolerance, associated with the philosophy of "live and let live," fails to acknowledge the need for mutual appreciation that enriches people's interaction in the same world or space. As Gutmann and Thompson insightfully observe, "in seeking political consensus in the face of fundamental moral disagreement, we need to attend not only to the nature of the positions but also the way in which people hold or express positions." Surely, toleration is not enough; mutual respect is needed. "Like toleration, mutual respect is a form of agreeing to disagree. But mutual respect demands more than toleration. It requires a favorable attitude toward, and constructive interaction with, the persons with whom one disagrees. It consists in a reciprocal positive regard of citizens who manifest the excellence of character that permits a democracy to flourish in the face of (at least temporarily) irresolvable moral conflict."[61]

Liberals are not likely to resist Gutmann and Thompson's proper insistence on mutual respect as an important civic virtue, but one may wonder whether they are conceding or advocating enough. It seems no coincidence that, while Gutmann and Thompson speak of "reciprocal positive regard of citizens who manifest the excellence of character that permits a democracy to flourish," Galston lists the civic virtue of "respect for individual excellences and accomplishments." This view reflects the traditional liberal notion that respect is deserved only by persons, that is, individuals, who are active and reflective agents of their actions. This being the case, will there be any respect for the helpless young, the sick, the mentally challenged, those whose circumstances have led them to passivity and acceptance? Liberalism has stressed freedom in the pursuit of happiness at the expense of equality in society. Associating liberalism with capitalism, communitarians and critical theorists, in particular, have made some of their most telling criticisms of liberalism in relation to the damage it does to community and its lack of concern for the weak and disadvantaged. Although D. Conway has made a valiant effort to exculpate capitalism of its alleged sin and to blame it on big government,[62] one fact remains obvious: liberal commitment to individual freedom to pursue the good life needs to be balanced by the egalitarian insistence that those who cannot avail themselves of the same freedom are given adequate assistance to equalize opportunities and outcomes in society.[63] Despite the attempts of liberals like Macedo and Gutmann to accommodate the communitarian demands for greater concern for the well-being of the community, particularly its weak and helpless members, the liberal preconception of the person gets in the way of a genuine regard for the human being as worthy of respect, irrespective of lack of agency or ability.

The virtues under category II should not be contentious. The need for citizens actively to rule or be ruled in intelligent ways is a given in a democratic society. In fact, for critical theorists, Galston's list might need more virtues. As we have seen, critical theorists and, in particular, its proponents in education, speak of emancipatory citizenship which will usher in the transformation of society. Such transformation will require not only the capacity to engage in public discourse but also the commitment and the ability to critically and intelligently examine the presuppositions underlying public discourse and its context. The citizen is not only to accept the discourse as framed by hegemonic public institutions, but to transform the discourse itself to allow for the critical evaluation of the predominant social, economic, and political forces shaping society. Unless liberals are simply paying lip service to the development of individuals who can think for themselves in the pursuit of their goods, they cannot avoid coming to terms with the kind of critical thinking demanded by critical theorists. Indeed, in this age dominated by the global economy, we are in dire need of citizens who are able to participate in societal transformation geared towards the elimination of inequities in the status quo and away from the relentlessly acquisitive, self-centred ethos pervading our capitalistic, technological society.

Further Steps towards Citizenship Education

Needless to say, Galston's list, including the additions and revisions raised by our analysis and evaluation, will be far from complete. A fuller analysis of the virtues needed for active, participatory citizenship in a plural society, in which individuals are encouraged to responsibly pursue their goods in cooperation with one another, awaits concerted effort. Thereafter, it will be necessary to determine curricular content, teaching methods and strategies, supporting co-curricular activities, and environmental conditions, including interpersonal relationships. Obviously, the preparation of educators, who are capable of developing virtuous citizens well suited to take on different roles in society, cannot be neglected.

Fortunately, the effort does not have to be undertaken in a vacuum. As Butts points out, citizenship education, in one form or another, has been undertaken in the United States since the founding of the American republic. The form has varied, however, owing to the interplay of persistent themes in American life: (1) the cohesive value claims that undergird the overall democratic political community; (2) the differentiating value claims of pluralisms that give identity to various groups in society; and

(3) the modernization process that has been gathering strength through-out the world for two centuries.[64] In Canada, some notion of citizenship education developed early. Through his notion that education is "of civil interest" and of importance to a "free people" interested in maintaining their freedom, and that "it was a requisite to social well-being,"[65] Egerton Ryerson contributed to the development of citizenship education. An incipient conception is apparent in his thought, as follows: "the school does not teach political science; but it may and ought to teach those elements of it which are within the limits of school teaching, and within the time of school attendance, and within the capacity of youth; and the application of which involves their several duties as members of the state."[66] Yet, notwithstanding demands for a new, progressive education in the late nineteenth century and well into the twentieth, schooling practices and content changed little. Didactic teaching, typically accom-panied by memorization, recitation, and passive learning, remained the rule. Kenneth Osborne discusses the history of citizenship education in Canada by distinguishing four identifiable periods. The first period is marked by the assimilationist nation-building effort in the country dur-ing the 1890s until the 1920s. The second, from the 1920s to the 1950s, emphasized preparation for democratic living without abandoning na-tion building. The third, from the 1960s to the 1980s, stressed pan-Canadian understanding and increased knowledge of things Canadian. The most recent period is marked by a lack of emphasis on citizenship in favour of preparing students for the global economy.[67] H. McKenzie encapsulates the earlier development of citizenship education by noting that the prevailing concerns relating to early civic education "shifted from notions of a generally passive loyalty to the ideal of belonging to and participating in the operation of an increasingly democratic state." In her view, the notion of citizenship education had developed some history by the 1950s, comprising four elements: "the civil element, con-cerned with the rights necessary for basic individual freedoms; the politi-cal element, incorporating the right to participate in political activity; social rights, relating to standards of economic welfare and security; and finally, the moral aspect, symbolized by the term 'good citizen.'"[68]

Certainly these elements could easily be related and linked to the expanded version of Galston's list and could serve as prospectively valu-able inclusions in the elaboration of the details of citizenship education. If citizens are to respect one another (virtue under category II), they must know what to respect about persons, and thus the first three elements – their civil, political, and social rights – come into play. The moral element – the good citizen – invests the characteristics of the citizen with the moral quality that accompanies the notion of virtue. Indeed, these elements could serve as valuable guidelines in the specification of the content and processes of citizenship education. Also useful are McKenzie's suggestions on its substantive content.[69] Equally valuable are the works of, among others, Conway, Conway and Osborne, and Sears.[70] Though they have addressed political or civic education in some of their works, these authors are closely linked, if not synonymous, with citizenship education. In any case, the eclectic approach suggested in this paper makes consideration of materials under slightly different labels eminently sensible.

Undoubtedly, much remains to be done if we are to implement a well-conceived, well-formulated citizenship education program in our schools. Nonetheless, we need to respond to insightful concerns raised in political theory about the current problems in our society and about the corresponding urgency in promoting citizenship education. Educators cannot but address this challenging endeavour.

Notes

1 As noted in chapter 1, see appendix A for a view of fourteen models of citizenship.
2 Sears, "'Something Different to Everyone.'"
3 Butts, *Revival of Civic Learning*, 24.
4 Galston, *Liberal Purposes*, 242–3, 250.
5 Beiner, *What's the Matter with Liberalism?* 105.
6 Pocock, "The Ideal of Citizenship," and *The Machiavellian Moment*.
7 Ibid., 35–6.
8 Ibid., 38–40.
9 Riesenberg, *Citizenship in the Western Tradition*, xxi.
10 Bellah et al., *The Good Society* and *Habits of the Heart*.
11 Berthoff, *Republic of the Dispossessed*; Pocock, *Machiavellian Moment*; Riesenberg, *Citizenship in the Western Tradition*; Zuckert, *Natural Rights and the New Republicanism*.
12 Bellah et al., *Habits of the Heart*.
13 Resnick, *Twenty-First Century Democracy*, 4.
14 Crispo, *Making Canada Work*, 200–10.
15 Cairns, *Reconfigurations*, 157–85.
16 Ibid., 120.

17 Ackerman, *Social Justice in the Liberal State*; Dworkin, *Taking Rights Seriously*; Nozick, *Anarchy, State and Utopia*; and Rawls, *A Theory of Justice*.

18 Sandel, "The Procedural Republic."

19 See, for example, Bellah et al, *Habits of the Heart* and *The Good Society*; Etzioni, *The Spirit of Community* and *New Communitatian Thinking*; MacIntyre, *After Virtue*; Sandel, *Liberalism and the Limits of Justice*; as well as Selznick, *The Moral Commonwealth*.

20 Osborne, "Education and Citizenship."

21 Beiner, *Theorizing Citizenship*, 12–16.

22 Bellah et al., *The Good Society*, 9.

23 See, for example, Galston, *Liberal Purposes*; Kymlicka, *Multicultural Citizenship*; and Macedo, *Liberal Virtues: Citizenship, Virtue, and Community*.

24 Beiner, *What's the Matter with Liberalism?* 36.

25 See, for example, Paul, Miller, and Paul, *Communitarian Challenge to Liberalism*.

26 Bellah et al., *The Good Society*, 8–9.

27 Hutchinson and Green, *Law and Community*.

28 Pocock, *Machiavellian Moment*, viii.

29 Zuckert, *Natural Rights and the New Republicanism*.

30 Sandel, *Democracy's Discontent*, 5–6.

31 Ajzenstat and Smith, "Liberal-republicanism," 1, 2.

32 Smith, "Ideological Origins of Canadian Confederation," 47–78.

33 Smith, "Civic Humanism versus Liberalism," 135.

34 Harvey, "The First Distinct Society," 79–108.

35 See, for example, Sunstein, "Beyond the Republican Revival"; Michelman, "Law's Republic," Pettit, *Common Mind*; Sandel, *Democracy's Discontent*.

36 Sunstein, "Beyond the Republican Revival."

37 Pettit, *Common Mind*.

38 Michelman, "Law's Republic"; Sunstein, "Beyond the Republican Revival."

39 See the *Yale Law Journal* (1988).

40 Calhoun, *Critical Social Theory*, 1–42; Giroux, *Theory and Resistance in Education*, 7–41.

41 Calhoun, *Critical Social Theory*, 20.

42 Giroux, *Theory and Resistance in Education*, 17.

43 See ibid., also *Schooling and the Struggle for Public Life*, *Teachers as Intellectuals*, and *Border Crossings*; Apple, *Education and Power*; Freire, *Education for Critical Consciousness*; and McLaren, *Life in Schools*.

44 Giroux, *Theory and Resistance in Education*.

45 Giroux, *Schooling and the Struggle for Public Life*, 14.

46 Giroux, *Teachers as Intellectuals*, 127.

47 Ibid., 170–6.
48 Chambers, "Discourse and Democratic Practices," 255.
49 Callan, "Discrimination and Religious Schooling."
50 Nieto, *Affirming Diversity*, 6.
51 Canada, An Act for the Preservation and Enhancement of Multiculturalism in Canada.
52 Macedo, "Charting Liberal Virtues," 208–9.
53 Hutchinson, *Waiting for Coraf*, 215.
54 Ibid., 214–15.
55 Sandel, *Democracy's Discontent*, 350.
56 Michelman, "Law's Republic," 1531.
57 Hutchinson, *Waiting for Coraf*, 216.
58 Galson, *Liberal Purposes*, 245–6.
59 Beiner, *Philosophy in a Time of Lost Spirit*, 33, 169.
60 Macedo, "Charting Liberal Virtues," 224.
61 Gutmann and Thompson, "Moral Conflict and Political Consensus," 134–5.
62 Conway, "Capitalism and Community," 137–63.
63 Waldron, *Liberal Rights*.
64 Butts, *Revival of Civic Learning*, 51–88.
65 McLeod, "Exploring Citizenship Education," 9.
66 As cited in ibid., 10.
67 Osborne, "Education Is the Best National Insurance."
68 McKenzie, *Citizenship Education in Canada*, 2.
69 Ibid., 4–10.
70 Conway, "Theory and Practice of Political Education in Canada"; Conway and Osborne, "Civics, Citizenship, State Power and Political Education"; Osborne, "Political Education and Participant Citizenship" and *Educating Citizens*; and Sears, "Conceptions of Citizenship and Citizenship Education."

Recognition of Cultural and Religious Diversity in the Educational Systems of Liberal Democracies

GUY BOURGEAULT, FRANCE GAGNON,
MARIE McANDREW, and MICHEL PAGÉ

Introduction

In liberal democratic societies, the management of the State's public institutions gives rise to the question of the delicate balance to be established between recognition of a multiplicity of values on the one hand, and the necessity of maintaining the coherence of the institutions on the other. This problem has been placed on the public agenda by the discussion around the hijab controversy in France, Belgium, Denmark, and Québec, about the Sikh's turban and kirpan in Great Britain and Canada, as well as around the public prayer and the teaching of history in the United States and in Canada.[1]

From a perspective that rejects the two extremes of State neutrality and absolute cultural relativism, the search for an appropriate management of differences within educational establishments leads to the formulation of three major questions. The first two are as follows. What are the basic arguments that can be put forward to legitimize the obligation to take cultural and religious diversity into account in the public institutions? On what foundation can we argue that the State must sometimes impose limitations on recognition of diversity? The answer to these questions must clearly flow from three fundamental principles for managing cultural diversity within educational institutions.

- The State has an essential role to play for the management of cultural and religious diversity within public institutions.
- The respect of the moral independence of individuals constitutes the fundamental value which should be used as a guideline to the State's interventions towards diversity.

- The place of diversity has to be limited by democratic values and procedures.

We expand upon these three principles in the first part of this chapter.

The third question is as follows: What ought to be the role of public school in regard to the obligation of taking into account the cultural and religious diversity of the students and the necessity of educating them to respect the common norms of their society? The answer to this question must follow three guidelines in the search for balance between cultural diversity and a common culture:

- first, a just balance between the exercise of parental authority, the children's rights, and the State's responsibility regarding the definition of the place of cultural and religious diversity;
- second, a civic instruction which educates the young to live in cultural and religious diversity; and
- finally, a common base of education constituted by a curriculum and school regulations which take diversity into account in order to educate the young to be integrated into the society.

These guidelines are considered in the second part of this chapter.

Political and Ethical Guidelines for the Recognition of Cultural and Religious Diversity

The Role of the State in the Management of Cultural and Religious Diversity within Public Institutions

The difficulties which confront the State regarding the coexistence of diverse cultural or religious minorities have brought certain authors to adopt the concept of axiological neutrality as the solution, one that permits the State to act as an impartial arbiter in the midst of conflicts.[2] According to one of the principal arguments of the liberal tradition, this duty of neutrality with respect to different conceptions of the "good life" is founded on the observation that none of these conceptions requires the adhesion of all the citizens. This neutrality applies to that which is from the State itself, its institutions, its policies, that is, everything that belongs in the public sphere. Classical liberal theory attributes to the State, however, the duty of assuring each individual a space of freedom – space in private life or sphere – that he could manage, without interference, according to his own conception of the "good life."

This distinction between the public and the private spheres allows the limitation of the field of expression of values and beliefs linked to the belonging of individuals to diverse groups, without harming individual freedom and while satisfying the requirements for social cohesion. From this perspective, State neutrality seems like a requirement of justice, assuring equal chances to each citizen to live according to his conception of good of his own impartial choice and hence without favouring the adoption of one conception of the "good life" rather than another.[3]

This theory has been subjected to numerous critiques. It has been judged inadequate and of little use in dealing with the struggles of diverse cultural and religious groups.[4] In spite of its pretention of justice, it leads to different ways of reinforcing inequalities for three major reasons. First, the neutrality of the State is apparent and illusory in as much as it contributes to the consolidation of cultural priviledges of one group to the detriment of others. As Nagel has observed, when the State plays the neutrality game, which forbids it to take sides in favour of any group whatsoever, it results in a "cultural laissez faire," which actually sanctions the cultural hegemony of one group, the same group which dominates the political and socio-economic scene.[5] It also gives greater importance to the conceptions of the "good life" which are linked to or are compatible with the dominant group.

Second, the State's claim to impartiality is impossible, because State neutrality can mask the fact that dominant groups illegitimately arrogate to themselves, through the medium of the State and its institutions, the right to establish common rules according to their particular interests.[6] It seems to us that the State cannot abrogate its role as guardian of the social order and is thereby the bearer of a collective vision of society. State intervention is thus imperative, not to ensure the equality of cultures within institutions, but rather to guarantee liberty and the right to dissidence to those citizens who don't share space taken up by the dominant ethos and who don't have power to have them acknowledged.

Finally, the most popular argument in the justification of the non-interference by the State, that of protecting individual equality, is today largely discredited, particularly by adherents of the communitarian school. For example, Charles Taylor has rightly pointed out that, in order to grant everyone in a given society real equality of opportunity, the State must compensate for specific handicaps experienced from the outset by some individuals disadvantaged because of their membership in specific groups.[7] The communitarians claim that in the name of social justice the cultural and religious differences must be recognized in the "public sphere" and, more precisely, in public institutions.

This demand is founded, among other things, on the importance of community attachment in forming personal identity. The communitarians consider that identity develops through a dialectical process constantly associating the individual with the community by which and in which he experiences his social integration.[8] The recognition of community identities, however, should not necessarily be equivalent to the enhancement of the community to the detriment of the individual.

Other scholars bringing a new liberal perspective to the debate believe that individual enhancement, one of the basic premises of liberalism, necessitates the preservation of the cultural context in which each individual may exercise his capacity to choose.[9] Consequently, the interest of the individual demands that minority cultures be allowed to express themselves in the public sphere and that certain measures effectively supporting the expansion of pluralism be implemented for societal equality. Nevertheless, the State should not consider itself responsible for the maintenance of particular communities or even accord them official recognition as intermediary structures between citizens and public institutions. Between a communitarian vision which clearly emphasizes on the maintenance of cultures and communities and a new liberal vision which insists on the protection of the moral independence of the individual, we prefer the second perspective for the reasons that we will develop in the next section.

Cultural and Religious Diversity and Moral Independence of Individuals

Many arguments lead us to reject the communitarian vision as it applies to the State's recognition of differences. The majority of ethnic communities are self-defining through an assortment of empirical, historical, and contingent factors which are in constant flux.[10] Moreover, the now dominant trend in the sociology of ethnic relations is to reject an essentialist perspective in the study of ethnicity by stressing the fact that ethnic relations are "constructed" and that the boundaries and cultural markers which define different groups are shifting over time.[11] In this regard, researchers increasingly validate the concept of multiple identity, especially in the migratory context, where concurrent adhesion to various cultural subgroups seems more the norm than the exception.[12] It follows that it would be illegitimate to force the individual to adhere to a single cultural or religious group in order to determine the role of the State with respect to him. There would then be the risk of subordinating individual liberty to the morality of the group.

As a result, the State should ensure high priority for the protection of the moral independence of individuals by recognizing that they belong to groups with diverse traditions. From a liberal perspective, each person has the right to give purpose to his existence by making plans and modifying them throughout his life according to his ideals.[13] The individual, therefore, should have the opportunity to choose what he deems to be "the better life" as well as the instruments necessary to the revision of this choice.[14] This capacity to live his life according to his designs appears partly dependent on adherence to his cultural community and thus to its viability.

It seems to us that the duty of protecting the individual's moral independence may justify recognition by the State's institutions of differences arising from membership in diverse groups. This duty raises the following question: how should we determine the limits of the place of cultural and religious diversity?

The Limits of the Place of Cultural and Religious Diversity

Within the framework of a democratically conducted public debate these questions can be resolved. It will be possible in this deliberation to take into consideration the consequences – positive or negative – for each of the parties concerned as well as for the society as a whole. The State must guarantee that these debates take place within clear guidelines in order to assure the utmost recognition of pluralism while maintaining the cohesion necessary to democratic life and proper institutional functioning.

The legitimacy of setting limits to pluralism have been well established by Chantal Mouffe.[15] If we adhered to pluralism as some sort of absolute ideal, no kind of coherent conceptual and organizational framework defined by laws can ever be established for a viable political regime. Thus, it is our view that the corpus of constitutional dispositions adopted to assure the functioning of democratic life should be protected, thereby imposing a limit to the changes which might emanate from the public debate. In this respect, there exists in every country fundamental principles which therefore are said to be constitutional; these dispositions are protected from the potential excesses of a democracy defined only by the rule of the majority. Almost unalterable norms, they even condition the legitimacy of other laws while reflecting certain basic values generally characterized as human rights. Thus, this human rights "culture" can present arguments in favour of an institutional adaptation to pluralism as well as a non-negotiable guideline for taking differences into account.

Beyond these boundaries, other laws, judicial norms, and regulations may set limits to decisions taken as a consequence of resolutions adopted in various forums. Indeed, given that democracy is also based on the principle of delegating power, it is obvious that certain legal guidelines cannot be modified in forums at an inferior level in the decision-making process. There should be no systematic encouragement of civil disobedience or individual anarchy.

In the more immediate future, however, legal norms should not serve as a pretext for injustice. It is the very essence of the democratic system to adapt itself, within the limits outlined above, to the continual redefinition of the social consensus on a variety of issues. Moral issues raised by these norms and their negative consequences, unresolved in the first type of forum, must be taken to a higher level of public debate, and, if necessary, they should be modified.

Clear rules are required to guarantee that the public debate will take place according to a fair and equitable procedure. For example, from the start, the parties concerned ought to be in a situation of equality; the discussion should take place on the basis of rational arguments and reasonableness;[16] the procedure adopted and carried through should render the debate as free as possible and the participation as widespread as possible.[17]

Another important rule is the non-exclusion of certain questions from the public agenda. It would seem to us preferable to submit the demands of cultural and religious minorities to the debate than to exclude them a priori from the public agenda. One of the objectives of democratic debate is to permit an extensive and equitable participation, so that each individual recognizes the legitimacy of the process which led to its adoption. This holds, even if the decision finally reached is not in accordance with his conception of the good or of his interests. Thus, it follows that in order to reach this objective, the fewest possible number of topics should be excluded from public debate.

Application of Political and Ethical Guidelines to the Recognition of Cultural and Religious Diversity within Public Institutions

The acceptance of demands from minorities in the schools seems to raise greater conceptual and practical difficulties than from those within other institutions whose narrower mandate is to dispense services "adapted to the clientele." Because of the special position occupied by the school at the boundary between public and private spheres, minority-group parents' claims must be accorded particular attention: their values must be respected and their special needs recognized. Thus, it is important to have a clear position on the sharing of authority over schools.

Parents' Rights and the State's Responsibility within the Democratic School

The position we endorse, inspired by Amy Gutmann,[18] states that none of the partners can claim a controlling authority, and, as a result, educational policies will be the consequence of a negotiation between them. In the establishment of the delicate balance necessary between the various partners, all serving "the child's interest," we propose two major reference points. On the one hand, the school is mandated by the State to give the child the knowledge and skills necessary to choose his life freely and to re-evaluate his choices throughout life. On the other hand, it is legitimate to maintain the cultural framework in which the individual can continue to construct his identity and thus conserve his ability to choose his life in the private sphere while participating in a creative manner in public life.

In agreement with Rawls,[19] we see two main reasons for rejecting the claim of parental primacy in education. First, by yielding up to the parents all authority and thus all educational responsibility, the State would relinquish its fundamental responsibility for social cohesion, even for social peace. Owing to its intrinsic social mandate, the school must assure instruction in the rights and civic skills needed for the maintenance and development of a democratic society.

In other respects, the right of parents to transmit their cultural and religious heritage to their children is not limitless. It has to be exercised within guidelines, mainly the respect and the protection of the moral independence of individuals and their freedom. Additionally, as Rawls notes, children have to know that their liberty of conscience is recognized in such a way that apostasy or a change of beliefs does not constitute a crime.[20] If the School ought not to encourage children's systematic scepticism regarding their parents' way of life, it nonetheless must intervene if the development considered as "normal" for the child seems impeded or to make sure he receives the education necessary to exercise his future rights and responsibilities as a citizen. Parents do not have an exclusive right to control the education of their children. They must exercise their educational rights and responsibilities according to the principles of a liberal democratic society.

Should one then come to the conclusion that the State holds all the authority? Certainly not. Indeed, a State which would propose a definition of the "good life" and impose it almost universally would lapse into totalitarianism.[21] Taking the diversity of beliefs, convictions, and opinions into consideration, the State should respect, to a certain extent, the wishes of the parents as they relate to their children's education and the school. The limits come from the proper role of a State in its duty to consider not only parental rights but also the requirements of the common good and, especially, the rights and interests of the children themselves as persons with rights and future citizens. It must be stressed here that when discussing the legitimacy of taking into account differences within the school setting, psychological and pedagogical understandings of the various stages in the child's moral development prove just as necessary as politico-ethical guidelines.[22]

Instruction for the Civic Culture

Supporters of civic instruction propose that education in a democratic society should encourage the development of the kind of aptitudes and abilities requested for life in a society respectful of cultural and religious differences. It should also assure a clear understanding of the principles as well as the structures, rules, and procedures characterizing a democracy, with the aim of assuring each citizen the possibility of participating in public life.[23] Beyond fostering the development of personal autonomy, the school has to guarantee the acquisition of the knowledge and skills needed to participate in democratic decision making.

Acquisition of other "virtues" and other competences remains a compelling prerequisite for complete participation in the public life and thus for the proper operation of democracy. To assure that everyone's point of view is taken into consideration in the debate over the establishment of norms of existence recognizing cultural and religious differences, each should learn to distinguish between what he is permitted in the private sphere and what he cannot impose on others in the public sphere. He must also recognize that not everything can be submitted to the rule of the majority alone and that minority points of view must be taken into account when it results in no inconvenience to others.[24] Civic education must favour equally the development of the ability to evaluate and incisively criticize the competence of political representatives as well as their performance in carrying out their given mandate.[25]

Additionally, the educational process must concern itself with the ability of citizens to recreate a society which, in order to remain vibrant, must be able to transmit its heritage and, at the same time, tolerate a condition of constant mutation.[26] Thus, the citizen's devotion to the society in which his being and belonging are intimately interwoven comes simultaneously through attachment and allegiance to institutions inherited from the past and through the critical faculty required to effect the necessary rectifications in the future.

The Place of Diversity and Its Limits within the Educational Systems

Introducing young people to the realities of the society into which they will participate is accomplished at school through a variety of ways. For the sake of brevity, only two will be emphasized here: (1) instruction in the compulsory subjects; and (2) the definition of school regulations that corresponds to the school's mandate of socialization. The democratic model does not question the right of a democratic State to determine, by legislative or administrative means, a compulsory minimum content in the various school subjects. Indeed, one can maintain that mastery by all students of a variety of scientific, technical, and cultural fundamentals and the skills to use, manipulate, and transform them are essential to the common good, to the maintenance of a democratic system and to the pursuit of a more egalitarian society.[27] Moreover, subjects with a loaded cultural content (such as languages, literature, history, geography, personal and social development) represent an important component of the double initiation into a particular society and into the emerging world society which integrates the future citizen.

Accommodation of cultural and religious diversity within the school cannot be actualized by exempting certain students from basic school subjects in societies where such subjects are compulsory by virtue of democratically adopted laws. From an ethical viewpoint, the debate thus focuses more acutely on the content to be emphasized within the framework of this common instruction. Choices on curriculum content are made periodically regarding the general framework defined by national and local decision-makers and, on a daily basis, regarding the educational strategies and activities favoured by teaching professionals.

Those debates do not deny the existence of a dominant culture within institutions. Contemporary educational research is a long way from demonstrating that the equality of individuals belonging to different cultural groups necessitates a rigorously egalitarian representation of their cultures in curricula and school practices.[28] Nevertheless, the educational literature clearly shows the necessity of a certain accommodation of differences in order to ensure the relevance of school instruction for minority group students as well as the validation of their previous experience.[29] This adaptation of the curriculum thus should be fostered more from a pedagogical rationale than from an ethical one and should be implemented more often on the basis of professional judgment than of State regulations.

Moreover, pluralism of instructional content could well become imperative under the impact of other factors: the debates currently taking place within the disciplines themselves (consider, here, the multiple interpretations of history or aesthetic points of difference in literature or the arts); the realities of national societies (always marked by a variety of social cleavages); finally, considerations of public interest (for example, the necessity of multilingualism and international education in the face of planetary challenges). All those factors act, to different degrees, in favour of an ever greater complexity in school subject content.[30] The production of knowledge and the adoption of public policies within the liberal democracies are such that the minimal content to be universally transmitted of necessity, can only be largely pluralistic.

Even if students have no alternative to being exposed to this content once it has been defined, they retain the right to react to it differently, to accept or reject it, all of which can offer excellent opportunities to put both the civic culture and the consciousness of diversity into practice in class. Furthermore, by virtue of the principle respecting the moral independence of individuals, teaching content with a higher political and cultural load carries an important obligation for teachers to abstain from imposing their own sociopolitical options.

The second important aspect in the process of initiation into the particular society where future citizens will have to make their way is the adoption of regulations governing the sharing of the common school space by its various inhabitants, especially the contacts among students. Initiation of young people into society through adoption of rules of conduct within the school does not mean the universal imposition of a uniform code. It is quite normal in liberal democracy that the regulations inside various institutions and even within the same institution may not be uniform. Regulations may be flexible enough to allow students to live according to a different culture or religion in every situation where flexibility does not endanger the common life.

Finally, the initiation of young people into the particular society where they will live includes awareness that the habits and customs with which they are familiar do not carry the same significance for all and that it is possible to live together without adopting identical life choices. By participating in deliberations aimed at bringing about changes in the norms of common life, and in making a certain opening for cultural and religious diversity while maintaining the means necessary for the school to carry out its mandate, young people engage in a practical course of civic education. They learn to respect individuals for their own distinct identities, to recognize diversity without marginalizing it, and to develop their critical reasoning with regard to their own and others' choices.

Notes

1 See, for example, Martineau et Laville, « L'histoire »; Sears, "Social Studies in Canada"; and Laville, "History Taught in Québec Is Not Really That Different."

2 Ackerman, *Social Justice in the Liberal State*; Larmore, *Patterns of Moral Complexity*; Rawls, *Political Liberalism*.

3 Rawls, *Political Liberalism*.

4 Kymlicka, *Liberalism, Community and Culture*; Taylor, *Multiculturalism and the "Politics of Recognition."*

5 Nagel, *Égalité et partialité*.

6 Young, *Justice and the Politics of Difference*.

7 Taylor, *Multiculturalism and the "Politics of Recognition."*

8 Ibid.

9 Kymlicka, *Liberalism, Community and Culture*; Walzer. "Comment."

10 Schermerhorn, *Comparative Ethnic Relations*.

11 Juteau-Lee, *Frontières ethniques en devenir*.

12 Camilleri, « Identité et gestion de la disparité culturelle »; Oriol, « Les communautés culturelles et la recherche ».

13 Williams, *L'éthique et les limits de la philosophie*.

14 Kymlicka, *Liberalism, Community and Culture* (1989).

15 Mouffe, *Dimensions of Radical Democracy*.

16 Callan, "Discrimination and Religious Schooling."

17 Habermas, *Morale et communication*; Pourtois, « La démocratie délibérative ».

18 Gutmann, *Democratic Education*.

19 Rawls, *Political Liberalism*.

20 Ibid.

21 Gutmann, *Democratic Education*.

22 Janine Hohl and Michèle Normand, *Développement moral, dynamique*

identitaire et adaptation au pluralisme en éducation (Montréal: GREAPE, Centre d'Études Ethniques de l'Université de Montréal, to appear).

23 McLaughlin, "Citizenship, Diversity and Education"; Gutmann, *Democratic Education*.

24 Gutmann, *Democratic Education*.

25 Galston, *Liberal Purposes*.

26 Gutmann, *Democratic Education*.

27 Carens, "Difference and Domination."

28 Ravitch, "Multiculturalism"; Abdallah-Pretceille, *Quelle école pour quelle intégration?*; Grinter, "Multicultural or Antiracist Education?"

29 Charlot, « L'intégration scolaire des jeunes d'origine immigrée »; Lynch, Modgil, and Modgil, *Cultural Diversity and the Schools*.

30 Conseil Supérieur de l'Éducation, *Les défis éducatifs du pluralisme*.

First Thoughts on First Nations Citizenship: Issues in Education

MARIE BATTISTE and HELEN SEMAGANIS

Citizenship issues in education for First Nations peoples in Canada historically have concerned civilization, assimilation, and colonization. The early formal educational experiences of First Nations peoples in boarding and federal schools were founded on forced citizenship and false belonging to an alien concept of Canada in which loyalty and allegiance to Eurocentric civilization and oppression were glorified into daily curricula. This colonial baggage continues to inform current curricula in public schools, forging conceptions of citizen rights, privileges, and responsibilities as defined within modern liberal society. The neglect of Aboriginal conceptions of society, individual roles, and responsibilities to the collective consciousness continues to yield a curriculum biased towards colonialist views of individuals and societies. When Aboriginal peoples are called to address issues like citizenship, particularly how they define citizenship from their own perspectives, what citizenship means, if anything, from an Aboriginal perspective, and how membership and responsibilities should be derived from that perspective, they are forced into the colonial paradigm to which they have difficulty linking their experience. What appears as resistance to colonization is frequently questioned, even challenged. Current issues of citizenship in Canada carry baggage that again drives First Nations relationships, treaties, and self-determination to a bias towards Eurocentric perceptions of citizenship and governance.

In current Eurocentric thought, citizenship is the state of being vested with the rights, privileges, and duties of citizens. To be a citizen and entitled to these certain rights and privileges with corresponding protections, one also becomes subject to corresponding responsibilities and duties embraced in values of loyalty to its government, state, or king.

Citizens achieve unity of the state not by impartial reason but rather by their emotional attachment via patriotism and nationalism. As history shows, such attachments can also legitimate an undemocratic, authoritarian government. In most monarchies, including the United Kingdom, citizens are usually referred to as subjects, meaning that they owe their allegiance to the sovereign in return for protection but not necessarily for rights of self-governance. These ideas signify a symbolic intersection between new post-colonial rights consciousness with the older idea of living under the rule of a sovereign.

Citizenship is a conceptual tool of the governing state that calls for an acquiescence to an ideology that the government creates. Usually, that ideology serves to eradicate dissimilarity or diversity of thought and propagandizes common values that support identity building and unity. Acquiescence in the imposed civic culture becomes the norm, or the universal, and the standard of vesting the rights, privileges, and duties of a citizen. Aboriginal peoples who comprise the First Nations[1] of Canada have experienced and still live in the uneasy gaps of these ideas.

From the Aboriginal perspective, citizenship is an idealist fiction. It is another impossible standard, like civilization and assimilation. Citizenship education is another manifestation of cognitive imperialism, another artificial category that renders the Aboriginal peoples and their perspectives invisible. It is built on the Eurocentric linguistic conception of individuality and its relations to the aristocracy and the state. It universalizes the colonizer's experience and power and establishes an unrealizable norm for others. While citizenship is a device for interpreting and communicating the experience, values, and achievements of the immigrants, it is also a subtle tool of domination and oppression when wrongfully applied. By the broad dissemination of "being a citizen" and the promise of rights against the state, the immigrants project their experiences as the highest achievements of humanity. Thus, citizenship is an idea that seeks to reinforce the particular position of the immigrants by bringing other groups into loyalty with their artificial institution. As Darlene Johnson states: "The political status of the First Nations within the Canadian Confederation has never been satisfactorily resolved. The prevailing Canadian mythology portrays a transition from ally to subject to ward to citizen. In First Nations circles, this is often referred to 'the Big Lie.' This theory of transition constitutes a denial of the inherent right of First Nations to be self governing. Such denial is characteristic of the practice of colonialism."[2]

The ideology of citizenship forces the colonized to yield towards an experience of double consciousness. Our colonial education in Eurocentric paradigms of knowledge has created the experience of double consciousness "the sense of always looking at one's self through the eyes of others, of measuring one's soul by the tape of a world that looks on in amused contempt and pity."[3] Given such normality of citizenship in double consciousness, typically the colonialists constructed the difference with Aboriginals as the savage Other. Being the Other made Aboriginal thought and society uncivilized. Aboriginal life became surrounded by a spider web of imported meanings that have been incontestable and oppressive. Aboriginal experiences and interpretation of life were ridiculed and ignored or openly attacked through colonial education. When Aboriginals refuse to validate dominant stereotypes of their cultures or of themselves or to validate the necessity of Eurocentric paradigms, they find themselves marked as deviant and invisible, deviant because they are different from the artificially created norm and invisible because they are not recognized as a viable human full of potential and ability.

The ideal of a civic public attempts to transcend particularities of interest and affiliation to seek a common good. Transcending particularities means attaining the universality of a general will that replaces difference (particularity) and the private realms of family. The concept of citizenship encompasses notions of individual rights, responsibilities, and privileges as well as assumes a relationship of reciprocity to a nation/state that are carved out from philosophical assumptions of the relationships the individual has with others, including the collective of individuals called the state.

The policy issues of citizenship of Aboriginal people have been blurred by historical events and perceptions created by colonialist propaganda filtered through colonial education, media, and politics. In order to understand the issues of citizenship from within an Aboriginal context, we must define and discuss Aboriginal consciousness about self and community and contrast the tenets of this view against liberalism that grew out of colonialism and that defines contemporary views of Canadian citizenship. In this chapter we intend to bring our thoughts and analysis of Aboriginal and Canadian concepts of society to the debate by offering contrasting conceptions of citizenship. This contrast should be understood from the perspective of the current constitutional order, not from the rejected colonial order. Finally, in this chapter we seek to identify the educational challenge for balancing diverse paradigms of citizenship and seek a socially just process for enabling First Nations to develop autonomously and equitably within Canada as they strive to continue their quest for self-determination.

First Nations Citizenship

Prior to creating colonial governments in Canada, the king entered into treaties with the First Nations of North America, which created the controlling relationship, rather than subjectship or citizenship, of First Nations with the Crown and its subjects. It is the free association with the imperial Crown. These treaties created the hidden constitution of Canada or treaty federalism that is the foundation of provincial and federal authority in North America.[4] Treaty federalism protects Aboriginal order of kinship, and turns the issue to free and equal association of First Nations with provinces within Canadian federalism. It is important to survey the historical framework of the treaties, since most curricula neglect it, to the detriment of the Aboriginal children and to the prejudice against any alternative vision of relationships.

Canadian Citizenship and Aboriginal Consciousness

Canadian citizenship is a new, ambiguous state created from British subjectship in 1976. Since a Canadian citizen can have dual citizenship, an immigrant's original nationality is not exhausted or extinguished. Immigrants can be citizens of both Canada and their homeland. Canadian citizenship, however, has a priority over all other responsibilities. The pursuit of particular interests must take place in the public framework of citizenship. It has incorporated a respect for particularity and differences. Yet the concept of citizenship supports a colonizer's view of universality.

In addressing the issues of citizenship from First Nations' perspectives, we must attempt to unravel the assumptions of self and society, or individualism and collectivism in society, from both the paradigms of modern liberal theory and the Aboriginal consciousness. Because of space limitations, this review will be partial. It is sufficient to say that these different world views hold different conceptions of government, citizen, and individual. They also have been the source of contagion and debate in whose context the issues of First Nations self-government and self-determination have been viewed by non-First Nations people.

Aboriginal people share an alternative vision of society. While it is compatible with universally recognized human rights, its stress is upon wholeness and relationships, particularly the responsibilities among families, clans, communities, and nations. At the minimal level, Aboriginal thought teaches that everyone and everything are part of a whole in which they are interdependent. Each person has a right to a personal identity as a member of a community but also has responsibilities to the other life forms and to the ecology of the whole. Thus, Aboriginal thought values the group over the individual and the extended family over the immediate or biological family. It was and is inconceivable that a human being could exist without a family or a kinship regulation. There are no strangers in Aboriginal thought. "Guests" within their territory were typically assigned to a local family or clan for education and responsibilities. Such kinship was a necessary part of aboriginal peace and good order. Aboriginal diplomacy and treaties with the Crown dramatically illustrate this point, since they were modelled on kinship. Within the vast fabric of families, clans, and confederacies, every person stood in a specific, personal relationship to every other person.

The Aboriginal order of kinship implies a distinct form of rights. Everyone has the right to give and receive according to his/her choices. Those who give the most freely and generously enjoy the strongest claims to sharing, and these claims are directed to their relations, not to a Eurocentric community, state, or nation. Aboriginal thought does not recognize these entities, since this is an artificial construct of Eurocentric languages. Instead of a state, Aboriginals recognize a web of reciprocal relationships among individuals. There can be no state or external political authority separate from your relatives. Leaders did not shed their kinship responsibilities but remained tied to their clans. This tradition renders the rights of citizens against the state as meaningless, because there is no state to argue against; there are only relatives. This situation, however, is changing as the education systems entrench the notion that states and citizens are necessary and essential to society, thus fostering a belief in authoritarian governments.

In the Aboriginal order, rights are the freedom to be what each person is created to be. Because no individual knows what that path is for another, each has the independence and security to discover that path without interference. From infancy, children are born into a family, surrounded by relatives and friends who are considered "uncles" and "aunts." The actual blood kinship may be worked out in time, but everyone appears related. Children are constantly reminded to respect and respond to the feelings of all of their kin. They are praised for showing sensitivity and generosity to others, teased for being self-centred, rude, or acquisitive, but are rarely punished. Childhood experiences of intense collective support and attention combined with self-discipline and responsibilities create a personality that is cooperative and independent, self-restrained yet individualistic, attuned to the feelings of other people but non-intrusive. At the same time, individuals are left free to discover their gifts and talents and choose their course of action by personal choice and integrity. Such a personality is compatible with a certain kind of social order that strives for consensus but tolerates a great deal of diversity and non-conformity.

An order is established where leaders seek to persuade through example, but do not command.[5] Within this order, personal safety and economic security are assured by linguistic solidarity, ritual, socialization, and kinship, rather than by external power or law.[6] People continue to understand and to trust those who have always loved them.

The depth and individuality of this trust make it possible for Aboriginal peoples to tolerate a degree of non-conformity that may distress "civilized" and authoritative societies. A non-intrusive, autonomous personality is inconsistent with the demands of a state, however, whether it is governed by a "democratic" majority or an authoritarian minority. To Aboriginal people, a "state" is a group of strangers who demand obedience through coercive and restrictive measures. This demand is a challenge to Aboriginal order and its intimate realms of relationships.

Treaty Federalism

The treaty relations between First Nations and the English sovereign are understood best as a branch of international law as well as customary constitutional law of Great Britain.[7] From the beginning of treaties with the First Nations, the Crown recognized their autonomy. From the Eurocentric viewpoint the treaties recognized the sovereignty of the First Nations, but from a First Nations perspective they recognized the self-determination of Aboriginal peoples. Without this dual understanding, treaties make no sense. Treaties brought First Nations under the protection of the prerogatives of the imperial Crown of England based on the will of Aboriginal peoples. This protection is similar to the individual citizen's entitlement to protection in rights and privileges derived from the Crown. Yet it is not a birthright: it is a *free and voluntary choice* of the Aboriginal peoples to ally themselves with alien nations as a means of protecting their Aboriginal values.

These prerogative treaties created two sovereigns of a shared territory.

Principles of trust, promise, and protection, rather than geographical unity, race, or political ideology, were the foundations of the nation-to-nation relationship.[8] Two general models of treaties exist in British jurisdictions of North America: Georgian treaties of Eastern Canada and Victorian treaties of the prairie provinces. Georgian treaties of peace and friendship were signed before Confederation, while Victorian treaties of peace and goodwill (the numbered treaties) were signed after Confederation. There are also a number of treaties in Upper and Lower Canada and British Columbia that share certain attributes of these models. These written agreements between First Nations and the imperial Crown created the nation-to-nation relationship. Together, these relationships are often called treaty federalism. Treaty federalism was the original Aboriginal-prerogative federation with Great Britain. It was an indispensable step that had to occur before the creation of colonial authority in North America.

Each treaty illustrated the spirit and intent of treaty federalism and its outline. The terms of some of the treaties clearly affirm the Aboriginal political tradition. According to their ancient customs, the Aboriginal peoples selected the chiefs and headmen who negotiated and signed the treaties, but they did not surrender any of their inherent right to self-determination. This tradition is confirmed in the Georgian treaties. In the ratification conferences for the Wabanaki Compact of 1725, the spokesperson for the Wabanaki Confederacy objected to the terms of the written treaty. In particular, he challenged the addition of a statement that the Wabanaki acknowledged King George to be their king and had "declared themselves to the Crown of England." The Wabanaki spokesperson wrote that, during the treaty negotiations, "when you have asked me if I acknowledged Him for king I answered yes butt att the same time have made you take notice that I did not understand to acknowledge Him for my king butt only that I owned that he was king of his kingdom as the king of France is king of His."[9]

The Míkmaq delegation at the Wabanaki Treaty Conference had asserted the same position. On 1 December 1725, when Lieutenant Governor Mascarene read to the Míkmaq delegates a proposed ratification treaty (often labelled Number 239) to the Wabanaki Compact, the Míkmaq delegates stated their own understanding of the words. They said they would "pay all the respect & Duty to the King of Great Britain as we did to the King of France, but we reckon our selves a free People and are not bound."[10]

At the pre-treaty conference in 1750 Nova Scotia Council asked the grand chief about the process of making a treaty with the Míkmaq Nation. He replied "That he would return to his own people and inform them what he had done here, and then would go to the other Chiefs, and propose to them to renew the peace, and that he thought he should be able to perform in a month, and would bring some of them with him if he could, and if not would bring their answer."[12] The council accepted Cope's authority to carry the treaty proposal to the other Míkmaq chiefs. The Míkmaq Compact (1752) marked the acquisition of a separate legal personality for them in the Law of the Nations and in Great Britain.

Under the protection of the Royal Proclamation of 1763, the First Nations in the Victorian treaties expressly affirmed their right to self-determination under the imperial Crown. The Victorian treaties recognized that the Aboriginal peoples properly selected Headmen and Chiefs to negotiate the treaties and these chiefs and headmen would, through the internal structures of each First Nation, maintain the duty to see that the treaty was fully performed.[12] These indispensable acknowledgments are crucial in understanding the context of Aboriginal free association with the Crown and the limitation of the citizenship. As protected nations under their prerogative treaties, Aboriginal peoples were never subject to the authority of the imperial Parliament, but remained as foreign jurisdictions under the prerogatives of the Crown rather than as subjects of the Crown.

Moreover, all the treaties distinguish between Her Majesty's other subjects and Her Indian people. These categories affirm that the Aboriginal peoples are distinct from other subjects. It affirms a basic constitutional distinction that recognizes their political relations with the Crown as a distinct character of the peoples living in a distinct geographical territory. The treaties affirm the distinct society from the colonizers and their political relationship to the Crown and thus affirm the Aboriginal peoples' right to self-determination from other governments or administrative agents.

In this regard, of crucial importance in the Victorian treaties of "peace and goodwill" is the acknowledgment of the First Nations' obligation to maintain "peace and good order" in the ceded land among all other subjects. The common and controlling article of the Victorian treaties provides

> the undersigned Chiefs and Headmen, on their own behalf and on behalf of all other Indians inhabiting the tract within ceded, do hereby solemnly promise and engage to strictly observe this treaty, and also to conduct and

behave themselves as good and loyal subjects of Her Majesty the Queen. *They promise and engage that they* will, in all respects, obey and abide by the law, that they *will maintain peace and good order* between each other, and *between themselves and other tribes of Indians and between themselves and others of Her Majesty's subjects, whether Indians, Half-breeds, or whites, now inhabiting or hereafter to inhabit any part of the said* ceded tract; and that they will not molest the person or property of any inhabitant of such ceded tract; or the property of Her Majesty the Queen, or interfere with or trouble any person passing or travelling through the said tract, or any part thereof, and that they will assist the officers of Her Majesty in bring [sic] to justice or punishment any Indian offending against the stipulations of this treaty, or infringing the law in force in the country so ceded.[13]

This treaty article affirms the inherent right of self-determination of the Aboriginal peoples and government by the chiefs and headmen. It also affirms that Aboriginal authority was a vested prerogative right to govern the ceded land and was inviolable. The exercise of Aboriginal authority did not require any association with the imperial Crown.

The coherence of the treaties was a customary order that the Aboriginal peoples reserved to themselves. Provided they did not transgress the treaty or infringe on the treaty rights of others or violate their customary law, under the treaties Indians could do anything they pleased in their reserved or ceded territories. Conversely, the imperial Crown and its agents or other subjects could do nothing but what they were authorized by some positive delegation from the First Nations in the treaties. Further, the treaties created the boundaries that confined alien political control.

These rights negotiated by Aboriginal leaders accrued to the collective Aboriginal peoples from which individuals within Aboriginal society could continue their relationships as they were conceived from the Creator and practised in daily life through language, culture, spirituality, and community. Under the idea of free association of the Crown, Indians were protected from the laws of the domestic body politic of provincial governments. Indians owed no loyalty and allegiance to domestic European governments, nor were they subject to their laws. As such, they were not viewed as citizens of provinces or of Canada, and thus they did not exercise the rights and privileges of Canadian citizenship. Although they did not vote nor hold office within Canada, the fluid boundaries of their land base fostered mobility, which enabled Aboriginal peoples to choose residency within their natural territorial boundaries. Although

Canada has since imposed artificial boundaries and defined their citizen advantages, Aboriginal peoples continued to live by custom and tradition within these boundaries, without any colonial rights or advantages.

Aboriginal self-determination was affirmatively recognized in the treaties by the first principle of the rule of law in the United Kingdom that all peoples, regardless of race or ethnicity, are to be secure in what the Crown has recognized as their liberties and entitlements. Canada and the provinces have only such power as delegated to the Crown by the First Nations in the treaties. Additionally, these promises and terms of the treaties created a fiduciary duty in the Crown to protect the right of self-determination.[14] This order was distinct from the colonial order.

Canadian Citizenship

Provincial Federalism and Colonialism

In 1867 Canada defined its collective imagined identity in the British North America Act and under section 91(24) assumed from the Crown legal authority for "Indians and lands reserved for Indians." Under section 132 the Imperial Parliament further delegated to the federal government the necessary and proper authority to carry into effect treaty obligations of the Imperial Crown within Canada. These administrative powers implemented Prerogative Treaties in the newly confederated Canada with First Nations. Although the Constitution [British North America] Act of 1867 recognized the historical identities of the colonists as participants in the newly forged nation, it recognized Indians not as individuals but only as a continuing responsibility to the collective under the treaties.

Since 1867 the colonialists have never allowed participation of treaty delegates or Indians in their political process. These constitutional voices have been excluded from debate on public policy. The failure of the existing electoral system to provide for true democracy is demonstrated by the fact that only twelve self-identified Aboriginal persons have occupied the 11,000 available seats in federal Parliament.[15] Recently, some Aboriginal leaders have represented the colonial riding system as individual representatives, but none has been delegated the authority to speak for Aboriginal and treaty rights of the treaty areas or Aboriginal nations.

While the fact remains that Aboriginal peoples cannot be excluded, the excuses for this exclusion have changed over time. The original justification was that the treaties created separate jurisdictions between the colonialists and First Nations.[16] Then the excuses shifted to the alleged racial and cultural inferiority of Aboriginal peoples. The next argument was their status under the federal Indian Act and the historical use of the federal franchise as a means of assimilating them. Currently, it is the lamentable fact that they constitute about 5 per cent of the population, and, although they now have the right to vote, because of their geographical distribution they have, regrettably, little voice in the political affairs of the country. Moreover, inmates in federal penal institutions are disenfranchised under the Canada Election Act.[17] Similar impediments to the exercise of the franchise by immigrants have not existed.[18]

Using this enumerated power, the Canadian government asserted its purposes and authority to create new categories, rather than following the treaties' grant of broad power of the chief and headmen over subjects within the ceded lands. In 1876 the federal Indian Act created new categories and definitions of Aboriginal peoples. Under the policy of divide and conquer, the federal government defined "Indians" in order to destroy communities by arbitrary criteria of residency, marriage, employability, education, and military service. These definitions, conceived without consent of the Aboriginal peoples, segmented Aboriginal societies into categories of status and non-status, treaty and non-treaty, urban and reserve, and enfranchised and disenfranchised Indians. By virtue of these definitions, First Nations peoples either retained or lost the rights and privileges contained in the treaties without gaining rights and privileges as Canadian citizens, and thereby diminished if not destroyed their connectedness with their original families and communities.

Contemporary categories affirm the colonizer's categories in identifying Aboriginal men, women, and children as non-status, non-treaty, or even Métis, which has weakened Aboriginal unity and fractionated the political power recognized in the First Nations under the "peace and good order" clause of the treaties. In addition, the federal government's restrictive definitions have created a dilemma over provincial and federal jurisdiction. By validating these categories, the first ministers of Canada have further complicated the issue of self-government, since governments typically presuppose a territorial base. Most of the Aboriginal population (75 per cent), by virtue of the newly created categories and mobility to urban areas, are located off reserves, most without a recognized land base from which to exercise their collective rights under the treaties.

For most of the post-Confederation period, status Indians were viewed as wards of the Crown, as dependent on the federal government and socially, linguistically, and economically incompetent to exercise full citizenship rights and duties. For Indian women, however, enfranchisement was a more traumatic and automatic consequence of marriage to a non-Indian man. Their dependent status as Indians could be transferred to their newly defined dependent status as wife of a white man. Since women were believed to be dependent on men, Indian men could not gain citizenship by marriage to white women, since they had no livelihood to be independent as did their white counterparts. Indian men could demonstrate their independence and competence by receiving an education, serving in the military, or joining the clergy. In other words, their right to vote was thus conceived as an earned attribute.[19]

Treating Indians as wards of the state, the federal government carved out the rights and opportunities of Aboriginal peoples from the limited colonial conceptions articulated in the Indian Act. Because they were not allowed to vote, hold office, or manage their own affairs, Indians held negligible political power. They were confined to reserves and held hostage to the economic whims of the colonial government and powers, thereby held in bondage to poverty. In addition, they were provided with an education that actively sought to destroy the language, culture, and foundations of Aboriginal consciousness. Those who did opt for enfranchisement had their status and rights defined by provincial and federal regulations and were forced to explore their economic and social identity outside the realms of tribal life and consciousness. Those who did not choose enfranchisement were subject under the Indian Act to limited and constricted rights and opportunities as issued by the colonial government, which decided the degree of power, prestige, and authority they would have over their own lives and within the larger society. In addition, the Indian Act created new political agencies funded and supported by the federal government, which would administer the locally defined limited powers and monies extended to them. In providing for elections of Chiefs and Band Councils, the federal government sought to erode traditional government bases that refused to be linked to the federal government and be limited by arbitrary or foreign visions of shared values of authority.

The Electoral Franchise

Against the background of the decolonization and the civil rights movement, in 1960 the Canada Elections Act accorded all Indian peoples the right to vote in federal elections.[20] Often this action is confused with the conferring of citizenship. In extending the franchise to all Aboriginal persons, the prime minster promised, "I say this to those of the Indian race, that in bringing this legislation the Minister of Citizenship and Immigration [Ellen Fairclough] will reassure, as she has assured to date, that existing rights and treaties, traditional or otherwise, possessed by the Indians shall not in any way be abrogated or diminished in consequence of having the right to vote. That is one of the things that throughout the years caused suspicion in the minds of many Indians who have conceived the granting of the franchise as a step in the direction of denying them their ancient rights."[21] Symbolically, this electoral equality offered a new relationship, but the cost would be high. In the 1969 White Paper Policy the federal government attempted to abolish all the unique and collective rights of the Indian people, the Aboriginal and treaty rights, and make them all provincial citizens.[22] The provinces would provide and deliver services as they did for all other Canadians. By granting the right to vote, the government argued, it was justifying the oppressive extension of the powers over Aboriginal peoples. Most refused this offer, and they continue to refuse to participate in electoral politics.[23] What is more important, Aboriginal people thought that by accepting the right to vote they would validate the existing colonial legislation limiting aboriginal and treaty rights passed before 1960, when they had no voting rights.[24]

Aboriginal people have negligible political power and influence in Canada. The primary reason for Aboriginal under-representation in Parliament stems from the failure of the electoral law to recognize existing constitutional rights of Aboriginal peoples. Additionally, current electoral law fails to recognize Aboriginal and treaty rights that define new constitutional communities of interest. Their constitutional rights are distinct from the "group interests" of others. Of special importance is their right to cultural association.[25] While the federal Electoral Boundaries Readjustment Act allows for group interests to be taken into account in the drawing of electoral boundaries, it has not been responsive to the constitutional interest of Aboriginal peoples. These facts show a violation of the essential core of modern democratic thought. All democratic ideals follow the principle that governments must never fall permanently into the hands of a faction, however broadly defined, in any society.[26] Democracy in Canada has been totally controlled by the colonialist-immigrant faction at every level. Canadian democracy has fallen permanently into the grasp of the colonialists and their interests.

Tenets of Collective Consciousness

Treaties recognize the collective rights of Aboriginal peoples. Integral to these treaties is the right to promote, develop, and maintain their Aboriginal consciousness, language, customs, and rituals. Treaties primarily yield not to individual rights but to collective rights, among which are the rights to live according to their collective consciousness, to maintain their connectedness with one another, to live by no artificial standards that exclude individuals but instead enable each person to develop his/her gifts and talents in order that the whole might be renewed and rekindled by continuing contributions. It is a consensual paradigm, in which the ideals of self-discipline and tribal self-determination can be manifested. Treaty relationships are governed by a collective consciousness of what is good because of shared philosophies of the animacy of all things that are interrelated and interdependent. In this way, each person is connected in a multitude of reciprocal relationships, some derived by birth and others by socialization to a holistic world view or consciousness.

Imbued within this consciousness, the Aboriginal individual is seen as vital to the collective, and the consciousness of that collective is vital to the sustenance of the whole. Culture, then, is the collective agreement of the members of the society on the prescriptions and circumscriptions about what is accepted, valued, sanctioned, both positively and negatively, and what will be the protocol and beliefs. Their informal agreement says, "This is how we are going to run our society." Their philosophy and world view are the theoretical or esoteric side of culture, while customs and ways are the practical applications of philosophy and belief systems.[27] Language is vital to that whole, since it is the repository of the collective knowledge and awareness of society.

In this collective each person has both rights and advantages stemming from being part of the whole but also has obligations and responsibilities that define membership and citizenship. The rights and advantages of being Aboriginal in the modern context have been seen only in terms of material and economic advantages, that is, the right to an education, housing, or tax exemptions. Beyond the Indian Act's rights and opportunities, however, the treaties offer each person within Aboriginal society the right to culture, consciousness, and continuity. Further responsibilities build from one's relationships to oneself and to others embraced in the whole. To oneself, one is responsible for recognizing and developing talents and gifts, of cultivating and mastering these gifts in order to build a secure foundation for the attainment of self-realization. As one understands oneself, spiritually, mentally, physically, and emotionally, s/he becomes centred and thus is a vital force in enabling others to become the same. Similarly, those who are troubled, addicted, disconnected, or impaired cannot contribute to self or the whole: "If a person is whole and balanced, then s/he is in a position to relate and carry out his/her responsibilities in a wholesome manner."[28]

Wholeness speaks to the totality of creation, in which the welfare of the group is the locus of the consciousness as opposed to that of the individual. Non-interference is respect for others' wholeness, totality, and knowledge, and each person therefore must be allowed independence to find his/her path and purpose. These ideals yield, then, to an appreciation of a person's individuality and independence, as well as of his/her need for long absences from the group, for not asking for assistance when in trouble, and for being a jack of all trades.[29]

To others, each person has responsibilities and obligations. These responsibilities support social values of sharing and of contributing to the good feelings of the group through humour and support for the sustenance and maintenance of the interconnected and interdependent whole. This whole necessarily contains many concentric circles, among which are those that embrace the cycles of nature and the life that it supports. Since everything is more or less animate, everything has spirit and knowledge. The social value of sharing manifests in relationships of the whole. Relationships result from interactions with the group and all of creation. Since all things in nature are interrelated and interdependent, it is vital that each person views his/her relationships not only with each other as humans but within all of nature. One is then responsible for the sustenance and maintenance of the renewable resources that enable the whole to survive. The four elements of water, fire, air, and earth are seen as vital forces or animates that command respect, and ceremonies renew and respect these forces.

Within Aboriginal self-government, the issue is not one of creating an entity or a body politic, constrained by borrowed criteria from non-Aboriginal systems, but rather one that embraces or is forged by the needs of those who have and continue to maintain the consciousness. Further, self-governance must define the process and means to facilitate the sustenance of this consciousness. Language and culture, then, are vital cornerstones of this consciousness, and a body politic embedded within treaty relationships requires not standards of arbitration but rather processes of discovery and exploration which will validate the life experiences and enrich others so that they may contribute to the growing whole. From this perspective, in First Nations consciousness citizenship balances the reciprocal individual and collective relationships and forges shared values within their own political system. Citizenship must be defined within a consensual paradigm which operates from a basis of respect and cooperation, not of coercion and propaganda.

Conclusion

The contagion of modern liberal theory among Aboriginal peoples has created confusion and doubt among many sectors of Aboriginal society. Among them are the categories of individual created from the relationship defined in the Indian Act. The non-status, Bill C-31, Métis, and some "Indian" bands have been thrown into a quagmire of ideological dilemmas between individualism and collectivism. On the one hand, many have accepted these colonial categories and conceptions of self as individuals and thus press for the individual rights advanced by the Charter of Rights and Freedoms within the Constitution Act of 1982. On the other hand, many seek to ensure their collective Aboriginal identities within culture, language, and community.[30] For those whose identities have been affected by colonial legislation and who have been excluded from community life and consciousness, consideration within First Nations societies must be given to a process of repatriation of Aboriginal consciousness. Whatever process is chosen, it is first and foremost a First Nations responsibility to define their inclusiveness founded upon an understanding of community, consciousness, and continuity. It is a process that cannot be legislated, coerced by external forces, or defined outside that inner circle.

In North America, it is an undisputed fact that colonization has profoundly affected and interfered with Aboriginal society and families. Residential schools, television, poverty, intrusive government, social-welfare programs, and urbanization all have contributed to the increased breakdown of Aboriginal families, cultures, and languages. Perhaps compulsory school education has created the greatest alienation of Aboriginal peoples because of its Eurocentric biases and prejudices in the curriculum. Since over half of the Aboriginal school population attends provincial schools, public schools are defining and validating the roles, relationships, and responsibilities of First Nations students, whose history and treaties define a totally different relationship with Canada and the provinces. Despite the inclusion of Aboriginal content in some schools, the provinces are prescribing the knowledge, the skills, and the values for Aboriginal children, largely thought to be effective for non-Aboriginal society but not for Aboriginal society. Inclusive Aboriginal content, as prescribed in some provinces, does not seem to resolve the dilemmas, since exclusion of Aboriginal children in education has been seen as an equity issue: enabling Aboriginal students to obtain the current forms of education, matching styles of teaching to student socialization patterns and preference, including not more than 20 per cent adapted content to the current curricula, and incorporating fragmented Aboriginal knowledge in Eurocentric curricula.

Public education has not sought to address the more complex issues of treaty relationships and the responsibilities of Canada and of Aboriginal peoples to those relationships. Perhaps this choice of exclusion is based on Canada's ignoble history of broken promises, presumed superiority, and conscious attacks on Aboriginal peoples and reflects a history that does not live up to the righteous values assumed to be at the core of Canadian citizenship. If there is to be some balance to the relationships and to the future relationships of First Nations and Canada, there must be a respect for the Aboriginal consciousness that treaties recognize and affirm. Queen Elizabeth II has eloquently provided the best standard for Canadian citizenship: "Canada asks no citizens to deny their forebears or forsake their heritage, only that each should accept and value the cultural freedom of others as he enjoys his own. It is a gentle invitation, this call to citizenship, and I urge those who have accepted the invitation to participate fully in the building of the Canadian society and to demonstrate the real meaning of the brotherhood of man."[31] The question is whether Canada can live up to this standard.

Notes

1 First Nations, Aboriginal, and Indian are used in this chapter as they refer to various conceptions of indigenous peoples in Canada. First Nations refers to nation/state bodies; Aboriginal refers to all Natives, including Métis, non-status, and off-reserve, while Indian is referenced to the specific policy and practices of the federal government towards the people as issued in the Indian Act.
2 Johnston, "First Nations and Canadian Citizenship," 349.
3 Du Bois, *The Souls of Black Folk*, 45.
4 Henderson, "Implementing the Treaty Order"; "Empowering Treaty Federalism."
5 Barsh, "Nature and Spirit of the North American Political System.

6 Henderson, "First Nations Legal Inheritance in Canada."

7 Brownlie, *Principles of Public International Law*; Henderson, "Empowering Treaty Federalism," 248–50.

8 Wildsmith, "Treaty Responsibilities."

9 Baxter, *Documentary History of the State of Maine*, 208.

10 National Archives of Canada, NS A: MG11 CO 217 Vol. 17:2 December (1725).

11 Atkins, *Selections from the Public Documents of the Province of Nova Scotia*, 671.

12 Treaties 1, 2, 3, 4, 5, 6, 7, 9, 10, 11. Treaty 1923 (Ottawa: Queen's Printer, 1966); "And whereas the Indians of the said tract, duly convened in Council as aforesaid, and being requested by Her Majesty's said Commissioners to name certain Chiefs and Headmen, who should be authorized on their behalf to conduct such negotiations and sign any treaty to be founded thereon ... And thereupon in open council the different bands, having presented the men of their choice to the said Commissioners as Chiefs and Headmen, for the purpose aforesaid, of the respective bands of Indians inhabiting the said district hereinafter described ... *to become responsible to Her Majesty for their faithful performance by their respective bands of such obligations as shall be assumed by them*" (emphasis added).

13 Treaty 6, in Henderson, "Empowering Treaty Federalism," 261; emphasis added.

14 *Sparrow v. The Queen*, S.C.R. 1075; 3 C.N.L.R. 178 (1990); Cairns and Williams, *Constitutionalism, Citizenship and Society in Canada*, 29.

15 In the 1870s three Métis were elected in Manitoba. In the twentieth century, nine Aboriginal persons were elected, but only three have been elected in districts where they do not constitute a majority. From the Northwest Territories, six Aboriginal peoples were elected where they form a majority in a constituency. See Royal Commission on Electoral Reform, *Path to Electoral Equality*, 241.

16 Ibid., 242. In particular, treaty payment and annuities were used. This is discrimination on political consciousness, since Aboriginal sovereignty was considered inconsistent with Aboriginal participation in Parliament.

17 Ibid., 237, 244.

18 Kaplan, *Belonging.*

19 Cairns and Williams, *Constitutionalism, Citizenship and Society in Canada*, 29.

20 Hawthorn, *A Survey of the Contemporary Indians of Canada.*

21 Canada, *Canada Elections Act.*

22 Weaver, *Making Canadian Indian Policy.*

23 Johnston, "First Nations and Canadian Citizenship."

24 In *Path to Electoral Equality*, it was stated, "The problems with the electoral

system cannot be viewed in isolation from the historical difficulties that Aboriginal peoples have had with Canadian political institutions. The failure of the Canadian government to work out constitutional accommodations recognizing inherent collective Aboriginal and Treaty rights, coupled with Canada's history of assimilationist policies, have had an adverse impact on Aboriginal perceptions of Parliament andvalue of participating within it. This has created a dilemma for many Aboriginal Canadians. Not wanting to legitimize the constitutional structure in place in Canada, many Aboriginal leaders have argued against assuming voting rights" (242, n347).

25 *Lovelace v. Canada*, United Nations, Human Rights Committee.
26 Unger, *Critical Legal Studies Movement.*
27 Littlebear, "The Criminal Justice System and Aboriginal Men."
28 Ibid., 12.
29 Ibid.
30 *Lovelace v. Canada*, United Nations, Human Rights Committee.
31 Canada, *Symbols of Nationhood,* 1.

Citizenship and Schooling in Manitoba between the End of the First World War and the End of the Second World War

ROSA BRUNO-JOFRÉ

In the last few years there has been a renewed interest in citizenship education and in a reformulation of educational aims in the light of some kind of ideal of a polity in a global society. With the exception of Ken Osborne's work, however, there have been few historical studies in relation to the understanding of citizenship and schooling in Canada.[1] In this chapter I examine the official discourse of Canadianization as expounded in the *Western School Journal* and by the Department of Education in Manitoba and then analyse examples of the intersection of the official discourse and life experience in school and beyond. I will focus mainly on Manitoba between the end of the First World War and the end of the Second World War.

By 1918 the impact of immigration had already been felt, while large movements of urban workers and farmers had grown in importance.[2] Education, character formation, and citizenship were both local and national concerns. Anglo-conformity was the central principle permeating the dominant notion of citizenship that sought to make proper members of the national polity. In addition, in the early 1920s there was an emphasis on a notion of citizenship mostly based on service to the community, duties, responsibilities, and social integration, while by the end of the decade the dominant discourse was beginning to be influenced by progressive education notions of education and democracy.

The end of the Second World War (1945) provides a historical breaking point, because it brought a new international reality that in the long run would affect Canada's view of itself. The war also led to a questioning of racist and ethnocentric ideas, and theories of cultural relativism emerged, which, along with internal developments, made imperative a reconstruction of the understanding of citizenship formation and its principles.

Through the examination of the official discourse followed by the exploration of oral testimonies and case examples like the public schools in Franco-Manitoban communities, I show that the official discourse was not necessarily taught and learned in schools. I also demonstrate that people frequently develop a sense of being Canadian in their own terms in an often contested process of resistance and negotiation.

Main Components of the Official Discourse of Citizenship in Manitoba

Public schooling was created as an integral part of the modern state, one of its functions being the shaping of a moral citizenry. Outside Quebec, the geopolitical framework for citizenship education was English Canadian. French Canada was neglected, loyalty to Britain and the British Empire was emphasized, and the colonization of the First Nations was treated as a matter of fact. The framework had unique connotations, however, given by the situation of Canada within the British Empire, its preoccupation with its place in North America, and the nation-building motif persistent in education. Furthermore, education was and still remains under provincial jurisdiction, although schooling for the First Nations had been left as a federal responsibility.

The aim of public schools in English Canada was to create a homogeneous nation based on a common English language, a common culture, identification with the British Empire, and an acceptance of British institutions and practices. The British Empire and its values and institutions were seen as an indispensable support for a distinctive Canadianism because of Canada's place in North America. Thus, before the Citizenship Act of 1947 there were only British subjects resident in Canada; there were no Canadian citizens as such.

At the end of the Great War, as evidenced by Canada's signing the Peace Treaty at Versailles in its own right and by its separate membership in the League of Nations, there was a growing feeling among Canadians that their country was a distinct national entity, but also an important component of the British Empire. Business leaders and political leaders also had an urgent concern with "education and the national spirit." They were motivated by the massive presence of so-called "aliens," the Depression after the war, and the growth of the Canadian labour movement, including 428 strikes in 1919 across the country and the Winnipeg General Strike in the same year.[3] In addition, the war and its sacrifices could be justified only by a new emphasis on community and duty.

Schooling was the state agency that was expected to generate unity of thought, to teach English to the children of new immigrants, to educate them in Canadian ways, and to generate a civic culture based on service, duties, and responsibilities. Social integration and cohesion were major objectives. In 1918 the minister of education, Dr R.S. Thornton, in his public address to the Manitoba Educational Association identified a need to bring newcomers more quickly into Canadian national life and into the life of the province. He said: "Our aim is to plant Canadian schools with Canadian teachers setting forth Canadian ideals and teaching the language of the country."[4] He quoted the 1916 census, which shows that 42 per cent of the population of the province represented thirty-eight nationalities. His concern was also related to the issue of social and labour unrest. The public school was conceived as an agency for national unity and social harmony. In the case of Manitoba, a major step had been taken in 1916 when, at Thornton's initiative, the legislature repealed the section of the Public Schools Act, which permitted bilingual instruction in schools supported by public funds, and unanimously approved the School Attendance Act, which made school attendance compulsory and instruction unilingual in English.

Tom Mitchell has recently argued that the Great War evoked a sense of national identity among members of Canada's English-speaking middle class, while Canada as a country in 1919 was fragmented along ethnic, social class, and regional lines. In his view, the middle class sought to address the post-war crisis "by casting the post-war order in a particular idiom of nationalism informed by a common Canadianism rooted in Anglo-conformity and a citizenship framed in notions of service, obedience, obligation and fidelity to the state."[5] The National Conference on Character Education in Relation to Canadian Citizenship that took place in Winnipeg in 1919 was an example of efforts made after the war to advance this idiom of citizenship. The conference was funded by the lieutenant governor of Manitoba, himself a Winnipeg investment banker, by other business and professional individuals, and by the Rotary Clubs of Canada. The organizers tried to move the service spirit of the war years to stimulate and guide post-war reconstruction. It is clear from its final recommendations that those who left room to accommodate diversity received little or no attention at the conference. Such was the fate of Professor Carrie Derick, vice-president of the National Council of Women, and first woman faculty member at McGill University. She envisaged an evolving unified Canada that did not suppress diversity and placed great emphasis on equality of opportunity through education and compulsory schooling.[6] Winnipeg labour organizations decided not to send delegates, but there were participants willing to voice the workers' view, without, however, making an impact on the audience. The One Big Union condemned it as nothing more than propaganda of patriotic imperialism.[7] Delegates from Québec, especially the Francophones, politely dissented from the national enthusiasm of the conference. They tried, with little obvious success, to make participants aware that there was another view of Canada.

The Role of Teachers in Citizenship Education

Most participants perceived teachers as playing a powerful role in transmitting an ideology of Anglo-conformity, assimilation, service, social stability, and hostility towards radical change. At the time, the *Western School Journal* reached every school district in the province. Initially a fully independent publication, since 1916 it had contained a bulletin of the Department of Education in Manitoba and also of the Manitoba Trustees Association, and after 1919 there was news from the Teachers' Federation. It also included a bulletin from the Manitoba Educational Association. Dr William McIntyre, principal of the Normal School in Winnipeg, known for his reformist bent, was the editor for much of the period until his retirement in 1934. The editorials and articles of the *Journal* praised the objectives set for the conference in 1918 and applauded its final recommendations.[8] An outcome of the conference was creation of the National Council on Education, which attracted support from the Canadian Industrial Reconstruction Association.[9] The Council, a voluntary organization, hoped, but failed, to establish a national bureau of education. It sponsored a notion of citizenship based on character education and on a Canadian nationalism that endorsed British imperialism and opposed the American cultural influence in Canada. To this end, it produced surveys of textbooks and arranged for the publication of a number of books, including *This Canada of Ours*, and organized three more conferences.[10] The Council quietly faded in the late 1920s.

The *Western School Journal*, in its editorials and articles, devoted great attention to issues of moral character, citizenship, and patriotism. The school was seen as the agency through which the state could promote morality, good citizenship, and nation building. In the 1920s the *Journal* by and large emphasized service, work habits, Christian values, obedience to the law, defence of national institutions, and a willingness to serve the state as the main traits of a good citizen. The inculcation of the "right habits" of neatness, accuracy, thoroughness, and faithfulness was often seen as a necessary condition for learning.

Similar traits of good citizenship appeared in the 1920s in the Programmes of Studies issued by the Department of Education from grades 1 to 6. In the July 1927 *Programme of Studies for Elementary Schools*, there was an italicized "Note" in the grade 1 section under the heading "Manners and Morals": *"Teachers should not fail to inculcate in the minds of all children in the school, (a) Love and Fear; Reverence for the name of God; (c) Keeping of His Commandments."*[11] This governing of the soul (dispositions, sensitivities, enhancing of sympathetic feelings) was supported by the readers accredited for use in Manitoba public schools, and the selections for study in the upper grades. Pedagogically, oral reading, language enunciation, and grammar were emphasized in the early grades. Memorizing was considered essential in most subjects until the curricular and pedagogical changes of 1927–30 that, particularly at the elementary level, included practical knowledge and experimentation.[12]

Character formation concerned social order and the need to establish a framework to guide the transactions with the state. The approach was eclectic. Some *Journal* writers suggested that character formation emerged from strict mandates and the teaching of habits and manners. The Boy Scouts and the Cadet Corps were seen as auxiliary agencies to the school in the development of moral purpose. Other writings also reflected an active participatory approach. Character formation also was equated with being Canadianized; it was conceived as part of the process of nation building through the assimilation of the "aliens." This approach persisted to some degree over the years even as curricular changes provided new insights. In the *Report of the Committee on the Review of the Programme of Studies*, published in 1926, it was stated that the school should aim to give its children knowledge of the conditions governing health , knowledge, awareness of good habits (neatness, punctuality, industry, etc.), solid interests (both vocational and avocational), and healthy ideals. The objective was to create a good citizen with some degree of social efficiency at the economic, domestic, and civil level, and the ability to make worthwhile use of leisure, understood as constructive enjoyment. Character was seen as the essential element in personality and the principles determining the trend of life were outlined. Those principles were faith, reverence, obedience, truthfulness, a clean heart, thoroughness, justice, courage, self-reliance, judgment, power (intellectual and moral) and steadfastness.[13]

Teachers – in particular the teacher in the one- room school, who was normally a woman – were expected to play an important role in the process of Canadianization and character building. An editorial in 1927, entitled "Nation Builder," is illustrative of the *Journal*'s approach: "She is out in a one-roomed rural school. She has twenty children under her control. They range from six to sixteen years of age. They are poor, ill-nourished, half-clad. They are strangers to Canada. Their mothers speak no English and the fathers have but a few words used in trade ... They work with joy because the school is for them the finest place in the world. Physically they are cared for, their manners and morals are carefully observed, their taste is cultivated, right habits are built up, the home and the school are happily co-operating. Old customs, unsuitable to this land and age, are being dropped."[14] This is a statement of how things were ideally supposed to be rather than how they actually were. Inspectors' reports often pointed out that most one-room-school teachers were too young, too undereducated, and too temporarily employed in each school to be effective.

Curricular Contributions to Anglo-Conformity

Textbooks tended to be very British. This tendency was most marked in the content of the readers in the elementary schools and of the Literature – the so-called English Programmes – in the secondary schools. Examples noted by Sybil Shack were in a collection entitled *Narrative and Lyric Poems* (second series) for use in the lower school, published in 1914 in *The Victorian Reader*, many of the selections of which later appeared in *The Alexandra Readers* and in *The Manitoba Readers. The History of England for Public Schools*, published in 1910, which she used in 1922 as a student, was "a model of condensation and assurance" of Britain's role as ruler. A paragraph Shack selected with reference to India reads, "It seems almost beyond belief that one nation, with the aid of a few thousand soldiers and civil servants, should be able to rule a people made up of many nations and numbering three hundred millions of souls ... But it is well for India that she is under British rule. Without the firm control of a guiding power, she would torn by internal strife and exposed to the greed and trickery of powerful neighbours." History books for young children were upholders of the rightness and goodness of leaders. *The Britannia History Reader*, published in 1909 and reprinted many times and designed for grades 4 and 5 children, is illustrative. Under "The Ideal Explorer," Champlain "was a good man and wished to serve God even before the king. He worked hard to teach the natives to worship God, saying 'that to save a soul was more than to found an empire.'" Opponents were portrayed as misguided or wicked: "in Lower Canada the leader of the rebellion was Louis Papineau, a man high in office in his own province. He did much mischief among the French by his fiery speeches in Parliament. After several riots he, with a few followers, escaped to the United States."[15]

There were, of course, special days and occasions that were also part of the process of Canadianization, Empire Day celebrated just before Victoria Day, Armistice Day, Queen Victoria's birthday. The Union Jack, a symbol of Canada's place in the empire, was flown outside every school during school hours. It seems clear, as Ken Osborne has pointed out, given the nature of Canada's History, that pride in Canada was relatively outward looking. Canada looked to Britain but also to the wider tradition of western civilization.[16] "After the War, the place of Canada with reference to the British Empire was also influenced by the notion of international citizenship since the Empire was seen as a good model compatible with the League of Nations."[17] There was some emphasis on international peace and cooperation.

In an editorial of the the *Western School Journal* published in 1927 patriotism was carefully defined as loyalty to "the ideal for which the Empire stands in what may be called qualified or ordered freedom for every one within the Empire." Loyalty to the king-emperor was also expressed through respect for the flag that symbolized the ideal, the system, and the person of the king.[18] The role of education in securing a democratic society appeared side by side with the overall notion of the empire.[19] Understanding patriotism as a feature of being a citizen was also linked to the idea of nation building and the realization that Canada was, indeed, a nation. An interesting example is the high-school textbook published in 1926 written by G.J. Reeve, who taught in Winnipeg, entitled *Canada: Its History and Progress, 1000–1925*. In his introduction, he stated his hope that the text would "instill into those who read the book a thorough spirit of patriotism which while not wholly ignorant of the mistakes of the past, may yet express itself in a proper and predominant love of country, based on a healthy belief in its future greatness."[20]

The ideal of citizenship as expounded in the *Journal* was a gendered ideal that reflected the educational leaders' understanding of women's and men's places in society and their responsibilities. Women's experiences and values were largely ignored. The emphasis on service (voluntarism) rather than active political participation gave citizenship a depoliticized slant, while education was seen as a way to counteract radicalism, especially in the early 1920s.

The principles of progressive education reached a number of Canadian provinces in the late 1920s and early 30s.[21] These principles influenced the notion of citizenship held by educational leaders but seldom affected school practice. In Manitoba, the curricular changes of 1927–30 reflect progressive influences, especially at the elementary levels. There was an emphasis on the development of the life of the child, on participation in purposeful activities, on relating the school to the community.[22] These changes were due, in part, to the long-standing influence of progressive-education-minded leaders like William McIntyre. In addition, politically relevant pressure was also coming from rural constituencies that had long been complaining about a bookish education which they perceived as having little practical value.[23]

Progressive ideas were reflected in curricular content and pedagogical guidelines, for example, in the emphasis placed on students' individuality and their future role in a democratic society. In 1939 the principal of the Brandon Normal School, Clarence Moore, wrote that the objective of education was "to produce a generation of informed, thinking, and socially disposed citizens." He went on to say, "It no longer suffices to teach the bare facts of geography and history. Complex and varied situations demand radical variations in materials and teaching methods."[24] The progressive discourse showed an interest in Canada's place as a North American nation, although it also contained a justifications of colonialism within the British Empire, of suppression of the Aboriginal peoples, and of sexual division of work. It also featured a continuing attempt, although sometimes questioned, to Canadianize students within the framework of Anglo-conformity. The discourse, as expounded in the *Journal,* which emphasized the virtues of liberal democracy, reflected anxiety about the rise of fascism and Stalinism in the interwar years; when war broke out in 1939, it was explained as a struggle for democracy. Citizenship education in the economically depressed 1930s was expected to generate social harmony.[25]

The Second World War brought into the discourse the elements of unity, patriotism, and service through war efforts by children. The Manitoba Education Department Act of 1937 prescribed a revised set of patriotic exercises, which became part of the public school program in 1941. In 1942 the Advisory Board recommended that citizenship be included as part of every school subject and other school activities. During the war Empire Day was organized around the war theme. The unity of the English-speaking world was featured in the program for Empire Day 1941: "it is no exaggeration to say that the future of the whole world and the hopes of a broadening civilization founded upon Christian ethics depend upon relations between the British Empire, or Commonwealth of Nations, and the United States of America."[26]

At the end of the war the process of Canada's self-definition began to take on new shapes. The Canadian Citizenship Act was adopted on 1 January 1947, and Empire Day was changed to Citizenship Day in 1951. Moreover, the place of Canada in what began as the British Commonwealth and developed into the Commonwealth of Nations provided a point of reference for Canada's identity in the international context. After 1945 the focus was on the United Nations, where Canada was accepted as a recognized state in its own right. The collapse of the British Empire and the assertive presence of the United States as a leading world power had a tremendous influence on Canada's perception of its role in the world.[27] Canadian Anglo-conformity continued to influence the social dimension of schooling for many years, but Canada was increasingly inclined towards the United States as the Cold War intensified. Some educational and community leaders tried to resist the ideological re-accommodation that began to be seen as a necessary alternative to the status quo.[28]

Exploring the Intersection of the Official Discourse with Life Experience

For many children, building an identity as Canadians meant having to deal with the intersection of contesting views, customs, and values sustained at home, in the community, and in the school. There was a great gap between official policies and statements and the lived experiences of teachers and students. In rural Manitoba, the impact of the official discourse in the classroom was mediated through the multitude of school districts, each with its locally elected board of trustees controlling one- or two-room schools, and by poorly trained and frequently changing teachers. The model for this system came from Ontario, the former home of many of the western settlers of the late nineteenth century. At the end of the Second World War, the Manitoba educational system had the same structural problems it had had in 1916, when compulsory schooling was legislated. By 1945 Manitoba's school population was

118,390, and there were some 1,450 one-room schools, located in rural areas and in small towns, among the 1,875 school districts scattered across Manitoba.[29] The districts controlled hiring, salaries, and working conditions. The situation did not change until the recommendations of the *McFarlane Report* (1959) were implemented in the 1960s.[30]

In Winnipeg, Brandon, and various smaller towns, the impact of the discourse was also conditioned by the classroom composition and the community of memory to which the minority children belonged. Sybil Shack, who started school in 1917, recalled that, when she was in grade 9 at Aberdeen School in north Winnipeg, there were thirty-two pupils in her class and all but three were Jewish. The influence of the community of memory along with numbers made a difference in having to deal with non-Christian holidays, religious festivities, text interpretations, and the hidden curriculum in general. These children absorbed Canadian ways while keeping their cultural and family identities even if their efforts implied resistance and contestation. For example, Shack recalled that in 1922–23, when she was at William Whyte School, a school serving an area heavily populated with the children of new Canadians, mostly Jews and others from central Europe, she was one of a group of students who went to see the principal, Miss Redman, to protest their having to study *The Merchant of Venice*. Miss Redman was sympathetic but tried to convince them that Shylock was really the hero, not the villain, of the play. She quoted from memory Shylock's famous speech and told the students that Shakespeare lived in a period when there were no Jews in England.[31] Shack wrote about her experience at William Whyte: "We did not know at the time, but William Whyte School had been built specifically for children like us, immigrants, and children of immigrants. Accordingly on the advice of the then superintendent of Winnipeg schools, Dr Daniel McIntyre, the school board planned and had constructed a model of its kind, William Whyte, a school in which girls were to be trained to be good wives and mothers in the British-Canadian style." However, "It was not from Dr McIntyre's courses that we learned to be Canadian. It was from the teachers we loved, admired and imitated in speech and manner. We learned from the way they talked, dressed and gestured, from the songs they taught us – 'Rule Britannia' and 'The Maple Leaf Forever' – from the stories they told us, and of course, the textbooks they used."[32]

Shack's account of her perception of how she and her fellow pupils became Canadianized serves as an illustration of the relational and multilevel character of citizenship building. Her experience at William

Whyte School reinforces the notion that the teacher was expected to be a role model embodying Canadian ways. It is not surprising that teachers in Winnipeg were primarily of British background, although most of them might have been Canadian born. By the early 1920s, however, there were teachers of non-British background who were either naturalized Canadians or the children of immigrants.

Making Room for Alternative Perspectives

Teachers mediated the curriculum and could challenge official views and even generate a political space in the classroom by using a critical alternative perspective. Some of them, such as Fred Tipping and Arthur Beach from Winnipeg and James Skene from Brandon, all of them industrial arts teachers, were active in the labour scene. Others had or had had an involvement with the feminist organizations, including the Women's International League for Peace and Freedom. Yet others were related to the Grain Growers' Association, whose publications advanced critical views of schooling and citizenship. The composition of the classroom reflected the political involvement of the pupils' parents as well as their ethnic origins. Citizenship formation, in practice, had a dynamic relational character and was constantly conditioned by developments beyond school boundaries.

The rural boards preferred a teacher of their own kind, particularly in ethnically homogeneous communities, and they had the political authority to hire the teacher of their choice. The teacher was seen as embodying the community and was expected to be an authoritative and exemplary figure who demonstrated and instilled the "right values." Teachers often enlarged their pedagogical space in line with community values. The inspectors then became the mediators in the transactions between the state (the Department of Education), and the communities (board of trustees). The inspector represented the department in relations with the school boards, and the inspector's power was occasionally visible in disputes over educational control, in particular over issues of language and preservation of cultural values.[33] Here and there throughout the province inspectors reported the existence of teachers of Icelandic, Ukrainian, or Mennonite background, usually in school districts where these groups were in a majority and were also represented on or constituted the local school boards. Inspectors who made special mention of these teachers noted that they all spoke acceptable English.

Yvonne L. related two encounters she had in the 1940s with an inspector in a one-room school three miles east of Ste Anne, a French Catholic community:

> The inspector came one day and I had left my French books on the desk. He saw French on the board. I said, I am taking the letter "I" today, Sir. Some would be confused if I taught in English. It would confuse them. You wait. You come here in June and they will be reading English. I had an argument with him. He said, I could take your permit away. I said that there shouldn't be such a law. I had that inspector in Grade XII and I knew him. I felt I could talk to him and he would understand. The second time he came, he was angry. He started to throw those books on the floor. I was picking them up and putting them back on the desk. The kids were out for recess. When he was finished, he asked me if I was that stubborn about teaching against the law even though I would lose my certificate. He said it would be his duty to take my certificate away ... He reported to the trustees that I had a problem with language. I explained to the trustees and they said it's all right, we won't fire you.[40]

The trustees did not fire her because they wanted her to teach French. Most teachers in Franco-Manitoban areas (one-room and town schools) taught French during class hours and hid the books when the inspector came. The teachers had support from the boards when they resisted state demands that contradicted the community's dominant values.[34]

Michael Ewanchuk, born in 1908, a student during the First World War, then a teacher, and an inspector after the Second World War, illustrates the mediating role he played and the assumptions of the time – a time when paranoid attitudes about uniformity had started to relax: "Now when I went to inspect some of the areas that I inspected were solidly Ukrainian, and some teachers did teach Ukrainian after four. And I would look at their books and they would be scared because I'd find a Ukrainian reader in the school. Well, why make a fuss over it? And then after a while the teachers couldn't teach Ukrainian, it just all went."[35]

This personal assessment is in line with the conclusions reached by Marcella Derkartz in her analysis of the Canadianization and assimilation of Ukrainians. She noted that "through the conformist era [the dominance of Anglo-conformity] relative successes in both the 'preservation' and 'assimilation' movements occurred."[36] Ewanchuk's narrative also shows the contingent character of identification and community. He recalled intervening when a teacher wanted to punish a student who spoke Ukrainian, although it was forbidden on school grounds. The boy had refused to take the punishment and the teacher was upset because the boy was actually an Anglo-Saxon who had learned Ukrainian. He told the teacher, "Let the youngsters be happy, and we are not going to have any more trouble. The youngsters will talk German or whatever they know on the side."[37]

The Process of Canadianization as Negative for Minorities

Minority children placed in schools where the discourse of Anglo-conformity went hand in hand with a British environment may have encountered difficulties in the process of building identity by experiencing and representing various identifications. Different ethnic communities protected their identities and tried to overcome the difficulties encountered in public schools by creating after-school schools. For some children the process of Canadianization involved pain and oppression. Frances McColl referred in an interview to the dreadful experiences of some members of her family in the school system. When asked what kind of dreadful experience? She responded: "My cousin's mother-in-law, she had a Ukrainian name. And I don't know what her first name was, but I guess it was long, and she became Mary Smith or Mary Brown and she was that all through school, on the register. They would not call her by her name. And she still has an inferiority complex about that. And she was very pleased when her son and my cousin were thinking of moving over here perhaps, because that would be nice. And she was pleased to be invited to my home. Well, good grief! It's more of a treat to be invited to hers."[38]

Betty Gibson recalled her first years of teaching, between 1929 and 1933, in a rural school in Deloraine, Manitoba, attended by a large number of Belgian children. She resented "the sort of attitude that if you were white and English you were a better person than if you came from some other country." The textbooks irritated her because they fostered those attitudes.[39]

Emma Thompson, who started school in 1920, went along with total assimilation and so avoided difficulties that so many others faced. Hers was the only German family in a rural, English-speaking area, where memories of the "Great War" were still very much alive. She recalled: "It [the community, the school] was British; but we took it for granted because we had come to a country where there were no other German people around ... My parents came to this country with the understanding that "now we are Canadians; we are going to live a Canadian life." I don't know anything about German cooking, for example. Nothing about my background, absolutely nothing."[40] Once Emma and her brothers had fully adopted the Canadian ways, they could easily blend. She became a teacher in her own school district and two of her brothers served on the school board. This example of assimilation, however, raises questions regarding ethnicity and race that are beyond the scope of this chapter.

Some children suffered ethnic and racial discrimination often based on a Christian ethnocentric world view dominant in schools and in the wider community. Jerry Dorfman, who attended a Jewish religious parochial school in Winnipeg and then attended David Livingstone School for grades 3 and 4 in the early 1930s, said: "I remember being called 'dirty Jew' by the kids sitting around me, but I guess we sort of expected that I suppose." He then was asked: "Because of the fact that you had come from a parochial school?" Dorfman replied: "And also when we were still in the parochial school there was gang warefare between the students at David Livingstone and the Torah, and I remember vividly one day when I was in Grade 1 or kindergarten, there was a war between us, and we were all lined up in the back of the Talmud Torah with big wooden planks to protect ourselves from the 50 raids from across the street."[41]

The First Nations were excluded from the transactions with the state, and their children were forced into residential schools. It was an exclusion regulated by the parameters of colonization and was reproduced in the classrooms. Dora Rosenbaum, who attended St John's High School during the First World War explained her understanding of the otherness of Aboriginal peoples in the following terms: "As far as Aboriginal people go, we didn't talk too much about that either. I don't think we did because there weren't any around. They were tucked in their little reserves. And they were referred to in the history books. And we talk about that, for example, in the 1700s and 1600s, but not in the present day. I don't think that we were even aware that they were serving in the Canadian Army, and that they served the country well. It was just after the war and after school that I saw Native people coming in, and seeing them in what I would call the ghetto on Main street." The interviewer interjected: "You mentioned before we recorded that they were considered as heathens." Dora answered: "Yes, and this was from the history books. We did not relate the Indians, or Aboriginals of the 1700s or 1800s to those of the 1930s, 40s, or 50s. It never occurred to us, because

one of the most important reasons, we didn't see any. They were living
on reserves, or if they came into Winnipeg, they'd head for Main Street.
That was it. Now we see them in schools."[42] This testimony shows how
racism against the Native people was a component of the process of
building a Canadian identity.

This process has been complex and eclectic. I will use as an example
the public schools located in Franco-Manitoban communities to explore
the oppositional dimension of citizenship formation and the impact of
collective action in the classroom. Citizenship formation has an
oppositional dimension because it can involve resistance, contestation,
negotiation, and memories of oppression on an individual or a collective
basis.

While the official discourse was addressed by and large to immigrants,
and western French Canadians were not immigrants in the usual sense,
as J.H. Thompson has argued, "the problems with regard to education
that beset other minorities directly involved French Canadians." He goes
on to say that "including French Canadians among those regarded by
English-Canadian Westerners as 'foreigners' also seems to illustrate the
prevailing opinion that the French, far from 'partners' in Confederation, were simply another ethnic group speaking another foreign language. And indeed in the Manitoba curriculum, French was treated as
another 'foreign' language."[43]

*Identity and Attachment Issues and the Development of a
Parallel Curriculum*

The influence of Franco-Manitobans on school life, in particular in
Francophone rural areas, was facilitated by the provincial educational
structure, but it was also an integral part of the process of elaboration of
the identity of what Martel calls the French-Canadian nation (Québec,
and communities outside Québec). Martel explains that, thanks to the
initiative of the French-Canadian Catholic clergy and the support of
professionals, a set of institutions was created to preserve the identity of
French-Canadian communities.[44] The emphasis was on the French language and the Catholic faith. For their guidance, these institutions drew
upon ultramontane and agriculturalist ideologies in Québec and throughout Canada. Until the end of the 1950s language and faith were the
central elements of identity and attachment to tradition as it became
clear in national meetings held in Québec in 1937 and 1952.[45] The
identity construed at the time was similar to that prevalent in Québec

nationalist circles. However, each French-Canadian or Acadian community outside Québec created provincial bodies to promote its own particular interests.[46]

Franco-Manitobans (at the time, French Catholics) had a strong sense of being victims of injustice and a strong desire for recognition. Their actions took the form of a collective challenge to the Department of Education. Franco-Manitobans claimed the rights due them within a legal sphere. They were moved by common purposes and solidarity.[47] This collective action was the response to the aftermath of the School Question, specifically, the Education Act of 1916, which eliminated the bilingual system, made English the official language of instruction in public schools, and relegated religious instruction to hours before or after school. The teaching of French and teaching in French was banned from grades 1 to 9; at the high-school level French was taught as a second language. Thus, l'Association de l'Éducation des Canadiens-Français, with headquarters in Saint Boniface, was founded in 1916 with the mandate to protect the interest of French Catholics in Manitoba. The Catholic Church played a prominent role in this association.

What is important to note is that l'Association had as much control as the Department of Education over the education of Franco-Manitobans attending public schools. Taillefer has demonstrated that l'Association was both the French and the Catholic "Department of Education" in Manitoba, playing a role parallel to the official Department of Education. The Programme de l'Association (later the Programme d'Études françaises) created in 1922 was a French program with accompanying books, annual competitive exams (concours), the hiring of competent teachers, and the creation of an inspectorate.[48] In practice, it became a parallel curriculum, in particular with reference to French and to the values inculcated in the schools, and the history of Canada as dictated by the department was taught in French instead of in English. Francophone inspectors ensured the implementation of the program. At the same time, Franco-Manitobans were not opposed to their children's being fluent in English. Indeed, l'Association supported and encouraged teachers to teach the official curriculum along with the program from l'Association.

Although religious teaching took place early in the morning, religion was also a central part of both the overt and the hidden curriculum; in fact, the program taught until the 1960s was permeated with French-Catholic nationalism and a morality tied to Catholicism. The establishment of l'Action Catholique in Manitoba in 1934 generated a complex social infrastructure in Catholic communities and in the schools. A large number of the teachers were nuns, and female religious congregations played a vital role in the preservation of French and Catholic values in Manitoba and also ensured that women played the role envisioned by the Church. Colleen Ross recreated school life in Ste Anne in the 1940s and 1950s through oral histories and analysis of documents, bringing life to the many facets of the permeation of French nationalism and Catholic values. One of them was the role of the parish priest in relation to students. Not only did he teach catechism, but he also heard students' confessions, usually scheduled on the first Thursday of every month during the school year. Confessions were neither sanctioned nor forbidden by the Public School Act. Extracurricular activities were strongly related to l'Action Catholique. Evidence of fear and obedience within a pious authoritarianism were often apparent in Ross's study.[49]

The Church, the school, the community, and the official and parallel curricula generated in the children a sense of being French Canadians. Their identity developed within the overlapping parameters set by the state and the Church. The point of reference was given by the claim of the right to teach and learn French and to practise the Catholic faith in the schools. The *Bulletin des Institutrices* (1924), published by the Ligue des Institutrices Catholiques de l'Ouest, was the medium that provided curricular and pedagogical information. The newspaper *La Liberté*, founded in 1913 as an organ allegedly free from partisan politics and directed by the Oblate Fathers, also played an important role in the educational network.[50] In it was published a list of schools that participated in the concours (annual competition for French writing), and it contained many articles on education. In 1946 the founding of the French radio station CKSB became yet another medium for Franco-Manitobans.

L'Association encouraged trustees and teachers to be members of the Manitoba Trustees' Association and the Manitoba Teachers' Society, but it also expected them to be members of their French counterparts, la Ligue des Institutrices Catholiques de l'Ouest and l'Association des Commissaires d'Écoles (funded by Association). The influence was extended over time. Figures on identification with l'Association were as follows: in 1926, 73 schools (54.8 per cent of the total of 1916); in 1931, 82 schools; in 1936, 103 schools; in 1941, 106 schools; and in 1946, 96 schools. All of them, with the exception of those located in Saint-Boniface, were in rural communities.[51]

Conclusion

The object of the official discourse was to generate a common polity, based upon a shared identity, loyalty to common institutions, a common language, a common culture, and a homogenizing notion of citizenship. The discourse contained both conservative and liberal components, however, and some of the changes, like the curricular change of the late 1920s, were a response to complaints about a bookish education, especially from the rural areas. The progressive educational discourse dominant (but not new) in the late 1920s and 1930s, while encouraging experience and participation, kept a colonizing British core. To that end, the First Nations were placed outside civic life, and this idea was conveyed to the students.

The intersection of the official discourse – as expressed in statements, policies, and programs of studies – with lived experience within the school boundaries and beyond produced unintended outcomes. In the process of Canadianization, the school became a public site where consciousness of collective identity, family values and identity, political standpoints, and ways of talking intersected with the official discourse of how to govern the soul and become a good citizen. Where there was no collective action, dissension from the norm could be threatening for the children. The norm also included a gendered understanding of the role of teachers. It was highly acceptable to see a woman teacher at the elementary level but was not necessarily so at the secondary level.

The understanding of citizenship formation "as a series of transactions,"[52] as relational, and as often having an oppositional dimension helps to explain the relationship between communities like the Franco-Manitobans, used as an example in this paper, and the Department of Education. The Franco-Manitobans generated a social movement around language and faith understood as rights issues and through collective action were able to achieve their educational aims. Having a geographical basis gave Franco-Manitobans a stronger negotiating power with the Department of Education, and this fact was reflected in school life. The collective memory provided a sense of identity based on religion, ethnicity, and community history. This sense of identity was somehow articulated in public schools affiliated with l'Association de l'Éducation and expounded in the official curricula.

The oral narratives and case studies, such as the history of Franco-Manitobans and other examples given in the chapter, make it clear that people often became Canadians on their own terms, deploying various identities following attachments and identifications.[53] In many cases, Franco-Manitobans, Jews, Ukrainians, Mennonites, and other minority groups experienced a process of resistance, contestation, and negotiation, resulting in a combination of ethnic and Canadian identity, the balance of which is difficult to determine. It may be argued that a sort of proto-multiculturalism was at work, but not necessarily one cultivating a cosmopolitan world view.

Notes

1 Two of Ken Osborne's recent works are "Education Is the Best National Insurance" and "Citizenship Education and Social Studies." See also Axelrod, *Promise of Schooling*.

2 In the case of Manitoba, the *Grain Growers' Guide*, the farmers' magazine, contained much discussion of politics, citizenship, and education. An important source is Laycock, *Populism and Democratic Thought*.

3 In 1920 there were 459 strikes across Canada; see Kealey, "1919: The Canadian Labour Revolt."

4 "Address of the Minister of Education," *Western School Journal*, 5 (May 1918): 185.

5 Mitchell, "Manufacture of Souls," 21.

6 *Report of the Proceedings of the National Conference on Character Education in Relation to Canadian Citizenship (Winnipeg, 1919)*, (hereafter *Proceedings*), 29–30.

7 Mitchell, "Manufacture of Souls," 18.

8 Editorial, "A National Conscience," *Western School Journal* 13, 8 (Oct. 1918): 305. The *Western School Journal* was published until 1938, when the Department of Education discontinued the grant and started the *Manitoba School Journal*, which was published monthly until 1963.

9 Chaiton, "History of the National Council of Education" and "Attempts to Establish a National Bureau of Education," 122. Chaiton argued that the Industrial Association wanted a pressure group to promote anti-socialism and interest in vocational and technical training in schools.

10 Chaiton, "The History of the National Council of Education of Canada," 109.

11 *Programme of Studies for Elementary Schools*, July 1927, Manitoba Department of Education, 5.

12 The Murray Commission issued its report in 1924 calling, among other

things, for a "revision of the course of study by a committee of experts." The
Advisory Board accepted the report in 1924 and established a Curriculum
Revision Committee. William McIntyre of the Normal School was in charge
of the subcommittee for grades 1–6; for grades 7–11 subject committees
were set up; grade 12 was under university control. A pilot version of grades
1–6 curriculum was used on a trial basis in 1917–8 and was authorized in
1928. The full grades 7–11 program was finally approved in 1930 after some
partial applications. Documents and information provided by Ken Osborne.

13 *Report of the Committee on the Review of the Programme of Studies*, Winnipeg,
    Department of Education, 1926, 6–7, 36–8.

14 Editorial, "Nation Builder," *Western School Journal* 24, 9 (Nov. 1929): 327.

15 The collection, *Narrative and Lyric Poems* (second series), for use in the
    lower school and published in 1914, contained in the first section "Enoch
    Arden," "The Prisoner of Chillon," "Elegy Written in a Country Church-
    yard," and Elizabeth Barrett Browning's "My Kate." The second section,
    more advanced, consisted of four of Tennyson's longer poems, including
    "Ode on the Death of the Duke of Wellington"; three of Browning's poems,
    including "Home Thoughts from the Sea" and "The Patriot"; Goldsmith's
    "The Traveller"; Byron's "The Isles of Greece"; and Clough's "As Ships
    Becalm'd and Homes" and "The Chambered Nautilus." *The Merchant of
    Venice* was also required study. Sybil Shack, "Schooling in Early
    Manitoba,'speech, 28 March 1979, Danalvert, Man.

16 Osborne, "I'm Not Going to Think How Cabot Discovered Newfoundland," 5.

17 Harvey, "National Sovereignty and the League of Nations."

18 "Patriotism," *Western School Journal* 22, 6 (June 1927): 234.

19 Scott, "Democracy in the Classroom," 231.

20 Reeve, *Canada, Its History and Progress*, "Introduction."

21 See Patterson, "The Implementation of Progressive Education in Canada."

22 *School Curriculum and Teachers' Guide. Grades I–VI*, prepared under the
    direction of the Advisory Board, Manitoba Department of Education, 1928.

23 Ken Osborne, personal communication, September 1998. See also
    Osborne, "One Hundred Years of History Teaching."

24 Moore, "The Social Studies," 6.

25 See Osborne, "Citizenship Education and Canadian Schools," a paper pre-
    pared for the Conference on Canadian Citizenship within the Next Millen-
    nium, Citizenship Council of Manitoba, Winnipeg, 30 October 1998, 14.

26 Empire Day, 23 May 1941, Province of Manitoba, Department of Education.

27 See Morton, *The Canadian Identity*; Cook, "Nation, Identity, Rights."

28 See Milan, "Education and the Reproduction of Capitalist Ideology,"
    chap. 1, in particular 18–19.

29 Ibid., 62, 108–25.
30 Levin, "Struggle over Modernization in Manitoba Education."
31 Sybil Shack, personal communication, September 1998.
32 Shack, "The Making of a Teacher," 433, 435.
33 Bruno-Jofré and Ross, "Decoding the Subjective Image," 586.
34 Ibid., 586–7, 587.
35 Interview with Michael Ewanchuk by Sybil Shack and Helen Mendelsohn, Winnipeg, 9 February 1995.
36 Derkatz, "Ukrainian Language Education in Manitoba Public Schools," 183.
37 Ewanchuk interview.
38 Interview with Frances McColl by Sybil Shack and Helen Mendelsohn, Winnipeg, 4 October 1994.
39 Interview with Betty Gibson by Rosa Bruno-Jofré and Lois Grieger, Brandon, Manitoba, 30 September 1995.
40 Interview with Emma Thompson by Sybil Shack, Winnipeg, 8 February 1994.
41 Interview with Jerry Dorfman by Sybil Shack, Winnipeg, 15 March 1995.
42 Interview with Dora Rosenbaum by Sybil Shack, Winnipeg, 25 April 1994.
43 Thompson, *Harvests of War*, 74.
44 Martel, *French Canada*, 3–5, 4–5.
45 These were the second and third conferences of the French language in Canada. These meetings called for "the preservation of the essential elements of identity and condemned any divergence from the path of survival" (ibid., 5).
46 Ibid.
47 Sidney Tarrow defines social movement in this way. Tarrow, *Power in Movement*; cited in Tilly, "Women, Work, and Citizenship," 3.
48 Taillefer, « Les Franco-Manitobains », 263–4.
49 Ross, "Franco-Manitobans," chaps. 6 and 7.
50 It became *La Liberté et Le Patriote*, after merging in 1946 with the Saskatchewan paper. Taillefer, « Les Franco-Manitobains », 329, 267.
51 Ibid., 267–80. By 1946 the number of schools reflected migration to urban areas as well as some limited consolidation of school districts. The first signs of problems in the French-Canadian institutional network appeared in the 1950s. Martel wrote, "There were signs of trouble on the horizon for the propagators of the French Canadian idea. Whether it was the definition of French Canada as a political space and focus of collective action, the view of a nation made up of two founding peoples, or the space and focus of collective action, or the constituent elements of a national identity, a number

of events forced a reassessment and an examination of each aspect of the French Canadian idea" (*French Canada*, 14–15).

52 Charles Tilly defines citizenship as a tie. He defines a tie as a "continuing series of transactions to which participants attach shared understandings, memories, forecasts, rights and obligations." One can refer to citizenship as a tie "in so far as it entails enforceable rights and obligations based on persons; categorical membership and agents' relation to the state." Tilly, "Citizenship, Identity and Social History," 7, 8.

53 For a clarification of multiple identities, see ibid., 7.

Bridging the Boundaries for a More Inclusive Citizenship Education

ROBERTA J. RUSSELL

As a legal term, "citizenship" is a term of identification rather than of action. As a political term, "citizenship" means active commitment. It means responsibility. It means making a difference in one's community, in one's society, in one's country. Without citizenship, there cannot be that responsible commitment which creates the citizen and which in the last analysis holds together the body politic. Nor can there be the sense of satisfaction and pride that comes from making a difference. Without citizenship, the political unit, whether called "state" or "empire," can only be a power. Power is then the only thing that holds it together. In order to be able to act in a rapidly changing and dangerous world, the post-capitalist polity must recreate citizenship.[1]

Introduction

In this paper I want to illustrate with examples drawn from government citizenship-related activities what some of the challenges are of providing for a more participatory and inclusive approach to citizenship education.[2] Examples will be used to show how various elements of programming are linked by a participation objective to present a comprehensive approach to a broad definition of citizenship.

The State of Citizenship

Since the mid-1990s, citizenship is a topic of renewed interest among academics, educators, and the public at large. Its presence as a conference theme, the topic of newspaper articles, and so forth is higher now than it has been in years. Those who are involved in the current renewal efforts usually fall into one of two camps: those who see citizenship as being in a state of crisis and getting worse or those holding a more optimistic view who see it in a less bleak and more nuanced perspective. In the first camp is Robert Putnam, who argues that declining voter turnout, increasing distrust in government, soaring political alienation and disengagement in the last three decades, and falling numbers of volunteers for mainline civic organizations all are evidence that citizenship is in crisis.[3] Christopher Lasch, too, worries about America's democratic malaise, the decline of democratic discourse, and the loss of places which foster intelligent debate about common concerns, recognizes the need for an ethic of compassion and an ethic of respect and pines for the lost art of argument.[4] On the other hand, Pippa Norris argues for the growth of more critical citizens who value democracy as an ideal yet who remain dissatisfied with the performance of the American political system, particularly the core institutions of representative government.[5]

According to Novella Keith, there are two kinds of political participation: (1) actions that relate to the government and public policies, and (2) involvement in our communities and in issues that affect us personally.[6] She believes that democratic participation in the first is in a state of crisis, not because citizens are apathetic and irresponsible, but because they feel pushed out of political life. The second form of political action is not in crisis; it is increasing, but participants, she says, do not usually describe such action as political. Keith, along with a number of writers in the field, sees this arena as the one in which the notion of citizenship is being redefined. These concerns about civics and citizenship are not limited to North America. In June 1994 the Australian government established a Civics Expert Group to provide the government with a strategic plan for a non-partisan program of public education and information on the Australian system of government, the constitution, citizenship, and other civic issues. The Australian government's action was motivated by evidence of a "civic deficit" characterized by low levels of political participation, distrust of politics, and deficiencies in knowledge and civic confidence. Regardless of what is driving this renewed interest in citizenship education, activities in this area are on the increase.

Citizenship and the Federal Government

The federal government's role in the granting of citizenship is fairly straightforward and relatively well understood by most Canadians. Its role in support of participation may be less well known. As Pal explains, citizenship policy within the federal government first developed during the Second World War around the issue of ethnic identity, thus making explicit the link between identity and citizenship concepts, prior to the Citizenship Act of 1947.[7] Beginning in the 1940s, the Department of the Secretary of State was the federal department most often associated with citizenship-related activities. That responsibility changed with the reorganization of federal departments in June 1993 when the Department of Canadian Heritage and the Department of Citizenship and Immigration were created, and many of the responsibilities of the former Department of the Secretary of State were folded into these new departments.

The Department of the Secretary of State was one of the oldest departments in the federal government. David Cameron describes it as having displayed a "chameleon-like capacity to assume new shapes and mandates as the needs of the Canadian government evolved" over the generations.[8] Established by an act of Parliament in the first parliamentary session after Confederation, it served initially as the official channel of communication between the Dominion of Canada and the Imperial Government in London and as the official repository of state records. In a history of the department, G. Lewe has documented the department's role.[9] As Lewe describes it, the Department of the Secretary of State was always at centre stage in the development of the country. Far from being a "grab bag of disparate programs" as it was sometimes described, it was a mirror of Canada's growth and of those elements of maturation which emerged along the way. The following background portrait on the department is drawn largely from that history. A review of the history of its citizenship-related activities over the years provides a good sense of the development of thinking in this area.

From 1920 to 1960 the department consolidated a number of functions which remain with its successor departments today. Among them were citizenship registration under the 1947 Citizenship Act and responsibility for many of the visible manifestations of the State, such as royal visits and ceremonies and the integrity and promotion of official symbols (such as the flag and the national anthem).

During the 1960s the Department of the Secretary of State entered the field of innovative social programming for Canadian youth. The Company of Young Canadians, Opportunities for Youth, and Katimavik were implemented during that period. Programs oriented to particular social and cultural groups also had their beginnings in the 1960s and 1970s, serving women, ethnocultural groups, natives, disabled persons, and official language minorities. As Lewe expresses it, "the growth of a citizenship dimension can be seen in terms of the country's evolution from colony to nation. A distinctive Canadian citizenship gained in 1947 ushered in many new departmental programs stressing the growing social conscience of a new country which was very aware of the needs of its minorities."[10]

By the 1970s the focus of much of the department's work was on support to communities and to individual participation. The following description of these two main thrusts of departmental activity are drawn from Lewe's history.

Strengthening of Communities

The preservation (and expression of) cultural identity was fostered by support to aboriginal, ethnocultural, and official language minority groups as well as support for greater community participation by urban Native citizens and immigrants, and women and minorities generally. Intercommunity exchange and understanding were encouraged through race relations, cultural activities, and youth exchanges. An emphasis on youth had been included in the Speech from the Throne of October 1976 and was reflected in departmental programs through activities such as support to youth participation programs like Open House Canada.

Support programs for communities were designed to enable them to do for themselves as opposed to doing for them. Communities were seen in very positive terms as having important resources of their own that could be directed towards developing solutions to the problems and challenges they faced.

Individual Participation

The Department of the Secretary of State sought to foster equality of opportunity and motivation to participate and contribute to Canadian life. In the mid-1980s the concept of "active" citizenship was introduced. Program activities designed during those years were designed to foster the development of attitudes, skills, and knowledge needed for an informed and active citizenry. Active citizenship was encouraged through information, voluntarism, and promotion of the day-to-day practice of citizenship values. Support for human rights was promoted through education and monitoring compliance with international and national codes. Democratic rights (or needs) of representation, advocacy and access were aided by support to organizations, including those representing women, official language minorities, ethnocultural groups, natives, youth, and disabled persons. Social and economic participation, particularly through the reduction of barriers and disincentives, was facilitated for women and disabled persons, with increasing attention to the economic opportunities possible in the multicultural, bilingual, and aboriginal interests of the country. A good illustration of the department's approach was its definition of literacy as a citizenship participation issue rather than an employment issue. From that perspective literacy skills were seen as "necessary prerequisites for effective participation" in Canadian society.[11]

Participation and a sense of belonging characterized the work of the department during those years, and many of the activities of the Secretary of State were directed primarily to full participation and to a sense of belonging for all Canadians. Thus, over the years the department facilitated citizenship activities by promoting Canadians' knowledge and understanding of their country, fostering a greater sense of belonging, promoting social cohesion in a context of growing diversity, and enhancing the ability of all Canadians to participate in and contribute to Canadian society.

In addition to the citizenship-related activities of the former Department of the Secretary of State and the present Department of Canadian Heritage, others across the federal system are working in this area. For example, the Department of Justice is active in Charter literacy, and the Department of the Environment has done some interesting work in environmental citizenship.

Canadian Perspectives on Diversity

While diversity has been central to the federal government's approach to citizenship over the years, the concept has evolved throughout our history. There have been three basic perspectives on diversity in Canadian society.[12] Each one is based on different assumptions about the nature of Canadian society and the objectives of social studies and citizenship education which lead to different insights and conclusions and, hence, the hidden curriculum shaping policies and programs. These perspectives are usually labelled as assimilationist, bicultural, and multicultural.

The Assimilationist Perspective

For years, it was commonly accepted that to be Canadian was to be of British or French origin. Everyone else was expected to assimilate into either of those two majority groups and the educational institutions were seen by authorities as the primary agencies for ensuring that the assimilation took place. According to Cornelius Jaenen, "public schools were seen as the chief agencies for socialization or assimilation." To illustrate this point, he cites the superintendent of Presbyterian "home missions" in charge of schools for immigrants who, in a public interview in Winnipeg in 1898, said: "The interest of the state lies in doing all it can to assimilate these and other foreigners, and make of them Canadians. They should be put into the great Anglo-Saxon mill and be ground up; in the grinding they lose their foreign prejudices and characteristics." Thus, early in our history the educators' interest in cultural diversity was in its complete eradication, since it was perceived by many as detracting from national unity. As Dr J.T.M. Anderson, Saskatchewan's director of education for new Canadians, expressed it in 1919: "the greatest agency in racial assimilation is the common or public school. This is the great melting pot into which must be placed these diverse racial groups, and from which will eventually merge the pure gold of Canadian citizenship."[13] As these early examples illustrate, if educators, politicians, and opinion makers expressed any opinion about diversity in Canada, they usually saw it as a problem to be overcome, rather than a positive feature of Canadian society.

The Bicultural Perspective

Anglo-Canadian dominance had given way by the 1950s to a somewhat cautious acceptance of the "other founding nation," but it did not extend beyond to any widespread acceptance of the "others," as those of non-British and non-French heritage were often described. Although the "other ethnic groups" (as the Bilingualism and Biculturalism Commission referred to them) were acknowledged, Canadian studies flourished, and there was a great increase in Canadian-produced learning materials during the 1960s and early 1970s. It was, however, the Canadian experience in terms of the historical experience of the two major groups, those of French and British heritage. The existence of minority groups might be acknowledged, but those groups were not considered part of the mainstream of Canadian society. During this period, multicultural education tended to be based on the "difference-equals-deficit" model, and ethnicity was often seen as something to be tolerated for only as long as it took these "others" to become "real" Canadians.

Both the assimilationist and the bicultural perspectives served essentially the same purpose. Both viewed all other ethnic groups from a dominant position in which the non-dominant groups are interpreted and evaluated in terms of their similarity to the dominant groups. Thus, a discussion of Aboriginal peoples in learning materials might state that "their homes are becoming more like ours."

The Multicultural Perspective

By the mid 1970s mere tolerance of diversity was giving away to a more inclusive view, one involving reform in terms of policies and programs. This view was, in large part, shaped by the fact that the policy of multiculturalism was in place federally, and various provincial governments were moving to put in place their own multicultural programs or policies. It was based on a recognition that all Canadians did not have equality of opportunity to participate in Canadian society and on a commitment to work to ensure that they would have that opportunity. These policies of multiculturalism are seen by many as having introduced an openness to a diversity of perspectives that has facilitated the inclusion of a range of perspectives (gender, disability, etc.) in addition to ethnicity and race. Now in the twenty-first century the need arises to further clarify concepts and particularly to develop an expanded notion of inclusion in citizenship education.

Citizenship: Clarifying the Concepts

A number of terms are associated with citizenship, including civics, participation, active citizenship, and service learning. "Civics" usually refers to the study of a democratic government, its political structure, its judicial system and government institutions. This concept is focused on the principles of democracy and the need for informed citizens who exercise their rights and responsibilities (by voting, obeying the law, respecting the rights of others, and being loyal to their country). In the education field, the broader concept of citizenship is more commonly used in Canada and goes beyond civics to include Canadian studies, human rights, and multicultural and anti-racist education. It also includes literacy as an essential element of citizenship participation and voluntarism as an element of one's responsibility to fellow citizens and the community. In comparison, in the United States, an expanded notion is also used, and the original terms "civic education" and "civics" are retained generally, with the exception of the preparation of adult immigrants, which is termed "citizenship education."[14]

Management guru Peter Drucker has described patriotism as "the willingness to die for one's country ... But patriotism alone is not enough. There has to be citizenship as well. Citizenship is the willingness to contribute to one's country. It means the willingness to live – rather than die – for one's country. To restore citizenship is a central requirement of the post-capitalist polity."[15] As Theodore Kaltsounis describes it, citizenship education is designed to help individuals to develop the knowledge, values, and skills to participate in and contribute to society.[16]

Citizenship "entails a commitment to a wider realm beyond that of self-interest," according to a Senate committee that studied and reported on the concept, development, and promotion of Canadian citizenship. In discussing the importance of both knowledge, informed citizenry, and responsible citizenship participation, the committee concluded that "good citizen participation is not simply a matter of having the right to participate and the inclination to do so. It is also a matter of possessing the knowledge and skills that will allow one to do so effectively."[17]

"Service learning" is becoming a popular theme in citizenship education in the United States.[18] Based on the belief that participation in community service activities can play a vital role in civics and social studies education, service learning represents an effort to counter a "rights-based, minimalist approach" to citizenship. Its pedagogy has roots in experiential learning, career education, and school-to-work programs. Calling into question the deficit model of community service, proponents of the service learning perspective see communities as having assets and service as drawing on the resources of communities to solve community problems. An academic and researcher interested in "service" and "citizenship" revolving around the development of links between schools and the people in their neighbourhoods that promote community problem solving, Novella Keith argues for greater use of a "community building" model rather than a "service delivery" model as more positive and more in line with the agenda of the "new civics."[19]

Proponents of service learning argue that it provides students with a better understanding of the real world and better preparation for lifelong citizenship.[20] Through community-based activities, they develop more complex, reality-based approaches to problem solving, which it is believed, will better serve them in their role as citizens. They develop awareness, participatory skills, and the propensity for action. These projects also have potential for improving reading and other skills because they have the power to engage students, giving meaning to their learning.

The Concept of Inclusion

Citizenship is a dynamic, not a static, concept. This concept of citizenship is constantly evolving, constantly being redefined. Inclusion of new knowledge and understandings and the perspectives of various groups constantly reshapes our knowledge base. In recent years, a number of groups have provided powerful critiques of our traditional understanding of the concept of citizenship. There has been a growing understanding that gender, race, class, and so on are factors which shape the content and the meaning of citizenship. Inclusion of the perspectives of various groups constantly reshapes our knowledge of the rights and responsibilities of citizenship. As new perspectives reshape our knowledge base, more meaningful opportunities for participation become available.

The poem below, taken from an early handbook for new Canadians, illustrates how exclusionary the concept of citizenship was seventy years ago. While our definition of citizenship has broadened considerably over the years, there is still some way to go before we achieve real inclusion. As Noddings points out, male experience is the standard in all of public policy.[22] What is needed, she argues, is to reflect *both* women's and men's perspectives.

Citizenship

The good citizen
Loves God
Loves the Empire
Loves Canada
Loves his own family
Protects women and children
Works hard
Does his work well
Helps his neighbor
Is truthful
Is just
Is honest

Is brave
Keeps his promise
His body is clean
Is every inch a Man.[21]

As the Senate committee pointed out, "in a modern democratic society citizenship requires of us that we not only be law-abiding but that we also participate in our own governance" and that "the normative content of citizenship skills in a pluralist society will differ considerably from those of an earlier and socially more homogeneous era."[23] Again, according to the Senate committee, removal of barriers to participation is one of the most obvious ways to promote active citizenship. An example of how inclusion can reshape knowledge, values, skills, and practice is given by Nel Noddings: "If women's culture were taken more seriously in planning social studies and history, instead of moving from war to war, we might give more attention to social issues."[24] The concept of inclusion is one that everyone claims to understand and believe in but one which many find difficult to put into practice. It is usually equated with representation – if people are discussed or represented in papers and sessions, they are believed by some to be truly included. Several academics (e.g., James Banks at the University of Seattle in terms of race and ethnicity, Peggy McIntosh at Wellesley College, and Patricia Schmuck in terms of gender) have developed explanatory frameworks which help people to understand the implications of true inclusion – how the concept goes beyond simple representation.

Peggy McIntosh and her colleagues at the Wellesley College Center for Research on Women have been working on the issue of inclusion for a number of years.[25] They believe that degrees of change exist in the process of transformation and use history to trace the types of curriculum corresponding to five phases of perception. The phases include

Phase 1 Womanless History
Phase 2 Women in History
Phase 3 Women as a Problem, Anomaly, or Absence in History
Phase 4 Women as History
Phase 5 History Redefined or Reconstructed to Include Us All.

Analogously, one can have Womanless Political Science, then Women in Politics, then Women as an Absence, Anomaly, or Problem for Political Science (or in Politics); next, Women *as* Political (the study of women's lives in all their political dimensions; or the politics of the family, the school, the neighbourhood, and the curriculum; the politics of culture, class, race, and sex); and finally, History Redefined or Reconstructed to include multiple spheres of power, both inner and outer.

Patricia Schmuck presents a somewhat similar five-stage framework. In Schmuck's framework, Stage 1 is characterized by exclusionary or androcentric thinking in which the experiences of one group, men, is assumed to reflect the experiences of all human beings. Stage 2 is characterized by compensatory thinking, a consciousness that women are missing and women who achieve exactly as men do are included without any changes to structures or methods of enquiry. In Stage 3 women are seen as deficient, so they are encouraged to fit in (assertiveness training). In Stage 4 women are seen as oppressed by organizational practices which discriminate against them; and Stage 5 includes both men and women, provides alternative points of view, and places women at the centre of enquiry rather than at the margins.[26]

An example that illustrates the challenges posed by those working for inclusion and practising it is found in a paper by Valerie Ooka Pang, who uses an experience from her workplace to make her point. At a meeting of a university committee on which she serves as an adviser on policy issues, she was mostly silent and expressed her views in what she describes as a "diplomatic, nonconfrontive manner." After the meeting, a male colleague pointed out to her that she was being true to her Asian heritage by her "inscrutable" behaviour; she went on to say, "We live in a democracy and if you don't speak your mind, you aren't doing your civic duty." She was offended and argued that silence has a place in democracy, that there can be no dialogue without silence, that someone must listen. The inclusion of culturally pluralistic voices is becoming accepted, "giving voice to the voiceless" but "one aspect of culture which is often misunderstood is the art of silence as articulate communication." Verbal domination is seen as "good" and silence is associated with weakness, femininity, and passivity. She discusses the art of silence as it relates to social behaviour, then distinguishes between oppressive, submissive, defiant, dignified, and attentive silence. Her point is that when one is expected to behave as "First World males," one's real value is not being acknowledged and that biting and aggressive verbal expression should not be viewed as necessary aspects of citizenship. She argues that a diverse society should have room for a multiplicity of communication styles.[27]

Two scholars from the University of Amsterdam, Geert ten Dam and Monique Volman, present an analysis of the heated public discussion which preceded the introduction in 1992 of "Care" as a compulsory subject in Dutch secondary schools. They use this event as a case study to illustrate "the problems linked with feminist curriculum politics and argue that this discussion referred to fundamental issues concerning "citizenship" and the objectives of education." "Care" they describe as "health and well-being, consumer issues, and the basic necessities of life' – domestic and caring tasks. Opponents to the inclusion of elements of Care, they say, tended to be "adherents of a traditional educational model in which preparation for functioning in paid labor and as an independent responsible citizen is central." The "Care lobby," those in favour of the course, were found in the "more progressive education trade unions, in consumers" and environmental protection organizations, and in the women's movement." Referring to feminist critiques over the past fifteen years of traditional approaches to the concept of citizenship, they focus on the "assumed gender neutral definition of citizenship" at its base.[28] Like Noddings,[29] they call for a more diversified and pluralistic model of citizenship in which domains and values, the private sphere of family traditionally ascribed to women, as well as the sphere of politics are included.

Another feminist critique comes from an Australian academic, Victoria Foster, in a paper focussed on schooling for citizenship as a site of desire and threat for girls. She begins with the argument that in order for women to be active, full citizens they must become (like) men ... although women have demanded for two centuries that their distinctive qualities and tasks should become part of citizenship. Foster's argument is that when women and girls attempt to live the promise of equal rights of participation as citizens, they must negotiate conflicting, contradictory, and even destructive demands. "The neo-liberal framework of equality" she says, "is a framework which retains a masculinist subject at its centre."[30]

At an educational conference at the end of the 1990s Maxine Greene argued that educators and school systems must find ways to foster renewed recognition of the value of caring. It is important, she said, for schools to deal with the erosion of community, the "prevalence of privatism and self-involvement," and "to ponder curriculum grounded in a commitment to a civic conscience," to cultivate the "capacity to read the texts of the social world," to enquire into and understand "values like justice, equity and freedom and the multiple voices and multiple realities of a pluralist society."[31] How can citizenship education prepare humane citizens for public life in a democracy?

While many tend to "hold tight to the traditional canons that governed curricula in the humanities over the years," according to Greene, others have emphasized the need to open curricula to the "diverse perspectives" of ethnic minorities and women, to "the perspectives of the excluded and the derelict and the oppressed." A critical challenge, she says, is the emerging division of the global labour force into three distinct groups – professionals and managers involved in delivering symbolic-analytic services, routine production workers involved in repetitive tasks like data processing, and relatively unskilled workers in the service industry. This polarization suggests that the so-called symbolic analysts, the "fortunate fifth" who comprise perhaps 20% of the population, will ultimately bear much of the cost of educating children from economically disadvantaged backgrounds." But "the difficulty is that those very people are losing the sense of connectedness that might move them to deal justly with the bottom fifth, those with little or no power." How can education nurture people's responsibility to others? The most advantaged learners, she argues, must receive early orientation to "the basic values of a caring, humane world, to set aside self-interest now and again, in the interests of others, or in the interest of what ought to be."[32]

The hidden curriculum of citizenship education too often carries the message that some groups and their experiences are peripheral to citizenship. The focus of citizenship education in a pluralistic society should be inclusive and should empower everyone to participate.

Where To in the Future?

I have tried in this chapter to illustrate with examples the challenges of inclusion and to describe how the various elements of citizenship have been linked within a governmental framework by a participation focus. Recent developments involving the department in major initiatives hold promise of more comprehensive, well-informed policy approaches in the future as well as well-prepared implementation activities.

The Development of Multimedia Materials

While in our own work we are now moving from the production of print materials to the use of new technologies, such as CD-ROMs and the Internet, inclusion as a way of fostering a greater sense of Canadian identity to enhance the ability of all Canadians to participate in and contribute to Canadian society remains central to everything we do. For example, a current study aptly named the *Terra Nova Project*, a CD-ROM on citizenship, links voluntary action, Canadian studies, multiculturalism, Charter literacy, human rights, youth, justice, and other issues and concerns. To facilitate learning, this new citizenship education CD-ROM utilizes graphics; differing points of view about issues; a database about Canadian history, geography, and laws; comparisons with other countries' laws and traditions; and the opportunity to re-examine points of view in dramatized situations. For example, it enables students to embark on an interactive investigation of rights and obligations through the use of dramatized events and, by reshuffling the circumstances of each dramatic enactment, to examine the strengths and limitations of the Charter and statutes.

Through support for such learning materials development, our objective is to provide both content and a view of citizenship which is broad and inclusive to link the various elements that come together to shape our notion of citizenship. Through the process of developing these materials, we utilize a collaborative approach by involving educators, researchers, developers, and government – the many partners and resources needed to adequately address the complex subject of citizenship.

Interdepartmental Policy Developments

When this chapter was first conceptualized, it would have been difficult to predict a number of the very exciting citizenship-education-related activities within the federal system which have been developed in the past two years. Among them have been some of the projects initiated by the Policy Research Initiative (PRI), created in 1996, which was designed to enhance the capacity to create policy research that is horizontal, longer term, and more strategic through greater cooperation between university and government policy research communities. Within this initiative, several trends were identified which are germane to the federal government's role in citizenship education. They have been incorporated by the Project on Trends, in collaboration with the Social Sciences and Humanities Research Council of Canada (SSHRC), and are also seen in the work of the Social Cohesion Network. The policy research that emanates from the PRI defines social cohesion as "the ongoing process of developing a community of shared values, shared challenges and equal opportunity within Canada, based on a sense of trust, hope and reciprocity among all Canadians," a working definition acknowledging that "cohesion is achieved by consensus, that partnership is based on trust and that fairness should be the goal."[33] While recognizing measurements issues related to social cohesion, the Sub-Committee on Social Cohesion has organized its work along three themes: fault lines in society, axes of community identification, and implications of changes in social cohesion.

Another major interdepartmental activity is the Metropolis Project, initiated by the Department of Citizenship and Immigration in cooperation the SSHRC, as well as several other federal departments. Having as its objective the encouragement of dialogue among community people and university and government researchers, this project fosters research into immigration in cities. Four centres of excellence have been created in Canada to foster relevant policy research, through a national competition handled by the SSHRC, one in each of three metropolitan areas, Montréal, Toronto, Vancouver, and a fourth one in the Prairies, regrouping researchers in six universities and partners in five cities. National and international conferences are held annually, as are smaller events such as thematic symposia and regional workshops, and an informative website is maintained at http://www.canada.metropolis.net, all to encourage a dialogue and the dissemination of policy research on immigration and integration.

Having as an advantage an approach which brings together all the major stakeholders in a collaborative venture towards a common goal, both of these major initiatives have the potential of informing citizenship theory, policy, and practice.

Notes

1 Drucker, *Post-Capitalist Society*, 172.
2 The views expressed in this article are those of the author, who wishes to thank her colleague Jeff Bullard for his advice and suggestions on earlier drafts of this paper.
3 Putnam, "Bowling Alone."
4 Christopher Lasch, as cited in Putnam, *Bowling Alone*.
5 Norris, *Critical Citizens*.
6 Keith, "Relationship Building as the New Citizenship."
7 Pal, "Identity, Citizenship and Mobilization."
8 Cameron, *Canadian Studies in the Nineties*, ii.
9 Lewe, *Department of the Secretary of State*.

10 Ibid., 44.
11 Munro, "Literacy."
12 Russell, "Multiculturalizing the Social Studies in Canada."
13 Jaenen, *Canada as Diversity*, 12, 13, 14.
14 Torney-Purta, "The Second IEA Civic Education Project."
15 Drucker, *Post-Capitalist Society*, 171.
16 Kaltsounis, "Citizenship Education," 65.
17 Canada, Senate, *Canadian Citizenship*, 7, 9.
18 Sweeney, « La pédagogie du service ».
19 Keith, "Relationship Building."
20 See, for example, Sweeney, « La pédagogie du service ».
21 Fitzpatrick, *Handbook for New Canadians*, 56.
22 Noddings, "The Gender Issue."
23 Canada, Senate, *Canadian Citizenship*, 15.
24 Noddings, "The Gender Issue," 68.
25 McIntosh, *Interactive Phases of Curricular Re-Vision*.
26 Schmuck, *Women Educators*.
27 Pang, "Intentional Silence and Communication."
28 Ten Dam and Volman, "'Care' for Feminist Citizenship," 1, 6.
29 Noddings, "The Gender Issue."
30 Foster, "Schooling for Citizenship," 2.
31 Greene, "Educate the 'Fortunate Few' to care," 40.
32 Ibid., 40, 41, 42.
33 Canada, *Social Cohesion Research Workplan*, 3.

The Historical Context for Citizenship Education in Urban Canada

HAROLD TROPER

Democratic immigrant receiving states like Canada, which afford non-citizens the possibility of naturalization, cannot help but have shared interests in the immigrant integrative process and citizenship education. Nevertheless, they often differ in their understanding of citizenship education largely as a consequence of different understandings of the place of immigration and immigrants in their respective societies. The Canadian case, especially in urban English-speaking Canada, is shaped by a particular historical legacy, a shifting demographic reality, constitutional vagaries and uncertainty about any singular overarching national identity. In this chapter I will outline the century-long backdrop to citizenship education in English-speaking Canada, noting the historical vision of immigrant and citizenship, the role played by urbanization, and the way they combine to force a shift in the national consensus on citizenship in an increasingly pluralist Canada state.

Contemporary Canadian Heterogeneity

There is no denying that immigration and ethnicity are influential forces in today's urban Canada. While, according to the 1996 Census, over 17 per cent of all Canadians were born outside Canada, approximately 90 per cent of all the foreign born now live in Canada's fifteen largest urban centres. Toronto and Vancouver lead the way. Fully 35 per cent of all Vancouver residents and 42 per cent of those in Toronto were born outside Canada.[1]

By way of example, at the end of the Second World War, Toronto was a city of about 650,000 persons, most of whom could trace their roots back to the United Kingdom. Of course, those of different backgrounds also lived in the city: Irish Catholics and a sprinkling of Jews, Italians, and other southern and eastern Europeans and their children. Yet the dominant community imagination was so overwhelmingly Anglocentric that Toronto was commonly described as the "Ulster of the North," and Toronto proudly projected itself as a municipal guardian of Anglo-Protestant values and traditions. As much as mainstream educators thought about education of immigrants, it was as an instrument to turn *them* into *us* as quickly and as throughly as possible.[2]

If we could take a snapshot of Toronto in the new millennium, we would be looking at a sprawling metropolis of approximately 3,500,000 people. The "Ulster of the North" is gone. Toronto is characterized by a patchwork of contiguous ethnic villages. The once parochial Protestant town, where Sunday blue laws, draconian liquor legislation, and the Orange Order held sway, now has a Roman Catholic plurality and trades on its cultural diversity as an enticement to tourists. And it *is* diverse: more than 100 different languages are commonly spoken in this city. Included in the city's multi-ethnic mix are almost 500,000 recent Chinese immigrants, 400,000 Italians, and 250,000 Afro-Canadians, the largest component of whom are of Caribbean background, although a separate and distinct infusion of Somalis, Ethiopians, and other Africans is currently taking place. There are 180,000 Jews and a large and growing population from the Indian subcontinent, Greece, Portugal, Poland, Vietnam, Hispanic America, and Slavic countries, to name but a few. Many children born in Toronto enter public schools each year not speaking English well enough to avoid ESL class. It is estimated that the majority of those living in what was until recently an all but totally White Toronto are people of colour. This diversity shows no sign of lessening. Indeed, compared with the Toronto of tomorrow, the Toronto of today may be recalled as a city of relative ethnic and racial homogeneity.[3]

If Toronto might lay claim to being the most ethnically and racially diverse city in Canada, it is only by degree. Other Canadian centres like Vancouver also are characterized by a pluralism of origins and breadth of cultural forms, which gives credence to the often overworked rhetoric of multiculturalism. What is more, the unprecedented population mix represented in today's Canadian urban complex – a mix which obviously differs dramatically from city to city – is reshaping residential housing patterns, the delivery of urban services, the structure of class, the physical landscape, and even the definition of what it means to be a Canadian.

What makes this diversity so remarkable for any discussion of citizenship education is that certainly until after the Second World War there was little or no room in the dominant Canadian public imagination for urban-bound immigrants, especially non-Anglo-Saxon immigrants. That is not to say that there were no immigrants, or *foreigners* as they were often labelled with some derision in Canadian cities. Pre–Second World War Canadian cities had their foreign quarters. There was Mordecai Richler's Main in Montreal, Vancouver's Chinatown, the now legendary North End of Winnipeg, and even Little Kensington in Toronto. These areas were commonly regarded as neighbourhoods apart, however, perhaps threatening, perhaps exotic, but certainly not an organic part of the urban mainstream and, many hoped, no more than a temporary way station for *foreigners*, who would quickly move on to rural Canada or the United States. If some of these *foreigners* insisted on staying in the city, it was only on the assumption that they should know their place, which effectively meant they would remain the underclass of the labour force, doing jobs that "real" Canadians preferred not to do.

Thus, although immigrants did live in major Canadian cities in the pre-war period, these centres are not considered cities of immigrants in the way that urban geographers and historians might talk about American cities such as New York, Chicago, Pittsburgh, St Louis, or Los Angeles. Nothing of the sort. If American cities were the contact points between immigrant labour and domestic capital, where unskilled and semi-skilled immigrant workers stoked the furnaces of American growth in the decades before the turn of the twentieth century, what about Canada? Until almost 1900, Canada had no passable equivalent to New York or Chicago. Canadian cities were less industrial hubs than regional, administrative, and commercial centres, and in the early years of the nation Canadian immigration policy deliberately streamed immigrants – primarily British and western European – away from cities into agricultural labour, where an unforgiving Canadian climate, unstable markets for farm produce, and marginal lands unyielding to the plow too often drained resources and dashed hopes. As a result, in spite of hard work, it was not unusual for farm incomes to fall far short of what was necessary to sustain a family. Indeed, conditions were often so difficult that before the turn of the century tens of thousands of immigrants and Canadian born, unlikely to find substitute work in Canadian cities, eventually turned their backs on Canada and sought factory jobs or new lands in the United States. So pronounced was the outflow of population to the United States that one wag claimed Canada's story was foretold in the Bible: "It begins in Lamentations and ends in Exodus."[4]

Forces of Population Growth

All this changed at the turn of the twentieth century. The completion of the first Canadian transcontinental railway, built with borrowed capital and cheap imported labour, opened to agricultural settlement the vast Canadian prairie northwest. The time was right. A coincidental and seemingly insatiable world demand for Canadian raw materials and agricultural products, especially grains, coincided with a major population upheaval in central, southern, and eastern Europe, cutting loose millions to seek homes in the new world. The result was a fresh wave of immigration into Canada – immigration the government eventually encouraged to fill the vast agricultural hinterland of western Canada and supply workers to labour in consumptive, bush-based extractive industries.[5]

Priority remained fixed on encouraging the immigration of farmers; but this was not the only criteria for preferred admission. Unabashedly colonial, the government defined those from outside the British Isles as *foreign* and, unabashedly North American, it excluded White, English-speaking American immigrants from this *foreign* category. In so doing, government officials were no more racist in their thinking than was common in the culture of their times. Nonetheless, immigration policy was as racially selective as it was economically self-serving.

With a seemingly insatiable demand for agricultural labour and workers for newly expanding industries, however, immigration authorities gradually set aside their racial concerns – at least as far as Euro-ethnics were concerned. Confounded by a shortfall in the number of settlers of the "preferred types," the government approved the admission of other European agricultural settlers, albeit in a descending order of ethnic or racial preference. At the top remained British and White American agriculturalists, followed closely by northern and western Europeans. Then came eastern Europeans – the fabled peasants in sheepskin coats, and a little lower on the list came those who, in both the public and the government mind, were less assimilable and less desirable peoples: southern Europeans. Slotted in at the very bottom were Jews, Gypsies, Asians, and Blacks. Indeed, regulations strictly controlled Asian immigration and virtually barred Blacks from Canada. Jews and Gypsies, both European groups and seemingly not predisposed to agriculture, posed a very different problem.

It cannot be denied, however, that, overall, government programs encouraging agricultural immigration worked. Between the turn of the century and the First World War, Canada soaked up immigrants. While immigration into Canada never reached the absolute numbers of those that entered the United States, the ratio of immigrants to Canadian-born population was as much as 400 per cent higher. At first, passing through but rarely staying in Canadian cities, non-English-speaking settlers gradually filled the geo-economic niches reserved for them on the Canadian prairies and the rugged mining and lumbering frontier.[6]

As immigration fuelled economic expansion, it also raised social anxiety. For many Canadians, the continuing influx of strange peoples speaking strange languages – people so recently subject to foreign kings, czars, and kaisers, and who prayed to alien gods – raised fears that these *foreigners* were genetically impervious to assimilation into Canadian society. French-Canadian leaders, on the other hand, feared just the opposite, that immigrants *would* assimilate and tip the national political and demographic balance in favour of *les anglais*. So long as *foreigners* were content to remain in the rural hinterland, so long as they continued to play the subservient economic and social role reserved for them, and so long as they did not demand participation in Canada as Canadians, then anti-immigrant sentiment stayed more or less in check.

Urbanization and Xenophobia

Immigrants and their children were not about to live the lives others carved out for them. One measure of this resolve was found in immigrant urban drift. As immigrant numbers began to rise in Canadian cities, so did hostility to immigrants. But why were there immigrants in the cities? Wasn't there an unspoken agreement between immigration advocates and the urban polity that *foreigners* would remain tucked away in rural Canada? Yes; but the prosperity that opened Canada's western agricultural, mining, and lumbering frontier and attracted immigrants to Canada in the first place also precipitated industrial development and a burgeoning job market in larger cities. It was not long before immigrants, avoiding or escaping the land, ricocheted back towards Canadian cities and into waiting jobs in the expanding urban economy – paving streets, laying trolley tracks, labouring in the expanding textile factories, tunnelling the sewer systems, or working as household domestics.

Regardless of how effectively immigrants filled waiting jobs in Canadian cities, there would be no overcoming the mainstream English

Canadian urban mindset that regarded *foreigners* as a threat, often a biological threat, to urban social stability and incompatible with maintaining Canadian cities as the highground of a "British" way of life or the corresponding French-Canadian fear that immigrants undermined French-Canadian continuity. Looking south across the border at American cities, guardians of the Canadian city gate feared that unchecked immigration would hasten the onset of municipal blight, political corruption, and miscegenationist race suicide. Alarm bells were sounding. Weren't these *foreigners* starting to pile up in Canadian cities in seeming defiance of Canadian immigration policy? Didn't these *foreigners*, largely Catholics and Jews, cleave to their old-world ways and one another, showing precious little inclination to assimilate? It was one thing if *foreigners* were content to spend their lives in sweat labour. It was another to find more and more *foreigners* daring to compete, and compete successfully, with skilled native-born artisans and small businessmen. What about the children of immigrants, untutored in Canadian ways, who still excelled in the public education system and were beginning to demand access to universities, to professions, and to the political arena? If these *foreigners* did not know their place – and it wasn't in urban Canada – they should be denied admission.

As urban xenophobic sentiment racheted ever upward, it was impossible for government to ignore demands for immigration restriction. By the mid-1920s Canadian immigration laws and regulations were revised so as to restrict entry into Canada along racial and ethnic lines. Rules against Asian admission were already tight. Now the admission of eastern Europeans was made much more difficult, and the immigration door was pushed shut on southern Europeans and all Jews, irrespective of country of origin, except those few who might come to Canada from the United Kingdom or the United States.[7]

Following the market plunge of 1929, with mass unemployment in urban Canada and a collapse in farm income, any residual sympathy for immigrants evaporated. The immigration door was sealed. Immigration officials who had once beat the bushes for immigrants now stood vigil against any breach in the Canadian wall of restriction. So difficult was it to enter Canada during the 1930s and 1940s that the country arguably had the worst record of all possible receiving states in the admission of refugees from Nazi Germany. Even those *foreigners* already in Canada were not immune from anti-immigration hostility. The pointed stick of urban racism never dug deeper that it did with the internment of Japanese-Canadians during the Second World War.[8]

Forces of Industrialization

The Second World War and its aftermath also proved a critical watershed in the history of immigration, Canadian identity, and ultimately citizenship education. While many policy planners initially feared that the war's end would throw Canada back into the job-hungry economic depression of the 1930s, the exact opposite was the case. A surprisingly smooth transition from wartime to peacetime production found a new urban industrial base gearing up to satisfy pent-up demand for consumer goods and services denied Canadians not just since the beginning of the war but since the beginning of the depression that preceded it. In addition, a huge export market then opened up as western Europe began a massive post-war reconstruction. Rather than a shortage of jobs in Canada, especially in Canadian cities, within a year or so after the war's end there was a surging demand for urban labour. Labour-intensive industry demanded that Canada's doors to immigration be reopened, and before long Canada was back in the immigration importation business. When immigration was first reopened, however, the government attempted to hold the line against the immigration of non-British or western Europeans. Prime Minister Mackenzie King was only reflecting the national mood when he observed that "the people of Canada do not wish to make a fundamental alteration in the character of their population through mass immigration." Discrimination and selectivity in immigration must remain. "Canada is perfectly within her rights in selecting the persons whom we regard as desirable to our future. It is not a 'fundamental human right' of any alien to enter Canada. It is a privilege. It is a matter of domestic policy." But those who wanted to retain Canada's racial wall of immigration restriction were outflanked. The business lobby demanded more labour than Britain or western Europe could supply, and the government was forced to deliver. The immigration door was reopened to southern and eastern Europeans. What is more, unlike the rural-streamed, mass immigration of an earlier era, in overwhelming numbers this new immigration was systematically directed into urban industrial, service, and even professional employment. Overnight, it seemed, Canadian cities became immigrant cities.[9]

What about the bedrock of vitriolic and politically acidic xenophobia that so dominated Canadian urban thinking only a few years earlier? What of that mainstream certitude that, as if it was some kind of sacred trust, Canadian cities must stand guard over British civility in North America? How was it that in less than one generation the Canadian urban mindset shifted from a narrow defence of Anglo-conformity to a welcoming celebration of the mosaic?

Put simply, the past was cut loose, made dysfunctional both by the onslaught of urban bound immigration and the mediating force of government pressing a new urban liberal agenda. The result was something of a revolution of mind, which paved the way for citizenship education – education grounded in civic participation, respect for human rights, and the affirmation of the positive value of pluralism. Three lock-step public policy initiatives – the first redefined the national community, the second promised equality of access and participation, and the third symbolically affirmed the mosaic as a positive Canadian virtue – together afford a convenient framework for tracking the revolution.

The Right to Participate

The first policy change was Canadian citizenship itself. Little remembered today is the fact that until 1947 there was actually no official Canadian citizenship. Holding true to the mythical imperial connection, those living in Canada were legally designated as British subjects resident in Canada, not as Canadians. This situation changed in the post-war period, and the name most associated with that change was Paul Martin. Towards the end of the war, Paul Martin was appointed secretary of state. He claimed to have previously entertained the idea of a separate and distinct Canadian citizenship, but, as he later recalled, his total conversion to the idea came during an official visit to recently liberated Europe in 1945. While in France he asked to visited the Canadian military cemetery at Dieppe. Walking amid the rows of graves, some still fresh with wooden markers, he reported being deeply moved by the incredible range of names found among the Canadian fallen – names that spoke to the pluralism of Canadian society. As Martin later wrote, "Of whatever origin, these men were Canadians."[10] They had fought and died for Canada. They deserved to be remembered as Canadians. In their memory he championed a distinct Canadian citizenship.

It took several years, but Canadian citizenship became a reality on 1 January 1947. The adoption of Canadian citizenship turned out to be far more than patriotic puffery or flag-waving sentimentalism: it was a far-reaching act. By rejecting the notion of citizenship in layered degrees, rejecting status preference for those of British or French origin, Canada pronounced itself inclusive. Henceforth, individual Canadian citizens were promised, all would be regarded the same under law, whether Canadian or foreign born; of whatever heritage, religion, national origin; and irrespective of any proprietorial claim that any group might make to being more Canadian than any other. The first fundamental of citizenship education, the right to participate, was set in place.

The Affirmation of Human Rights

The adoption of a single and inclusive Canadian citizenship served as a necessary prerequisite to the implementation of human rights legislation in Canada, which is our second policy initiative. Canadian citizenship raised expectations about openness in civic society, about access to public institutions never before equally extended to Canadians regardless of origin or ethnicity and gave teeth to the demand for legislated equality before the law. The human rights agenda was already being pushed by a coalition of organized labour, liberal churches, the CCF, and older Canadian ethnic communities who had embraced the Canadian war effort, enlisted in the military in disproportionate numbers, and who, in the aftermath of war, refused to accept second-class status for themselves or their children. Alive with expectations of unfettered participation raised by Canadian citizenship, the coalition was also buoyed by widespread revulsion at the racial excesses of Nazism, an academic-led assault on social Darwinist and eugenic thinking, a gradual withering of Anglocentricity now rendered an anachronism by the collapse of the British imperial dream, and, of major importance, a need to clear away incumbrances to the smooth social and economic integration of new immigrants then moving into Canadian cities in large numbers.

Canadian human rights activists demanded tough legal protections against racial, religious or ethnic discrimination. If few believed social attitudes could change overnight, all agreed that the law could change. And the law did so. In the first decade after the war, Canadian provinces, Saskatchewan leading the way, enacted fair employment and accommodation legislation barring discrimination on account of race, religion, or country of origin. Courts, responding to the spirit of the day, used their powers to expand society's human rights thrust. In the international forum, Canada signed the Universal Declaration of Human Rights, giving symbolic voice to the new Canadian human rights agenda. The second fundamental of citizenship education, affirmation of human rights, was in place.

This rolling embrace of a singular citizenship and the legal guarantees of human rights for all Canadians mirrored a new spirit in urban Canadian thinking. It even remade language. Immigrants were no longer *foreigners*: they were New Canadians. For that matter, they were no longer in the cities by sufferance. They were there by right, and now by right of law. It was also only a matter of time before the domestic human rights upheaval affected Canadian immigration legislation and administration. Over a period of twenty years, ethnic and racial immigration barriers were chipped away. The last openly racial discriminatory provision – restrictions on Asian family reunification – was expunged during Canada's centennial in 1967. Four years later in 1971, for the first time in Canadian history, the majority of all immigrants entering Canada in one year were of non-European origin. This continuing fact of Canadian immigration life has effectively changed the face of major Canadian cities.

The Policy of Multiculturalism

Our third policy shift occurred in 1971. In that year the federal government articulated its policy of multiculturalism. I will not deal with the complex of political pressures that nudged the government towards a multiculturalism policy. Rather, let me point out that, as articulated by the government, multiculturalism served up a radical reconstruction of Canadian cultural definitions. It eschewed formal recognition of any overriding or primary national cultural tradition. In so doing, the multicultural policy statement affirmed bilingualism, English and French as the two official national languages, but it rejected biculturalism – a notion of Canada as a product of the nation-building efforts of two charter groups, the English (British) and French, who retain a proprietorial right to determine the boundaries of Canadian identity and a custodial prerogative to preserve the primacy of their respective cultural heritages. Instead, multiculturalism promised respect for diversity and pluralism as the true and only basis of Canadian identity.

Again, it might be interesting in another context to speculate as to whether multiculturalism was sound policy, or, for that matter, how and whether it worked at all. What is important for us is that the Canadian government, with wide support in urban English-speaking Canada, was signalling its view that no overriding national cultural consensus had taken root through more than 100 years of national development. As asserted in the policy statement, "there is no official culture, nor does any ethnic group take precedence over any other. No citizen or group of citizens is other than Canadian, and all should be treated fairly." Accordingly, the government declared that the binding force in the Canadian social compact henceforth would be articulated as a function of mutual respect for cultural diversity, the same cultural diversity which was now the reality of the Canadian city street.[11]

Multiculturalism has recently been under attack from many sides,[12] but at the time it struck a responsive cord especially in English-speaking urban Canada. Whatever else multiculturalism did or did not do, I suggest that it symbolically completed the circle begun with the enactment of a separate and distinct Canadian citizenship. If multiculturalism was not the Magna Charta for group rights, which some hoped and others feared, it did reassure Canadians of all backgrounds that a personal and individual cultural affinity was not antithetical to the common good. Thus, the mosaic as a positive article of faith arrived just as it was also becoming part of the lived experience of urban Canada. The third fundamental of citizenship education, respect for pluralism, fell into place.

In retrospect it is easy to by cynical about official multiculturalism and even to find fault with the promise of an inclusive Canadian citizenship. It is also unfortunately easy to find gaps in the net of Canadian human rights protections and to demonstrate that, if racism is not part of Canadian immigration law, it is too often part of Canadian public practice. Nobody can deny that the lot of immigrants in urban Canada is anything close to problem free,[13] but it is true that the Canadian urban experience is now an immigrant and ethnic experience and, equally important, is accepted as such by the larger urban civic society, in spite of the fact that less than a generation ago the very idea of urban-bound immigration – let alone immigration of non-Europeans – would have been dismissed as a nightmare vision. Any government advocating it would have been squashed by the wrath of voters. Yet so pervasive has been the reconstruction of the Canadian urban consciousness as inclusive of immigration and ethnicity that Toronto, for example, in 2001 marketed its bid for the 2008 Olympics around its image as the world in a city.

What do these three policy changes mean to citizenship education in Canada? Certainly, it must be argued that immigrants and immigration are central to the emerging definition of "Canadian," especially in urban Canada. As a result, any formal or informal educational mechanisms put in place to inculcate a sense of national belonging must be inclusive of the immigrant experience.

Notes

1 For a discussion of recent urban immigration figures, see Siemiatycki and Isin, "Immigration, Diversity and Urban Citizenship in Toronto," 75–7.

2 Harney and Troper, *Immigrants*.

3 Statistics Canada, "1996 Census: Ethnic Origin, Visible Minorities." *The Daily* (www.statcan.ca), 17 February 1998.

4 Hamilton, *Canadian Quotations*, 69; see also Hansen and Brebner, *Mingling of the Canadian and American Peoples*, 182–218.

5 Troper, *Only Farmers Need Apply*.

6 For the best study of Canadian immigration policy during this era see Avery, *Reluctant Host*.

7 Troper, "Jews and Canadian Immigration Policy," 44–61.

8 Daniels, "The Japanese Experience in North America."

9 Troper, "Canadian Immigration Policy since 1945."

10 Martin, *A Very Public Life*, 437–53.

11 Troper, "Immigration and Multiculturalism."

12 See, for example, Neil Bissoondath, "I Am a Canadian," *Saturday Night*, October 1994, 11–22.

13 For a discussion of issues related to multiculturalism at the street level see Troper and Weinfeld, "Diversity in Canada."

Democratic Research to Inform Citizenship

CELIA HAIG-BROWN

Warning

Some will say that this is not a piece of scholarly work. It is, however, a historically grounded, politically explicit analysis with implications for scholarly work. I engage primarily with two notions: citizenship and its shifting meanings in current Canadian society, and democratic research which could inform future reconceptualizations of citizenship which this changing world demands. I draw on the popular press, poetry, children's books, and other literature to argue my position.

Introduction

I want to begin with the abstract upon which this chapter is based, because it has taken on a new, problematic meaning since it was written.

> The hope for Canada – and the world – lies in the ability of its citizens to create a loose affiliation of associated states whose raison d'être will be the realization of regional, environmental, and *long term* economic interests and whose commitment will be to the possibility such contradictory loose-ness and connection affords. If we, as educators, are to embrace diversity in the classrooms of this country, we must be prepared to investigate thoroughly the local, varied meanings of being citizens in those places.

What kind of research will inform the education of citizens who will populate this ideal place where people are, in the words of the American theorist Marlo Thomas, "free to be"? It is not the practice of reductionist and depersonalized statistics like national indicators: it is research that

FIGURE 1   PeterSon cartoon. (Courtesy Roy Peterson, *Vancouver Sun*. Used with permission.)

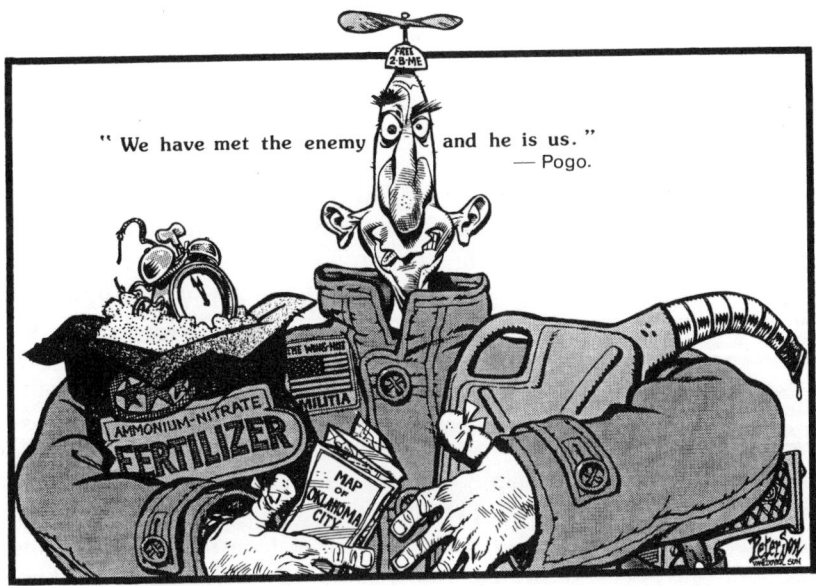

takes the time to delve deeply into people's wishes, hopes, and dreams for their children; their lives; and their search for justice. With its continuing focus on the populace, some people might call it democratic. It is research that acknowledges differences between people, not as flaws to be erased or aberrations to be tactfully ignored, but as complex and difficult riches with which to build and rebuild strong communities.

The cartoon depicted in figure 1[1] appeared in the *Vancouver Sun* the day after the federal offices in Oklahoma City were bombed out of misdirected vindictiveness. Despite a few pitiful attempts to say, "Oh, that's the United States, not Canada," PeterSon, it appears, would agree that it's a small world and a smaller continent. One could engage in a long analysis of the distinctions between my use of "free to be" in the abstract and the beanie-baby message "free to be me." The original book title is *Free to Be – You and Me*. I want to claim that my use implied concern for others as well as self; PeterSon perhaps wanted to give the message that the bomber omitted an important part of the title. Regardless, the presence of a "home-grown" white supremacist in Chilliwack,

B.C., a two-hour drive from my original home and formerly a long-time resident of the Caroline area in Alberta, speaks clearly of the enemy who is us and the need for limits on the freedom of those who brought us the Oklahoma bomb. Since then, the world has experienced 11 September 2001, and its ongoing effects. The question of the limits of freedom that democracy can accommodate has only intensified.

My second problem, as I rethink the notion of citizenship, is its unproblematic presentation of the "wishes, hopes, and dreams that people have for their children; their lives; and their search for justice." Nice idea, but far more complicated than such easy words suggest: white supremacists have wishes for their children too.

When people within the "general community" want to deny the rights of other people and their children – to read Margaret Laurence's *The Diviners*, to wear a turban, to adopt a child, to marry – the problems begin. Whenever I think of this struggle, I hear the words of a Kwaguelth chief in the U'mista Cultural Centre's video *Potlatch: A Strict Law Bids Us Dance*.[2] He says to the encroaching Europeans that he and the people dwelling in the land are happy to share the place, but that they should not be expected to become like the white men. We don't ask you to become like us, he adds. Where are the lines? How much "freedom to be" allows respect for others' ways of being? What about teaching creationism in science classes? Why did the ministry officials in British Columbia insist that the word "spirituality" not be used in the new First Nations 12 curriculum framework? Why did the Gender Equity Committee of the same ministry instruct its members not to use the word "feminism" in its documents? If Canada is to have a democracy peopled with "good" citizens, where must the boundaries of freedom be drawn? What does justice look like?

The corruption of the term *justice* is something in which Canada has some expertise. In 1950 my father, Roderick Haig-Brown, wrote: "Vicious exchanges between Ontario's Protestants and Quebec's Catholics lessen the nation. Prairie hatred of Ukrainians is often vicious and dangerous. Pacific Coast hatred of the Japanese, founded on economic jealousy, used the war to strip them of homes and property and liberty; there is no comparable shame in Canada's history ... Canada's treatment of Canadian Indians ... is hopelessly outdated, it is narrow, based on ignorance and misconception, and at this stage of the twentieth century it is oppressive."[3] When this essay was used in a textbook in B.C. schools in the 1950s and 1960s, the statement above and others deemed equally controversial were edited out without my father's knowledge or permission. The omission came to my father's attention after my brother Alan found himself reading the essay in an adult education class with a number of First Nations fishing cronies. They were taken aback at the following statement, which remained without its original context: Canada "will never accept domination or oppression."[4] Alan returned home and confronted his father with the quotation. The latter, after comparing the textbook version with the original, wrote to the Vancouver school board expressing his concern about the editing. Subsequently, board employees agreed to place a mimeographed sheet in the front of each text used in their schools with the restored version.[5] Although admirable, this move leaves disturbing questions. How many Canadian children learn similarly censored versions of history? What does that say of understandings of Canadian justice and citizenship in this so-called democracy? One thing is clear: responsible citizens must be vigilant about elected and appointed officials who are engaged in the business of education.

When such omissions are unquestioned, and when some people's wishes, hopes, and dreams include censorship, racism, white supremacy, sexism, heterosexism, and other violations of human rights, the proposed loose association of states and the people within them must be on guard. Responsibilities tied to human rights limit the freedom that local politics can allow. Problems come with who decides, who monitors, and ultimately who benefits from the decisions about these limits. These are questions to keep in mind as we consider democracy and its role in research to inform citizenship.

Citizens

As I began my work on this chapter, I continued to ask myself why the topic gives me pause; why I had ever agreed to write about citizenship. Ever conscious of Schutz's notion of the biographically determined self,[6] I cast back to see where this response originated. These were the images:

What is a good citizen? It's something we learned about in school, usually in social studies. Why do I feel my eyes glazing over? I see a white man in a grey suit with a white shirt and tie holding a briefcase and glasses; another man – tanned healthy-looking, also white; in carefully pressed work clothes – men contributing to the country, to development; voting; mowing the lawn. I see people bent over kitchen tables filling out tax forms before 30 April; a police officer – no, a policeman – congratulating some faceless person for obeying the law. I see white war vets, and only on Remembrance Day; never wounded or waking in a sweat with old nightmares. If there is a woman, she's looking like "Mother" out of a Dick and Jane reader.

Who is not a good citizen? Kids generally – they're always too young to vote; teenagers for sure, except in the assembly at which the principal issued the citizenship awards. There, the other students knew that you didn't have to be smart to win a citizenship award, but people had to like you and you had to have done something. Other "bad" citizens include people with brilliant red or blue hair and "immigrants" (not northern Europeans). These "bad" citizens are recognizable by skin shade, name, or accent when they speak; not by the length of time they, their parents, and grandparents have spent in this country. Then there are prostitutes and people wearing black leather: the latter are self-centred consumers, bikers, dykes, or all three.

I can't quite see myself – single parent, divorced, workaholic. Nope. My dad was a good citizen; my mum worked to have her children become citizens, but I'm not sure she was one herself – after all, she didn't give up her American citizenship until she'd been in the country for more than twenty years, and then it was so she could vote for Diefenbaker to try to stop the nuclear warheads coming to the Comox air base and, at the very least, to cancel my father's vote for Pearson.

A good citizen has become someone who abides by the laws; someone who doesn't disrupt the status quo; someone who contributes to society; someone who is happy; someone who cares about other people, usually just like him/herself, so that there is a common understanding about the limits and possibilities of that caring. A good citizen is not critical, difficult, or disruptive.

Non-Citizens

Ever anxious to disrupt binaries such as "good" and "bad" – which never seem to capture much of a true story – I would like to add a third consideration: those who would be non-citizens. The school superintendent at Peguis reserve in Manitoba says, "I am a member of the Peguis Nation and a Canadian citizen in that order,"[7] but Haida elder Lavina White proudly claims Haida Gwai as her country and is one of a number of her nation who has sent a letter to Ottawa revoking her Canadian citizenship.[8] The establishment of residential schools – one of the aspects of history that all Canadians should study in their schools – and subsequent moves to do away with "the Indian Problem" were and are attempts to create brown people who look and act like European Christians. In a speech I heard at the University of British Columbia in the late 1980s, an African-American academic, Angela Davis, presented her view of the melting pot: We were all to jump in and come out looking like white, middle-class men. While Canada wants distance from the melting-pot concept, Davis's words spoke to my understanding of significant portions of this country's immigration history: Ukrainian, Japanese, Doukhobor, Chinese, Indian ... the list goes on. Another African-American, poet Pat Parker, writes, "Where do you go to become a non-citizen?'

> I want to resign; I want out.
> I want to march to the nearest place
> Give my letter to a smiling face
> I want to resign; I want out.[9]

Again, one might try saying, "Oh, that's the United States; it's different in Canada." Of course it's different in Canada, but the poem was given to me by a Canadian of African heritage when I told her about this chapter – and I have barely mentioned Québec.

If we are sincere about citizenship within democracy, about reconstructing the notion of a "good" citizen, we can begin with defining what respect for one another might look like, engage in the difficult task of drawing some lines about dealing with lack of respect. "We" must also look to the even more difficult concern of making sure that "we" includes those Canadians who, in the past, have been excluded or ignored and who subsequently sought solutions by giving up on an unresponsive country. If we want education to address the notion of citizenship, we might start with the people and an examination of democracy.

Democratic Research: What Is It?

Democracy has not always been a popular notion. Raymond Williams writes: "with only the occasional exceptions, democracy, in the records we have, was until the 19th Century a strongly unfavourable term, and it is only since the late 19th and the early 20th Centuries that a majority of political parties and tendencies have united in declaring their belief in it. This is the most striking historical fact."[10] It is no wonder that current understandings of the term are varied to the point of incoherence. The

Greek philosophers whose ideas continue to permeate Canadian officialdom were not committed to the practice of democracy to which they were privy. Plato openly attacks democracy in the Republic. "Contrasting democracy with the rule of an aristocracy of the truly wise and virtuous, he can find little to say in its favour."[11] Plato refers derisively to democracy as "a charming form of government, full of variety and disorder, and dispensing a sort of equality to equals and unequals alike."[12] Aristotle, while finding the idea of democracy tolerable, also found "direct, mass democracy ... a perverted form of government, one in which the interests of the poor predominate over the general good of the community."[13] What should Canada teach its children about citizenship, the poor, and community "good"?

Since its first use, conceptualizing democracy has included a struggle between those who see it as rule by the multitude and those who see elected and/or appointed representatives in power. If we Canadians struggle with a commitment to democracy, we can certainly connect such inconsistencies with history. Clearly the second, passive definition has taken precedence in most current considerations: for most, the right to vote rather than any serious commitment to popular power is the defining attribute of democracy. The latter, liberal notion of open election leads to the establishment of what Williams calls "a temporarily absolutist body."[14] Even if one limits an understanding of democracy to open election, Canada has only a brief history of universal suffrage. It was not until 1918 that women (of European ancestry and with a number of other stipulations) got the vote[15] and until 1960 that Indians as defined by the Indian Act received complete franchise.[16] Resonating with the idea of a loose affiliation of regions or states, Williams goes on to claim that a serious reconsideration of democracy incorporates a shift "towards questions of autonomy and of the distribution of power and resources. Thus socialists should propose and begin acting to ensure that minority nations and existing regions prepare, by public commission and enquiry, their own proposals for institutions of self-government and representation."[17] Developing their own versions of government and representation holds a key to the possibilities which still lie with democracy, and continuous involvement of the people of a region or a locale in producing democratic organization is central.

If democracy is people's government, what are the implications for democratic research? Research conducted for the people, of the people and by the people is very different from research done to the people by others. It includes opportunities for the people – all of them – to play a part in defining what the research will be from the framing of the questions to the analysis and the eventual representations within the report which arises from the research. It is this continuous involvement which differentiates a truly participatory democracy from one in which only an occasional or even a single input is allowed. Sandra Harding suggests starting a consideration of democracy with John Dewey's claim that "those who will bear the consequence of a decision should have a proportionate share in making it." She continues, "Democracy advancing values have systematically generated less partial and distorted beliefs than others."[18]

A fundamental problem posed in this chapter may be reduced to the simple question: Who will benefit from this research? In considering democratic research, another important step may be to acknowledge a relationship between ethics and knowledge production. There are those analytic philosophers – proclaiming their allegiance to people like the anti-democratic Plato and Aristotle – who insist, quite rightly from their perspectives, that those who mix ethics and epistemology are making a category mistake. I actively seek this so-called mistake. What are the social and personal responsibilities academics and other study participants have in knowledge production games/work? Immediate utility is certainly not the issue. Despite their endless efforts to reduce the knowledge to one of utility, academic freedom is about more than allowing racist and sexist "old boys" to maintain the status quo in their words and actions. It is also about the possibility of investigations, deep and thorough, of ideas, dreams, and everyday worlds, investigations that may have no apparent utility and no direct applications to anything.

Indicators and Other Standardized Tests

In education, some researchers are working in places and on projects which they do claim will be of use. Perhaps one way to look at the possibilities of democracy in relation to research is to consider a couple of current examples. The Pan-Canadian Education Indicators Program (PCEIP) is one of the most comprehensive and expensive educational studies in Canada. In times of tightening budgets – since we Canadians refuse to accept that diminishing resources mean that corporations cannot continue to dodge taxes, claim social welfare in the form of government subsidies, and create endless and dangerous messes for our children and grandchildren to resolve – educational researchers engaged in social research which claims some form of utility might ask two questions: (1) Who will have input into the design and development of the research project? (2) Who is going to use the information produced and for what? An editorial in a recent issue of [*Canadian Society for the Study of Education*] *CSSE News* finds the results of the PCEIP "relatively comforting ... empirical evidence [which] indicates that schools work."[19] Is the comfort of academics a desired outcome of the program? One government bureaucrat told me that in Manitoba students' success on the national language arts exam threatened the government's re-election platform which had been built around a claim of falling standards in education. Instead of being comforted, it issued a press release stating that students did well because the exams were not rigorous enough. Is political point scoring a desired effect of the program? Where do the children's needs and interests come in?

Whenever I hear about national indicators, I recall a group at the Fortieth Annual Canadian Education Association's 1992 summer short course, for which I was one of the team leaders. A representative from Nova Scotia commented, with barely controlled emotion, "Go ahead, do the national indicators. We will rank seventh among the provinces and we will continue to focus on making our school system the best it can be for the children of the province." To think that national standardized testing will contribute in any direct way to improving education for children in schools or teachers is a naïve dream, especially when the people most directly involved have, to this point, little clear idea of their possibilities for ongoing input into the analysis of the results, the distribution, and use of the information.

Beyond the obvious expense and the doubtful gains to be made, there are other hazards to using the School Achievement Indicators Project (SAIP) assessments, one component of PCEIP. The impact on curriculum is obvious. Teachers, when faced with accountability based on exam results, often teach to the exam rather than focusing on students' needs or even on established knowledge appropriate to their context. In September 1995 a teacher who a week before was excited about her planning disappointedly reported to me that she had to make the course far more prescriptive when she realized that the class had to write the Provincial Learning Assessment exams mandated for all students at that level. The stated goal for the federal indicators' program is a focus "on the outcomes achieved by students, rather than on the inputs used or the services provided by institutions."[20] Such decontextualized emphasis bodes ill for any notion of local considerations. Teachers may feel the need to prepare children, not to take their place in the world and their homes as critical and productive citizens, but to score high on the exams.

The use of exam results is another concern. Once the information about individual classrooms, schools, and school districts is available, who will control its use? Despite all claims to the contrary, images of even bigger brothers watching children and teachers ever more carefully and ruthlessly flood in. Can we predict which provinces, which parts of town, which students will be found lacking? I am afraid, for the most part, that we can, and it won't be the schools in Shaugnessy in Vancouver or in St John's Ravenscourt in Winnipeg; it won't be Ridley or Upper Canada colleges in Ontario; and it won't be students in French immersion classes across the country. Should we spend the money to tell ourselves what we already know: that children in our country are punished for being poor, that the relationship between socio-economic status and school achievement remains constant? Or should we spend it on a more democratic form of research that begins with and builds on specific local needs and seeks ongoing local direction?

A *Globe and Mail* article exemplifies the problems that can arise with an over-emphasis on standardized testing, another form of assessment research that makes little or no allowance for democracy. The author, J. Lewington, documents the success in transforming the climate of a Chicago elementary school in an impoverished area of the city. A local school council chair and a principal, subsequently hired, addressed the issues of students' and teachers' low participation and achievement as well as a complete lack of parental involvement in the school. In short, they addressed the process of making the school a more democratic social institution. There have been significant changes: parent volunteers are now interviewed and selected from a list of applicants whose numbers exceed the number of positions; even achievement scores have climbed four points in the past five years. Yet the article ends with the comment that the principal must make more so-called progress: "with little time left before her next evaluation, the hunt is on for instructional innovations that, finally, will yield academic success for the students." Academic success in this case means still higher test scores. Instead of celebration of the changes that have been made in the form of increasingly democratic processes within the school, the emphasis is placed on what at least this reporter chooses to emphasize – "achievement" scores. That people in positions of control in educational institutions and business may judge these children on the basis of their test scores is no small matter, but their impact has grown out of proportion. Yes, they matter, but so does the community around the school and the daily existence of the people who dwell there. Why is the parents' increasing involvement in their children's education and the school itself, and the children's lives that are no longer spent "out of control in the hallways" with teachers who "arrived late and left early" so easily diminished in a comment about test scores? What of the fact that schools in Chicago undergoing similar changes showed signs of fundamental shifts in "school goals, teacher training and curriculum"? Perhaps those focused on assessment scores would do well to listen to a parent who has been central to the changes: "'You have to look at where we were before,' said Mrs. Price, now council chairwoman. 'We were in the basement and we couldn't see our way out. Now you see a little light at the end of the tunnel.'"[21]

While standardized test scores in the form of national indicators or of individual assessments will continue to play a role in children's lives, research which is to inform citizenship must do something more than measure what exists. Educational researchers may find more possibility in uncovering local concerns for the future of the community and dreams for the children of that community and in recognizing the need to negotiate the contested territory which constitutes all communities, including negotiation of their own views of appropriate research and its outcomes. A naïve view of community, or a country, as a harmonious whole is no more useful to building a critical understanding of citizenship or a democratic research process than are questionable measures which serve only the powers that be.

An example of research which at least moves in the direction of democracy is the Canadian Education Association's Exemplary Schools Project.[22] This study of twenty-one schools across Canada, funded by Human Resources Development Canada, was focused on local definitions of success.[23] The specificity of the investigations allowed for a wide range of answers to the question: What makes this a successful school? The answers from students, teachers, parents, administrators, and other community members demonstrated a diversity of local needs, interests, and emphases for the schools and the children of the communities. Most of them had little to do with success on national achievement tests.

Conclusion

What does the foregoing ultimately say about democratic research, schools and citizenship? Most important, to reiterate a statement from the abstract, "*democratic research is research that acknowledges differences between people, not as flaws to be erased or aberrations to be tactfully ignored, but as complex and difficult riches to explore thoroughly in order to build and rebuild strong communities.*" It is not research inscribed in a game of "majority rule," where numbers reduce people to faceless statistics. Good citizens do not end their involvement at the ballot box or at the appointment of "experts" to conduct research. They recognize that their responsibility goes beyond abdicating to either "temporarily absolutist body." Their participation continues long after votes are counted and contracts signed; they refuse assumptions about the ways their vote or their scores will count. Sometimes they are difficult and disruptive. This participation is something we can teach children in schools instead of taking a narrow focus on voting as some kind of terminal wish after which we cross our fingers or turn a blind eye until the next opportunity.

If academics are to conduct research which has consequences for schools and the people who dwell there, who are also citizens of this country we call Canada, the notion of democracy in the broad sense of continuous government by the people should play a part. In education, democratic research may simply be research which will benefit students, not simply tell us what we want to know, provide high salaries to researchers, and generate sensational media flashes to "the public." Those who will bear the consequences will want continuing involvement in deciding what research should be done, why, and how to make the results useful to the places where they dwell. There is much to learn from the words of Martha Flaherty, president of the Pauktuutit Women's Association: "If research is part of our own development and action plan for change, then the people being researched must be in control of the process from beginning to end."[24]

Notes

1 PeterSon, editorial cartoon, *Vancouver Sun*, Tuesday, 25 April 1995.
2 U'mista Cultural Centre, *Potlatch.*
3 Haig-Brown, *Measure of the Year*, 21.
4 Ibid., 361.
5 Personal communication with Alan Haig-Brown, May 1995.
6 Schutz, "Common-Sense and Scientific Interpretation of Human Action."
7 Thomas, "Interview with Celia Haig-Brown," Peguis School Board Office, Peguis Reserve, October 1993.

8 White, "Lecture Delivered to Education 474 Class," Simon Fraser University, First Nations Language Teacher Education Program, Prince Rupert, B.C., 15 March 1995.

9 Parker, *Movement in Black*, 61.

10 Williams, *Resources of Hope*, 94.

11 Blitzer, "Democracy," 522.

12 Plato, *Republic*, 447.

13 As quoted in Blitzer, "Democracy," 522.

14 Williams, *Resources of Hope*, 267.

15 Jackel, "Women's Suffrage," 2330.

16 Colombo, "Franchise," 193.

17 Williams, *Resources of Hope*, 278.

18 Harding, "Rethinking Standpoint Epistemology," 81, 71.

19 John Anderson, "Comfort from Assessment," *CSSE News*, 21 (November/December, 1995): 2.

20 Council of Ministers of Education, *Pan-Canadian Education Indicators Program*.

21 J. Lewington, "Parent Power Shakes up School," *Globe and Mail*, Saturday, 20 May 1995, A1, A6.

22 Gaskell, *Secondary Schools in Canada*.

23 See, for example, the case study by Archibald and Haig-Brown, "Kisti Notin."

24 Martha Flaherty, "Freedom of Expression or Freedom of Exploitation," *Bulletin* 8, 1 (February 1995), Social Policy Issues and Ethnic and Intercultural Relations Post-Baccalaureate Diploma Programmes, Burnaby, B.C., 1–3.

Paradoxes, Contradictions, and Ironies of Democratic Citizenship Education

CECILLE DePASS and SHAZIA QURESHI

Introduction

In April 1995 I attended a conference on "Citizenship Education: Canadian and International Dimensions" at St Thomas University, Fredericton, New Brunswick.[1] At the start of the conference, a group of boys dressed in school uniforms sang the national anthem in French and English. Listening to their proud voices and seeing them lined up so neatly, I wondered: Where are the youth of colour? Have they been selected to lend their voices to this choir of young Canadians? I looked around the room at the invited guests and delegates gathered together for what promised to be an international exploration of issues of citizenship, an exploration which promised to include and yet transcend differences in geography, cultural heritage, race, and politics. I looked and wondered: Who is represented at this gathering? Whose curriculum in social, political, and economic spheres will be reaffirmed? Whose presence and ideology will be placed at the centre, and whose will be simply tolerated? The sounds of the young boys broke through my thoughts and made me wonder: Whose voices are heard? Whose voices are ignored? And who is not even given the chance to sing?

The voices of the boys' choir at the Fredericton conference brought back flashbacks of several personal experiences I have had in Calgary since voluntarily migrating to Canada in 1977 from Jamaica. In this paper, I have selected some of the critical incidents as a resource to illustrate, in a very personal and real manner, the paradox of the multi-layered forms of inclusion and exclusion which underpin the notion of citizenship in Canada. It is through such lived experiences that people of non-EuroCanadian background, like us, learn and relearn the positive and negative meanings attached to the labels, "immigrant," "new Canadian," "ethnic," "visible minority," imposed upon us by the dominant voices of this society. The daily realities serve to educate us repeatedly to the discrepancies within the promises of the rhetoric of full citizenship and membership within Canadian society and to their dissonance with our lived experiences.

Our purpose in this paper is to bring to the forefront the contradictions, paradoxes, and ironies lurking beneath the concept of citizenship. We re-examine notions of who belongs and who does not belong by critically exploring the ideas of inclusion and exclusion. It draws on selected aspects of William Kaplan's work on belonging as the central theme which gives meaning to the concept of citizenship,[2] and it incorporates some of the main ideas from Frances Henry et al.'s study on the colour of democracy in Canadian society.[3] It examines the differential manner in which many of us are encouraged and some others are discouraged from playing vital roles in the communities in which we live and work. For it is within the communities that we learn the meanings of differentiated citizenship through the ongoing, non-formal, daily, educational experiences.

The paper is organized in three parts. In the first section we discuss what are generally regarded as inclusive perspectives of citizenship, held to varying degrees by states such as Great Britain, Canada, and the United States. This discussion is interspersed with critiques which serve to debunk some of the myths perpetuated by the dominant perspectives. In the second section we discuss what are termed exclusive perspectives of citizenship and explore what their implications might be within Canadian society. In the third section we examine in further detail two particular forms of exclusionary citizenship and their underlying assumptions.

At strategic points throughout the text of this paper, snapshots of some of the lived experiences of the first author appear in italic type. These critical incidents depict ways in which tensions within the larger social picture are played out at the individual level, and they contextualize what may otherwise remain an academic discussion. The critical incidents have been deliberately placed so as to appear to sever connections and threads in the paper. The aim of this strategy is to create dissonance and incongruity and thereby to parallel the discordant effect they had on the first author as she went about her daily life in the Calgary community.

Definition of Terms

In the *Shorter Oxford Dictionary* (1973) *to include* is defined as: to shut or close in, to shut up, or to confine; *inclusion* is defined as the act of closing in, the fact or condition of being included. In comparison, in *Webster's New World Dictionary* (1982) a somewhat softer definition is presented: *to include* means "to shut up or in; to enclose; to have as part of a whole; to contain; to comprise; to take into account; to put in a total." *To exclude* is defined in the *Shorter Oxford Dictionary* as: to shut out, to prevent the existence, occurrence, or use of, to refuse to admit, to shut out or off, to debar from, to banish, or to expel. *Exclusion* is defined as the act of shutting out an idea or a person.

The term *people of colour* is used in this paper instead of the federal government's euphemism *visible minorities*, which is used, for example, in demographic analyses. The latter term is considered by many people of colour to be demeaning, anonymous, and psychologically distressing, because it denies their particular histories, undermines their ability to define themselves, forces them to accept an externally imposed definition, and denies their human right to seek the essence of selfhood within their own being in the context of their personal history.[4] The term *people of colour* is preferred in this paper because it is a self-selected term for self-definition. It stands in opposition to the various labels imposed upon us by dominant groups, and it makes explicit the underlying notion of race.

The term *democratic racism* denotes an ideology, held by gatekeepers of the dominant culture, to maintain existing social and economic systems in which the majority of people of colour are systematically marginalized and excluded. It is a term coined by Henry et al. to explain the contradiction in Canada in which "two conflicting sets of values are made congruent to each other ... Commitments to democratic principles such as justice, equality and fairness conflict but coexist with attitudes and behaviours that include negative feelings about minority groups and differential treatment of and discrimination against them."[5] Despite state intervention to ameliorate the social and economic position of minority groups, such as policies and codes that attempt to promote fairer and more equitable employment practices, and to govern and regulate provisions for child care, schooling, housing, and health services, this contradiction nonetheless remains an inherent part of the western legacy of egalitarianism.

Inclusive Perspectives of Citizenship

As we enter the twenty-first century, issues of belonging, membership, and collective and national identity form an important part of the public debate in countries such as Canada and the United States that have attracted and continue to attract sizeable numbers of immigrants. The issues also have assumed importance in older industrialized European countries, such as Britain, France, and Germany, largely because catchment pools of labour have shifted to include more non-traditional sources of immigrant labour.

Calgary, 1977: A few months prior to the municipal elections, an enumerator knocked at the door of my apartment and asked if I was eligible to vote. On checking with him the criteria for voting, I was informed that to be allowed to vote in the municipal election one had to either be a Canadian citizen or hold a British passport, and also had to be at least eighteen years old. My husband and I were well over eighteen, but we were landed immigrants. Although we were from Jamaica, a country with strong ties to Britain which were forged during some 300 years of colonial rule (from the mid-seventeenth to the mid-twentieth century), we were not British citizens. We were both disappointed that neither of us was eligible to vote.

Inclusive perspectives view citizenship in an open manner. Working within inclusive perspectives, the social and historical constructs of race, religion, ethnicity, class, and gender are not seen as legitimate grounds on which state gatekeepers can grant or withhold citizenship. Inclusive perspectives argue that citizenship should be open, if not free, to everyone who lives in a society, and that all members of society should be treated equitably.[6]

The extent to which inclusive perspectives are upheld, however, varies not only across nations and political climates, but also within particular nations, with contradictions and discrepancies seeming to coexist at any given time. In the 1960s and 1970s, Britain attempted to close its doors to the post–Second World War flood of immigrants from its colonies by redefining citizenship. Race was used more explicitly as the criterion for either granting or refusing residency, and severe limitations were placed on the entry of dependants from the colonies. In effect, the British government created classes of citizens and, in so doing, moved away from a more inclusive model associated with being members of the British Empire and Commonwealth. Of importance to the discussion is

Kaplan's argument that for landed immigrants who have become citizens it is "incorrect to assume that citizenship necessarily brings with it social, political and economic equality, even when it brings security of residence ... Ethnically and racially distinct people still find themselves victims of discrimination."[7]

Countries such as the United States, Australia, and Canada have generally adopted more inclusive perspectives while having simultaneously constructed explicit and implicit mythologies of immigration, citizenship, and nationhood. These countries have tended to develop more effective ways to integrate immigrants, but specifically those who appear to be more like members of the dominant groups. In Canada, for example, full citizenship and acceptance are granted relatively more graciously by state and corporate gatekeepers to immigrants and their descendants from certain European countries, while the sphere of inclusion is extended far more reluctantly to immigrants and descendants of peoples from countries commonly classified as "the south."[8]

Expressing concern that the extension of citizenship on a broader basis has helped to reduce the national sense of community, Kaplan further feels that "if a state makes no distinction between citizens and non-citizens, then citizenship [becomes] meaningless ... [S]ome suggest that the erosion of differences has led to exactly that result."[9] Kaplan implies that the gradual erosion of distinctions between, on the one hand, men and women who are citizens by blood and birth and, on the other hand, men and women who are initially classified as landed immigrants/resident aliens and who later become legal citizens, is likely to diminish the symbolic meaning of citizenship. The concept of citizenship with its concomitant rights, privileges, and responsibilities has been devalued, in the eyes of some of the more conservative members of the population, because the state's gatekeepers have adopted policies which are progressively more expansive. In this discussion, however, Kaplan's actual position is not clear. Initially, he seems to say that the distinctions ought to be preserved, yet later in the discussion, when he expands on Walzer's ideas, Kaplan seems to fully endorse the right to full citizenship.

When the distinctions between citizens and non-citizens become blurred, the state loses its ability to use the concept of citizenship as a symbolic tie to bind its people into a community which is "meaningful, and emotionally satisfying."[10] Thus Kaplan, speaking mainly from a majority perspective, proposes a more ideal view of united citizens living in harmony within a state. However the amibiguity continues. Does the Kaplanic utopia consist of a single state with all its citizens restricted only to those who were born there? Is it only such a community that can be "meaningful and emotionally satisfying"? Both issues cut to the heart of the debate.

Calgary, mid-1980s: I stood in line at the polling station in the gym of the local elementary school, quietly chatting with my next door neighbour. By this time, I had become a Canadian citizen and was an active member of several professional and community organizations and groups. As we approached the scrutineers, the woman took one look at me, turned to her partner and said: "Well, we have just lost a vote." I was taken aback. Is one's political affiliation so visible?

In contrast, working within a minority perspective, the tensions and interplay between and within groups, and the associated challenges of living in a culturally and racially diverse environment are considered a vital part of the unfolding drama of Canadian citizenship in the 1990s. The minority perspective recognizes the existence of at least three groups of citizens: *Group 1* consists of the sectors of the population who share an attachment to historic Anglo symbols like the Union Jack and who became misty eyed when they hear the anthems and songs associated with the British Empire. This group of people are bound together in an emotionally satisfying manner,[11] and have vested interests in the existing social and economic structures. Group 1 may include members of the state, corporate elites, and gatekeepers. Group 2 consists of the sectors of the population who seek to join members of the dominant group and, in so doing, fully accept and promote the latter's world view. Group 2 offers a large catchment pool that trickles into the dominant group. Group 3 consists of the sectors of the population who actively and passively resist the ruling myths, dominant memories, and symbols because they represent the world view of the conquerors and colonizers.[12]

Critiques of the dominant myths of citizenship are a central part of some recent scholarly writings. Johnston and Bear-Nichols, for example, examine the negative experiences of colonization on Canada's First Nations peoples.[13] Historically, for the majority of First Nations peoples, citizenship has not been synonymous with concepts such as democracy, participation, representation, freedom, autonomy, respect, and equality. Instead, citizenship has meant subordination to an imperialistic culture, deculturation, alienation, and dependence. In contrast to suggestions made in social studies texts that indigenous peoples benefited immeasurably as they underwent a natural process of being initially allies, then subjects, and later wards, colonization was a two-edged sword of protection and coercion.[14]

In tracing the links between colonization and education, Bear-Nichols argues that formal education is an inextricable part of the process of assimilation. She reiterates the historical process in which education was used as a tool to dismantle indigenous cultures, to promote social and cultural dislocation and to break the reciprocal ties between the people, the community and the land. To become Canadian means to become assimilated: to abandon one's culture or to be stripped of one's culture and community. In both Bear-Nichols's and Johnston's analyses, cultural and structural assimilation as imposed by the state are, in effect, acts of systemic violence and even genocide.[15]

Strong-Boag, in this volume, applies the concept of differentiated citizenship to examine the lot of EuroCanadian women, Native peoples, and the working classes in the late nineteenth and early twentieth centuries. Her paper indicates that after Confederation, the Native peoples protested the abrogation of their rights. She states that a number of women formed various church groups and informal networks in order to oppose their legal, economic, and political disadvantages. She states that the appeals from these groups received less than a fair hearing from men of privilege and power who represented the interests of the colonial power. The commonsensical, popular interpretation of citizenship largely ignores the historical realities of women, native men and women, and working-class men and women in Canada.

The generational and gradualist myths which underpin public discussions on full participation of men and women of colour in Canadian society, for example, on public boards and commissions, need to be debunked. The demands of people of colour for inclusion in civic, cultural, political, and economic spheres as reflected in *Equality Now Report* often meet with resistance.[16] The demands are usually stalled by one set of gatekeepers who argue for incremental and gradual changes or squashed by the exclusionary arguments of "never!" from another group of gatekeepers, namely, those sitting at the other side of the decision-making table in public boards and commissions.

Calgary, 1978: Less than six months after migrating, three of us, a Jamaican man, my husband, and I, were entering a store in a single file. As I pushed open the door, a young EuroCanadian man came through the door, looked straight at me, and said: "Why the *@#$* don't you people go back to where you belong?!"

Summarizing the paradox of citizenship when it is extended to some people in a partial and differential manner, Walzer argues that "No community can be half-metic, half-citizen and claim that its admission policies are acts of self-determination or that its politics [are] demo-cratic."[17] Expanding on Walzer's ideas, Kaplan postulates that policy makers develop policies to govern membership and non-membership in a state.[18] These policies have been used legally as tools of tyranny and oppression, as is amply documented elsewhere.[19] Still, according to Walzer and Kaplan, the citizens of a state cannot claim geographic jurisdiction and the right to democratic rule over a people with whom they share the territory if the residents are not deliberately included in the policy and decision making processes and procedures of the state. "The rule of citizens over non-citizens, of members over strangers, is probably the most common form of tyranny in human history ... The denial of membership is always the first of a long train of abuses. There is no way to break the train, so we must deny the rightfulness of the denial. The theory of distributive justice, begins, then with an account of mem-bership rights ... It is only as members somewhere that men and women can hope to share in all the other social goods – security, wealth, honour, office and power – that makes communal life possible."[20] Thus is brought to the debate the manner in which a dominant group legitimizes and extends membership rights to some of its members while at the same time denying some minority women and men access to the prized social and economic goods. The voices who sing "O Canada" often do so in a differentiated hierarchy.

Exclusive Perspectives of Citizenship

Notions of one's ability to assimilate within the existing social and eco-nomic structures are central to exclusive perspectives of citizenship. Exclusive forms of citizenship, as practised in several industrial western European countries, tend to be restrictive. Large numbers of immigrant residents and their children are denied the "transcendental status" asso-ciated with becoming full members in a national community.[21] Exclusive models, by denying full citizenship and/or full participation, may effec-tively split the society into largely artificial divisions of people. This restrictive form of citizenship tends to segregate immigrants on the basis of country of birth, ethnicity, and race to living in a state of limbo called being a landed immigrant or a resident alien. The place of birth of a person's parents is used as a distinctive marker to determine which adults and children belong and which do not belong. Thus, many of the immigrants from countries to the south may be granted permission to enter the country and may be allowed to work, but primarily in the lower echelons of the segmented labour market. One is given permission to eat in the kitchen but it is understood that one will eat the leftovers and crumbs from the table.

When compared with the restrictive perspective of citizenship in most western European countries, Canadian policy makers have followed a far more inclusive model. This shift in focus, however, as reflected in social policies, has been fairly recent and seen only in the latter part of the twentieth century. On a continuum, the more inclusive perspectives of citizenship have given birth to social policies which range from support for pluralism and tolerance of diversity; to promotion of human rights and equal opportunities; and, more recently, to the promotion of educational and employment equity, anti-racism, and social justice. The irony is that this gradual trend towards policies which promote larger grounds of inclusion and embrace a more diverse citizenry are increasingly under attack from popular neo-conservative groups.

Despite the introduction of more progressive policies, the contradictions are apparent when viewed through the eyes of people of colour. The continued denial of access to real economic, political and social opportunities, and the continued resistance to efforts to remove artificial barricades which block meaningful acceptance and integration into the social institutions and structures of this nation, suggest that xenophobia and racism remain deeply seated problems in Canada. Thus, private institutions as well as the public arena continue to remain sites of contestation and challenge.

Within a narrow exclusionary perspective, citizenship becomes a prize to be guarded. Accordingly, the doors and gates to Club Canada, as well as the fences and boundary lines around Club Canada, present visible and invisible barricades that appear quite formidable to most people of colour. Once one is within Club Canada, an exclusive perspective means that full rights of citizenship, and the opportunities to partake of the social and economic goodies on the table in the dining room are jealously guarded. Either intentionally or unintentionally, some of us may be classified, ranked, and then granted somewhat more prescribed and limited rights and privileges in Club Canada. Some people of colour may be admitted into the house but relegated to eat in the kitchen. We are not allowed to sit at the table and eat in the dining room with relatives and guests. We suspect that some of us may be allowed into the dining room but primarily in the limited capacities of caterers, servers, maids, nurses, and cleaners.

In challenging the reluctance to accept people of colour as fully fledged members of the society, Simms reminds us that the Canadians who are marginalized have been actively involved in creating the country we call Canada. "These people descended from ancestors who helped to break the frontiers of Eastern, Central and Western Canada, worked on the railroads, fished in coastal waters, ploughed and gathered in wheat fields, potato plots and fruit vineyards, farmed in obscure communities in some of the harshest climatic conditions, and gave unconditional love to generations of 'white' Canadian children. In more recent times many of the 'visible minorities' have come to Canada as students, domestic workers, professionals, skilled trades people, sponsored spouses, and relatives, and as refugees. In short, these people are old and new Canadians and they have served and continue to serve this country in very positive ways."[22] In short, all of these people sing "O Canada" in voluntary and involuntary capacities. In the next section of the paper we will explore the manner in which dominant voices of gatekeepers attempt to curtail full and active participation of people of colour in the Canadian Choir.

Forms of Exclusion

In exploring the ideology of democratic racism, several forms of exclusion which are seldom made explicit in our interactions with members of the dominant culture and which are socially constructed may be identified: exclusion by definition, exclusion by principle, exclusion by whitewashing, exclusion by pacifying, and, paradoxically, exclusion by inclusion.[23] In this section of the paper we will discuss two related forms of exclusion.

Exclusion by Definition

Calgary, Winter 1995: After presenting a workshop at a youth symposium in one of the hotels in the northeast of the city, three of us women of colour were crossing the parking lot to take the supplies back to the car. Two young Euro-Canadian men who were outside the hotel watched us walk across the car park. One of them looked at us and deliberately spat on the ground.

Canada's national identity can be deliberately defined in a fixed, narrow, and bounded manner in which "O Canada" is sung by only one set of dominant voices. The criteria selected to demarcate, either implicitly or explicitly, who is admitted and whose voices are heard may be used to shut out the different and multiple voices of men and women of colour. In order to make the grounds of exclusion complete, gatekeepers and representatives of the dominant Anglo culture tend to draw on a conventional stock of often contradictory claims of "the others," the people of colour. The claims include but are not restricted to the following: that people of colour refuse to fit in; that they cannot fit even if they try to do so; that people of colour are a threat to the nation's identity and to its social and economic stability; and that the mere presence of people of colour endangers the physical and economic well-being of the other members of the community.[24]

Often an additional claim is made that some of the cultural values concerning, for example, beliefs, value systems, spiritual practices, family structures, and roles of family members, are incompatible and inimical to the ideal Canadian values and norms.[25] To support these claims all cultures are treated as monolithic, static, and rigid. As well, some exotic cultural practices are singled out and presented as typical examples of the culture. However, there is neither critical analysis of some of the more unusual practices and conventions nor scrutiny of dysfunctionalities and contradictions within the dominant culture. Thus, cultural differences of the others are emphasized and used to place entire groups of people outside of the social and political life of the nation.[26]

The implication of this and other forms of exclusion is that people of colour are not regarded as legitimate members of Canada. We are entitled neither to participate fully in the social and economic benefits associated with eating at the table nor to achieve the transcendental status of being a part of the national community. Our differences are polarized in the following manner: our origins are elsewhere, our families and children are usually labelled as deviant, and our cultural practices are viewed as aberrant behaviours. Thus, culture and identity usually become the focus of the public discussions. Sometimes the terms are used as code words to avoid an interrogation of the social construction of race. Paradoxically, one is able to deny one's racism and at the same time make overtly racist remarks about the "other" because of the assumption that racism is a problem caused by the presence of people of colour.

Could it be that the cultural insecurity of Anglo-Canadians may be part of the larger concern over national identity? In an effort to shore up the defence, gatekeepers construct a history of cultural nationalism which to a large extent ignores the effects of colonization and conquest,

implies that Canada has evolved somehow inevitably into a homogeneous national culture, and asserts that the Anglo culture is under attack by
the aliens, the racial minority groups. Thus, the members of Club Canada
have a very clear picture of the lines which demarcate who belongs and
who does not belong, who should be allowed to sing "O Canada" and
who should not.

Exclusion by Principle

*Calgary, 1992: I was conducting a survey for a provincial government depart-
ment on corporate initiatives "to manage diversity." As I waited for my interview
with a senior manager of human resources of one of Calgary's major Crown
corporations, the senior manager entered the reception area, took one look at me,
and said to his receptionist in an angry voice: "Who is that woman? What is she
doing here?"*

Exclusion by principle is a central component of the ideology of
democratic racism, according to Henry et al.'s analysis.[27] Exclusion by
principle may be practised by members of the dominate groups in the
following manner. Ideal living and working conditions associated with
key principles such as democracy, freedom of speech, and meritocracy
are promoted at fairly superficial levels and are assumed to be an integral part of everyone's lived Canadian experience. The principles tend
to be accepted at face value and presented as absolute truths. For
example, in public discussions, commonsensical claims about a democracy are used to deny the existence of systemic racism. The argument
often runs along the following lines: Canada is a democratic country
with the concomitant ideals of justice and equality for everyone; thus, it
cannot be racist. Yet in our daily lives democratic ideals may be neither
put into practice nor applied fairly. Contention often occurs if one
initially questions the commonsensical claims; then explicates the shifts
in the meaning and application of central concepts such as equality of
status, equality of opportunity, and equality of outcomes; and, finally,
maps the discrepancies between the ideals and principles and the lived
realities of many racial minority men and women.

The right to freedom of speech and complaints of censorship tend to
be used by members of the dominant groups to block discussions on
racism. Freedom of speech becomes a form of social control. It ensures
and guarantees "freedom of the affluent and the powerful, who have the

means of access to – and therefore control over – which speech is heard, what ideas are expressed, which money goes to support which projects or investigations, and ultimately, therefore, who gets to communicate what and gets to hear what in this society. So freedom of speech, though it sounds like the panacea, can simply be a method by which the rich and the powerful and those already in control remain in control."[28] Thus, key questions concerning whose freedom, freedom for what purpose, and to what end are seldom addressed.

It is a truism that when ideas and strategies for individual and institutional changes come from the centre they tend to be more readily accepted than when they come from the margins – in the latter case suggestions for significant changes tend to be discounted as being unnecessary and as lacking legitimacy.

Conclusions

Issues concerning belonging and membership underlie much of the public debate in industrial countries like as Canada which have attracted and continue to attract sizeable numbers of immigrants. An inclusive perspective, unlike the exclusionary perspective, supports pluralism and essentially rejects notions of structural assimilation as being the prerequisites for full citizenship. Working within an inclusive perspective, we have reviewed critiques of policy makers who define membership and non-membership in Club Canada in a particularly narrow sense. Men and women are members of a community in whose social goods, such as security, wealth, honour, and power, they can hope to share.[29] Even if citizenship offers security of residence to former immigrants, however, it is impossible to assume that citizenship synonymously offers social, political, and economic equality.[30] Within an exclusive view of citizenship, the discussion tends to focus on the abilities and inabilities of immigrants of colour to assimilate into the values and structures developed by the dominant groups. Yet many men and women of colour have made and are making significant contributions to Canada's economy.[31]

For the people of colour who continue to live at the margins, full citizenship is seen as an elusive prize which is jealously guarded by corporate and state gatekeepers. The related forms of exclusive citizenship can be identified as follows: exclusion by definition, by principle, by whitewashing, by pacifying, and, paradoxically, by inclusion. In this chapter we have shown that forms of exclusion can be used by members of the dominant groups and their gatekeepers, either deliberately or unintentionally, to deny access, to entrench privileges, and to control the corporate and state agendas in Canada.

The reliance in the literature on inclusion and exclusion as discrete analytical categories establishes false dichotomies and presents a limited view of the debate on citizenship. Different forms of privilege and oppression can and do exist within and between the different racial and cultural groups who live in Canada. The dichotomy fails to distinguish between historical and current patterns of dominance and subordination. The dualistic framework fails to identify the different racial minority groups that have undergone, at different times, forced cultural and linguistic assimilation, have experienced forced and voluntary inclusion at the lower rungs of the labour market, and generally have experienced systemic exclusion from the upper echelons of the labour market in Canada.

We suggest that the inclusive and exclusionary forms of citizenship should be analysed more carefully within the context of the formal and hidden curricula in schools and the workplace and within the context of differential relationships with the centres of power. Full membership within Canada means far more than being granted access to the premises or being allowed entry into the kitchen. Full membership means for some of us the unlimited freedom to participate, for others to redistribute, for others to create, and for still others the ability to transform the social and economic goodies – the food, drink, and spirit of community which we bring to the table; for we, too, are Canadians!

To conclude, we sing in harmony with the voices in an emerging Group 4. This group includes men and women of colour and, as important, First Nations women and men who work with members of the existing social and economic organizations and institutions to create a more equitable society. This group seeks to forge new agreements and new alliances at the tables of Canada – an evolving centre nation.

In developing more equitable agreements and alliances, men and women of colour accept fully the complex rights and responsibilities of civic duties which accrue to full citizenship. In creating more equitable agreements and alliances, the interests and rights of people of colour are valued, seen as legitimate, and actively defended. As members of Group 4, we seek to claim and reclaim our places within Canada. We seek full integration and acceptance, not assimilation. We seek to sit at the tables, at all levels of society, and to take an active part in creating, negotiating, and implementing the politics and the policies that touch our lives as Canadians. For we, too, are Canadians.

Notes

1 In this section and in the critical incidents reported in the body of the paper, "I" refers to Cecille DePass.
2 Kaplan, "Who Belongs?"
3 Henry et al., *The Colour of Democracy*.
4 Simms, "Racism as a Barrier to Canadian Citizenship"; DePass, "Centering on Changing Communities."
5 Henry et al., *The Colour of Democracy*, 21.
6 Kaplan, "Who Belongs?"; Abella, *Report of the Commission on Equality in Employment*.
7 Kaplan, "Who Belongs?" 255.
8 See, for example, Harold Troper, "Historical Context for Citizenship Education in Urban Canada," in this volume.
9 Kaplan, "Who Belongs?" 256.
10 Ibid., 257.
11 Cancelli, *Canadian Citizenship*; Kaplan, "Who Belongs."
12 Norton, "Ruling Memory"; Wright, *Stolen Continents*.
13 Johnston, "First Nations and Canadian Citizenship"; Bear-Nichols, "Citizenship Education and Aboriginal People."
14 See Johnston, "First Nations"; Bear-Nichols, "Citizenship Education"; and Strong-Boag, in this volume.
15 Bear-Nichols, "Citizenship Education"; Johnston, "First Nations and Canadian Citizenship."
16 Canada, House of Commons, *Equality Now*.
17 Walzer, *Spheres of Justice*, 61.
18 Kaplan, "Who Belongs?"
19 See, for example, Bear-Nichols, "Citizenship Education"; Johnston, "First Nations and Canadian Citizenship"; Lister, "Tracing the Contours of Women's Citizenship"; Okin, "Women, Equality, and Citizenship"; Owen and Zerilli, "Gender and Citizenship"; Simms, "Racism as a Barrier to Canadian Citizenship."
20 Walzer, *Spheres of Justice*, 61, as quoted in Kaplan, "Who Belongs?" 258.
21 Kaplan, "Who Belongs?" 257.
22 Simms, "Racism as a Barrier to Canadian Citizenship," 346.

23 Henry et al., *Colour of Democracy*; Bancroft, Willis, and DePass, *Civic Participation of Visible Minorities*.

24 See, for example, Kaplan, "Who Belongs?"; Andrews Phillips, "Lessons of Vancouver: Immigration Raises Fundamental Questions of Identity and Values," *Maclean's*, 7 February 1994; Joan Fraser, "Martin Sr. Would Not Have Approved," *Calgary Herald*, 3 March 1995, A12; n.a., "Reformer Backs U.S. Protesters," *Calgary Herald*, 10 May 1995, A3; n.a., "Close Doors, Speak English, Majority Tells Pollster," *Calgary Herald*, 18 May 1995, A13; Rick Mofina, "Reformers Face Critics on Immigration," *Calgary Herald*, 23 May 1995, A1; Todd Kimberley, "The Face of Racism," *Calgary Herald*, 27 May 1995, E6; Leila Nair, "India Lost a Jet: Canada Lost 278 of Its Citizens," *Calgary Herald*, 21 June 1995, A5; Henry et al., *Colour of Democracy*.

25 House of Commons, *Equality Now*; Phillips, "Lessons of Vancouver"; DePass, "Centering on Changing Communities."

26 Henry et al., *Colour of Democracy*, 24.

27 Ibid.

28 J. London "Word for Word," Toronto CBC Radio, 18 July 1993; as quoted in Henry et al., *Colour of Democracy*, 27–8.

29 As argued in Walzer, *Spheres of Justice*.

30 With a somewhat different twist to the discussion in Kaplan, "Who Belongs?" (1993).

31 As pointed out by Simms, "Racism as a Barrier to Canadian Citizenship."

Visible Minorities as Citizens and Workers in Canada

FERNANDO MATA

Introduction

Regardless of the theoretical model of citizenship that could be proposed for a cultural pluralist society, one critical question is that of the integration of minorities as both citizens and workers in the state.[1] Issues related to the political and economic integration of minorities are critical, particularly for the social democratic model of T.H. Marshall as well as for the new communitarian views of liberal citizenship. In European countries, the debate about the level of formal and substantive citizenship granted to immigrants and their descendants is a major point of debate in the social policy agenda.[2] Although Canada (like countries such as the United States and Australia) grants all its immigrants equal access to citizenship rights, there is no concrete evidence that this is accompanied by a corresponding political participation in the life of the country. The granting of formal membership in the civil society as voters or taxpayers to immigrants or ethnic minorities will not likely solve problems if they do not participate adequately in economic and political life. The interest in studying this type of issue has also become more evident in view of the current global economic restructuring, which is affecting the international mobility of labour and immigrant admission policies in all countries of the industrialized world.

Citizenship status acquisition constitutes the basis for the membership of the individual in the nation state.[3] Formal integration, however, does not often run parallel to social, political, and economic integration. Imbalances between these dimensions of integration may lead to the emergence of marginalization processes that will produce an negative impact on civic involvement and participation in political life. In Canada, visible minority groups (immigrants, in particular) are among those experiencing great difficulty in terms of socio-economic integration, and they may also be at greater risk of social and political marginalization. They are affected by higher unemployment rates and lower incomes and are more likely to be concentrated in manual jobs than other groups.[4] These problems are signs of the presence of systemic barriers, racial discrimination processes, and other structural causes that limit their participation in society.

If visible minorities or their descendants become marginalized and continue being targets of racism, the granting of formal citizenship will not guarantee political, economic, and social rights to which they are entitled under the concept of a modern "multicultural" citizenship in Canada.[5] Socio-economic marginalization presents a threat to democracy because it impedes the full participation of all citizens. It may lead to alienation, a sense of disenfranchisement and powerlessness, and political apathy. My purpose in this chapter is to briefly discuss some cross-linkages among labour force integration, citizenship, and visible minority status in Canada using recent demographic data. In the light of the empirical evidence, it is of particular interest to examine the characteristics of visible minority workers of different citizenship status in Canada and the extent to which predominantly visible minority groups, regardless of their citizenship status, performed in the labour market better, worse, or equal to predominantly non-visible minority groups. With data from the microdata files of the 1991 Census of Canada, selected socio-demographic and economic data on fourteen groups differing in their citizenship and visible minority composition are highlighted for analysis of and commentary on their labour force characteristics.

Visible Minority Immigrants as New Citizens of Canada

How are visible minorities legally defined in Canada? According to the Employment Equity Act of 1985, members of visible minorities are "persons, other than aboriginal peoples, who are non-Caucasian in race or non-white in colour." In describing visible minority members as non-Aboriginal, non-Caucasian and non-White, we are dividing the Canadian population, in fact, into three composite racial groupings: "visible" minorities, Aboriginal peoples, and Caucasians or "Whites." The status of visible minority is given by virtue of race or colour, regardless of the country of birth. Visible minority groups such as Blacks, Chinese, Filipino, South Asian, Japanese, Korean, and Southeast Asian now are special categories in the census counts, and their sociodemographic and economic characteristics are distinguished from those of non-visible minorities.

From a citizenship perspective, visible minorities may become citizens of Canada by virtue of their birth or their choice. Visible minority immigrants can become naturalized, keep the citizenship of their former countries or hold dual/multiple citizenships. Under the 1977 Canadian Citizenship Act, Canadians can hold citizenship of other countries, and this has allowed many immigrants to have or retain dual or multiple citizenship. Becoming naturalized means meeting certain legal require- ments: a minimum of three years' residence; knowledge of one of the official languages; knowledge of basic Canadian history and geography; and taking the oath of citizenship. The status of a Canadian citizen may be ascribed by birth or achieved by naturalization. Landed-immigrant status or permanent-resident status grants the individual similar privi- leges to those of a citizen, with the exception of obtaining the Canadian passport and access to some public service jobs. Some individuals admit- ted to Canada may be non-permanent residents. The status of non- permanent resident allows a person to stay in Canada for only a limited time. Examples of this legal status are student or employment authoriza- tions, minister's employment permits, and refugee claimant status.

In recent decades, there has been a dramatic shift in the sources of immigration to Canada. Since the 1980s two out of three people immi- grating to Canada come from Africa, Asia, the Caribbean, and Latin, Central, and South America. Close to 250,000 immigrants enter Canada every year, and this steady stream has been accompanied by one of the highest naturalization rates in the world. In the new millennium there is a rising trend in citizenship acquisition (see figure 1). Before 1952–3 the number of naturalizations never exceeded the 100,000 mark, but in 1978 it experienced a peak record high of 223,214 individuals. This figure reflected changes introduced by the citizenship legislation passed on February 1977, which reduced the permanency requirement in Canada from five to three years. Although the annual citizenship figures plum- meted in the late 1980s, by the early 1990s they had improved substan- tially. In 1995 and 1996 the number of Canadian citizenship certificates issued totalled 212,504 and 225,773, respectively, surpassing the previous 1978 peak. About 56 per cent of these certificates were granted in the province of Ontario alone. These record figures in citizenship acquisi- tion, which are closer to the annual intake of immigrants, are a reflec-

FIGURE 1 Citizenship certificates issued: Canada, 1952–96

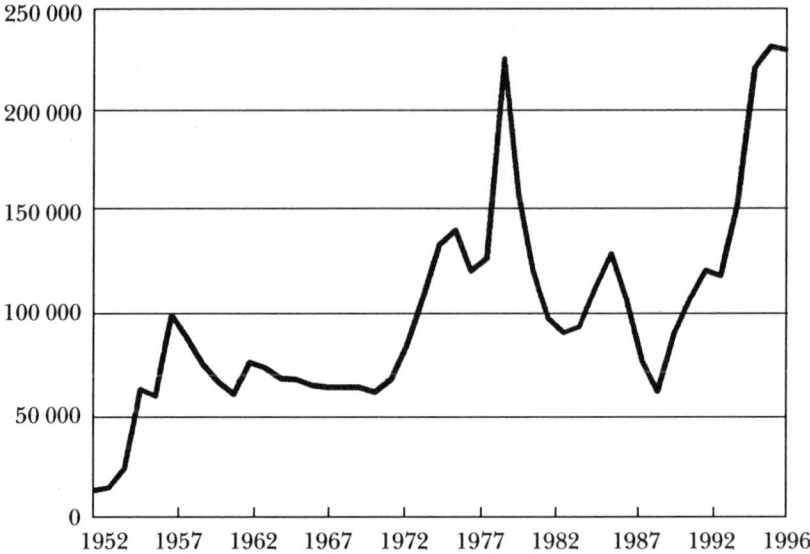

Source: *The 50th Anniversary of Canadian Citizenship: A Graphical Overview* (Ottawa: Integration Branch, Citizenship and Immigration Canada, September 1996)

tion of several factors, such as immigrants applying earlier, shorter processing time and the reduction of application backlogs. Changes in citizenship legislation abroad allowing immigrants to hold multiple citizenship also have increased the volume of applications for Canadian citizenship in recent years.

Table 1 presents the number of number of citizenship certificates issued in 1995 and 1996 as well as the top ten countries of last permanent residence of applicants. Visible minority immigrants from Asia and other parts of the world not only are becoming naturalized in large numbers but are doing so after a relatively short period of stay in the country. They have been described by DeVries as "early" naturalizers.[6] Hong Kong, which now has replaced the United Kingdom as the largest national group being granted citizenship certificates, topped the list in 1994. Immigrants from China, Sri Lanka, Iran, and Somalia spent less than four years in Canada on average acquiring Canadian citizenship. In contrast to these immigrants, nationals from the United States and some

TABLE 1
Citizenship certificates issued in 1995 and 1996: top ten
countries of last permanent residence

Countries of L.P.R	1995	1996
All	212,504	225,773
Top 10 countries		
Hong Kong	31,746	29,996
India	16,215	21,276
China	13,291	17,516
Taiwan	7,691	13,207
Philippines	15,149	13,132
Pakistan	3,966	7,753
Sri Lanka	8,926	6,151
United States	5,185	5,837
Iran	n.a.	5,828
United Kingdom	6,161	5,585
Bosnia/Hercegovina	6,270	n.a

Source: *Citizenship and Immigration Statistics 1996*, Cat. No.
MP22-1/1996, ISBN 0-662-64556-1, p. x (Ottawa: Minister of
Public Works and Government Services, 1999)

European countries, such as Portugal and the United Kingdom, spent
more than ten years on average before becoming citizens. The pool of
potential applicants for Canadian citizenship contains a fair number of
visible minority members, concentrated primarily in the major urban
centres of Toronto, Montreal, and Vancouver. Overall, the visible minority population of Canada is steadily growing. It "jumped" from 1.24
million in 1986 to 2.04 million in 1991 (a 64 per cent increase). According to the 1996 census, visible minorities accounted for 11.2 per cent of
Canada's population. With the tendency of recent immigrants to settle
in major Canadian cities, visible minorities now account for more than a
quarter of the populations of Toronto and Vancouver. Demographers
forecast that by the year 2000, they will constitute between 10 and 15 per
cent of Canada's total population and possibly a third of the population
in the major centres.[7]

Visible Minorities, Citizenship Acquisition, and Labour Force Status

Studies in the area of immigrant naturalization in North America as well
as in other countries of the industrialized world suggest that the rate and
timing of citizenship acquisition varies considerably among different

categories of immigrants.[8] Younger age at immigration, longer periods of residence, official language proficiency, and socio-economic status have been found in Canada to be positively associated with higher naturalization rates.[9] Immigrants admitted as refugees also have been found to acquire citizenship in larger numbers and faster than other groups. After undertaking a comprehensive review of the state of research in the area of citizenship status and socio-economic integration of immigrants and visible minorities, Jerome Black concluded that the study of differential propensities to naturalize by ethnic, racial and other demographic categories is still an unexplored research territory in Canada.[10] Data availability problems have also aggravated this research vacuum. Official citizenship statistics have been discontinued, surveys collecting citizenship related variables have been scarce, and census or ethnographic information often has lacked the necessary variables to undertake adequate empirical analyses.[11]

The cross-linkages that exist between citizenship, visible minority, and labour force status have been relatively under-studied in Canada. One major reason contributing to this situation is that the construction of the "visible minority" concept draws heavily upon notions relating to intergroup relations or skin colour that, in themselves, are seen by scholars as relatively independent of questions of formal membership status in the nation state or from work status. Both visible and non-visible minorities (immigrants or not), however, are individuals placed along different points of a continuum of citizenship, ranging from a status of a more permanent nature, such as that of a citizen and/or landed immigrant, to a status of a temporary nature, such as a non-permanent resident. Each legal status confers specific legal rights and privileges, including the right to work. From this triangular perspective, the visible minority population of Canada comprises individuals of a wide range of citizenship and work strata (i.e., recently arrived immigrants who have not yet acquired citizenship status, citizens by birth, visitors who may be allowed to work or not in particular occupations).

Both visible minority and non-visible minority workers of different citizenship status in the country are being integrated at different points of the Canadian occupational hierarchy. The specific form of this integration is the result of complex factors such as differences in their human capital, occupational segmentation processes, and patterns of adjustment to labour markets. Concern has been expressed, however, that some segments of visible minority workers (particularly more recent immigrants) become concentrated in sub-sectors of the labour force.[12] Over time, this process leads to the ethnic stratification of the labour force and the concentration of workers in particular occupations, branches of industry, and earning brackets.[13] Regardless of their citizenship status, some segments of visible minority workers will be among the most disadvantaged in terms of economic attainments as well as access and participation in Canadian labour markets.

Demographic Snapshot

Of the existing statistical databases in Canada, one of the richest to study simultaneously citizenship and visible status characteristics in the labour force are the census microdata files. The latest one, the 1991 Census Public Use Microdata File on Individuals (PUMF 1991), contains citizenship breakdowns for the Canadian population that may be cross-tabulated with other demographic, educational, and labour force characteristics. This file, which represents a 3 per cent sample of the total population enumerated in the 1991 Census of Canada, contains approximately 810,000 records. Several data breakdowns were required to distinguish visible minority and non-visible minority workers of different birthplaces and citizenship status in Canada.

Based on the PUMF 1991 information, estimates show that the total number of labour force members aged 15–64 who had not attended school in the nine months prior to the census day (4 June 1991) is approximately 11.6 million individuals. Of these, 9.6 per cent were visible minorities and the remaining 91.4 per cent were non-visible minorities. About 81 per cent of these workers were also Canadian citizens by birth, 13 per cent were naturalized immigrants, and the remaining 6 per cent were non-citizens.

The first data breakdown entailed separating visible and non-visible minority groups in the labour force. Visible minority groups in the labour force were defined as those whose membership was at least 75 per cent or more of these workers. In total, seven visible and seven non-visible minority groups were identified. With regard to the citizenship question, the PUMF 1991 allowed for an initial breakdown by workers who acquired Canadian citizenship by birth and those who did so by naturalization. Citizens were distinguished from those who were citizenship eligible, citizenship ineligible, or non-permanent residents. The year of immigration was used as a rough proxy for the eligibility to apply for and acquire Canadian citizenship. Canadian legislation requires a minimum of three years' residence before a landed immigrant may apply for Canadian citizenship. To allow for a reasonable period to apply and obtain citizenship status, 1986 was chosen as a rough cut-off point for eligibility. Thus, the citizenship eligibles consisted of those landed immigrants who held a foreign citizenship and who had arrived in Canada prior to 1986. Citizenship ineligible immigrants arrived in Canada in or after 1986, and consequently most of them had not met the three-year residency requirement.

A second data breakdown allowed us to distinguish citizens and non-citizens by broad geographical regions of birthplace, which varied substantively between the groups. "Late" naturalizers, such as those immigrants born in the United Kingdom, United States, Italy, Portugal, and Germany, accounted for 57 per cent of all citizenship-eligible immigrants (i.e., those who, despite being eligible for naturalization, decided to keep their old citizenship). Among citizenship-ineligible immigrants, the most numerous nationality groups were Hong Kong and the People's Republic of China (16 per cent), Caribbean and Latin America (15 per cent), Vietnam and South East Asia (11 per cent) and Southern Asia (11 per cent). The largest birthplace groups among non-permanent residents were Caribbean and Latin America (17 per cent), U.K./ U.S. (11 per cent), Hong Kong and the People's Republic of China (11 per cent), Southern Asia (10 per cent) and Southeast Asia (10 per cent). Naturalized immigrants had the longest stay in the country: 60.2 per cent of them arrived in Canada in 1970 or before.

Demographically, visible minority groups notably differed from non-visible minority groups. The former were, on average, younger, more likely to be married, and more residentially concentrated in Metropolitan Toronto than the latter. Citizenship-ineligible immigrants (recent arrivals) and non-permanent residents were found to be the youngest, while those non-naturalized and naturalized born in Europe and the U.S./U.K. were among the oldest. Male workers predominated over females among European groups, regardless of their citizenship status. About 54 per cent of those who were citizenship eligible resided in Metropolitan Toronto in 1991. In terms of university credentials, groups of visible minority predominance have a slightly higher proportion of individuals holding university degrees than those of non-visible minority predominance: 23 per cent to 20 per cent. About three out of ten Asian-born, naturalized, and citizenship-ineligible individuals had these types of degrees. Citizenship-ineligible persons born in the U.K/U.S. had the highest proportions of individuals holding university degrees among non-visible minority groups.

Five major labour force characteristics of these groups are presented in table 2. On average, visible minority groups comprised larger proportions of unemployed individuals than non-visible minority groups. As a reflection of the typical difficulties experienced by the more recent cohort of immigrants in adjusting to Canadian labour markets (i.e., their short periods of residence in Canada), citizenship-ineligible individuals, both those born in Europe and those born elsewhere, had higher proportions of unemployed workers and those who worked fewer weeks per year than other groups. They also displayed lower average total incomes than the members of other groups: $15,575 and $13,586, respectively. Among visible minority groups, naturalized immigrants born in the U.K./U.S. and Europe tend to work more weeks and earn higher incomes compared with other groups. While 43 per cent of naturalized U.K./U.S. born were employed in professional or managerial jobs, only 28 per cent of their European-born counterparts worked in these types of jobs. In fact, most of the European groups of the sample, regardless of their citizenship status in Canada, were manual workers (40 per cent +).

Visible Minority Citizens and Non-Citizens in the Occupational Hierarchy

A multidimensional scaling (MDS) analysis of the census of the PUMF 1991 data was undertaken to understand more clearly the patterns of labour force integration of the fourteen visible and non-visible minority groups of different citizenship status in Canada. A total of twelve indicators[14] of labour force integration were used, which included measures of age, gender, marital status, possession of a university degree, residence in Toronto, unemployment status, average number of weeks worked, self-employment status, managerial or professional types of occupations, manual type of occupations, and total incomes.[15]

Multidimensional scaling is a useful multivariate technique to identify "hidden" structures in the data by expressing relationships between indicators and groups as points in an R-dimensional space.[16] When non-metric MDS using the ALSCAL algorithm was applied to the fourteen group data, it revealed that improvements beyond an $R = 2$ solution were negligible. The Young's S-Stress statistics obtained for a two-dimensional solution was 0.073. This result was not as satisfactory as expected for the number of observations, but it fulfilled the minimal 20 per cent error

TABLE 2
Selected labour force characteristics of visible and non-visible minority-citizenship groups

Visible minority-citizenship groups[a]	Estimated N (thousands)	Percentage with university degrees	Percentage unemployed	Average number of weeks worked	Percentage working in manual jobs	Average total incomes ($ Can)
Visible minority groups[b]	1,019.9	23	15	41	33	20,684
Citizenship ineligible Asian-Born	140.6	30	17	38	32	14,740
Naturalized Asian-born	351.5	32	10	44	28	27,218
Citizenship eligible Asian-born	58.5	21	15	42	41	21,101
Naturalized non-Asian born	257.8	22	10	44	27	27,584
Citizenship eligible non-Asian born	46.9	11	14	42	38	22,419
non perm. residents	70.8	27	16	40	31	18,142
Citizenship ineligible immigrants	93.8	16	22	39	37	13,586

TABLE 2–(concluded)

Non-visible minority groups					
Citizens by birth	10,535.3	20	10	43	34	26,943
	9,000.5	31	10	43	31	26,144
Citizenship ineligible UK-U.S. born	23.4	25	9	43	25	23,075
Citizenship eligible UK-U.S. born	128.8	26	9	44	23	29,524
Naturalized UK-U.S. born	304.6	16	6	46	20	35,564
Citizenship ineligible European born	351.5	20	20	37	48	15,575
Citizenship eligible European-born	609.3	7	10	44	49	26,818
Naturalized European born	117.2	15	8	45	40	31,903

[a] Refers to labour force members aged 15–64 not attending school full time, excluding Atlantic and Territories.
[b] Groups where the number of visible minorities is >75 per cent of the population.
Source: Public Use Microdata File (PUMF) of the Census of Canada 1991.

level of the "elbow" criteria established by Wagenaar and Padmos.[17] Kruskal's RSQ statistic revealed an acceptable degree of fit between distances and proximities (0.970).

The dimensions where visible and non-visible minority groups are located represent labour force attributes capturing information of several variables at the same time. The first dimension (horizontal or x plane) contrasts groups of high economic performance (on the right) and low performance (on the left). The second dimension (vertical or y plane) contrasts non-manual (upper portion) and manual jobs (lower portion). In such a bidimensional plane, the quadrants represent combinations of attributes of groups.

The first dimension accounted for 53 per cent of the total variation in the data, while the second one accounted for an extra 24 per cent. Inspection of the first-dimension coordinates suggests that they distinguished mostly between high- and low-performance groups (i.e., between workers who earned more (less), worked more (less), had higher (lower) proportions of managerial and professional jobs, and/or were (were not) self-employed. The second dimension contrasted predominantly male and blue-collar workers of lower education from female and white-collar more educated ones.

The positions of the fourteen visible minority-citizenship groups are represented as circles and stars in the two dimensions in the MDS plot of figure 2. Indicators are presented as squares in the two-dimensional plane. Groups located at close proximity to each other are similar in their basic socio-demographic and economic attributes. Indicators situated at close proximity from each other in the plane are strongly correlated in the data. The location of each indicator in the plane defines a vector that traverses the plane and passes through its origin (point 0,0). The perpendicular projection of a group's position to this vector reveals the degree of correspondence between the group's characteristics and the particular attribute tapped by that indicator.

The only two visible minority groups found in the quadrants of high economic performance were those naturalized born in Asia and elsewhere (groups V2 and V4, respectively). They seemed to perform in the labour market better than other visible minority groups, such as non-permanent residents and citizenship-ineligible immigrants, and they were situated in relatively closer proximity to the "favourable" cluster of indicators of quadrant II than the other visible minority groups.

Naturalized and citizenship-eligible European born are the sole occupants of quadrant I (groups N6 and N7). Those who were naturalized

FIGURE 2   Coordinate positions of visible minority-citizenship groups
on MDS dimensions

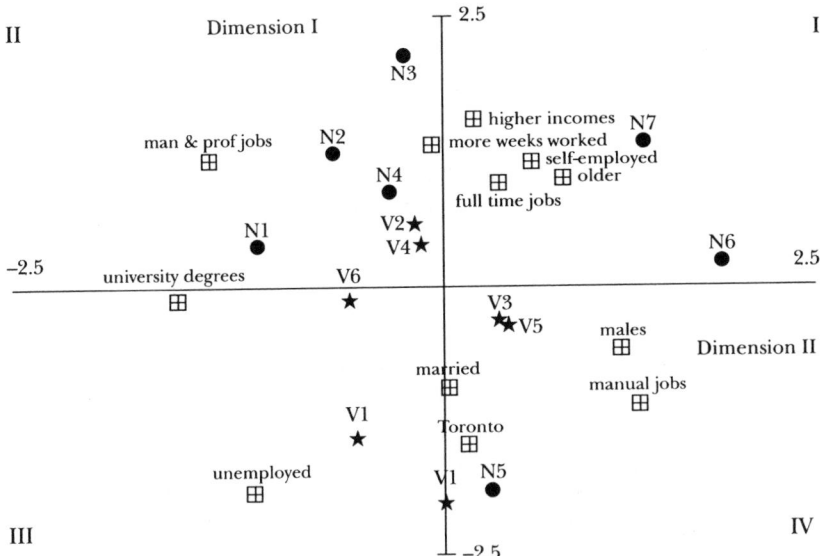

Symbols:

Stars: Visible Minority Groups
Circles: Non-Visible Minority Groups
Squares: Indicators
V1   Citizenship-ineligible Asian born
V2   Naturalized Asian born
V3   Citizenship-eligible Asian born
V4   Naturalized born elsewhere
V5   Citizenship-eligible born else-
      where
V6   Non-permanent residents
V7   Citizenship-ineligible born
      elsewhere

N1   Citizenship-ineligible UK/U.S.
      born
N2   Citizenship-eligible UK/U.S.
      born
N3   Naturalized UK/U.S. born
N4   Canadian-born citizens
N5   Citizenship-ineligible European
      born
N6   Citizenship-eligible European
      born
N7   Naturalized European born

European born (N7) were more likely to be older and self-employed
than the other groups, as indicated by their proximity to the location of
the older and self-employed indicators. The Canadian born (N4) occupied intermediate positions between European and U.K/U.S.-born
immigrants. Naturalized immigrants from Asia and other countries also

were located in quadrant II but appeared not to perform as well as the rest of the other visible minority groups occupying quadrants III and IV.

Quadrants III and IV were quadrants of lower economic performance. These quadrants were occupied by five of the seven visible minority groups. Citizenship-eligible Asian born and born elsewhere occupied almost similar quadrant positions (V3 and V5). Groups V1, V6, V7, as well as N6 experienced some degree of difficulty in view of their proximity to the location of the unemployment indicator. All these groups also had relatively greater proportions of married individuals and Toronto residents. The disadvantaged positions of citizenship-ineligible Asian born and elsewhere (mostly recent immigrants of visible minority backgrounds) and recent immigrants from Europe in the MDS space indirectly reflect the recency of their arrival in Canada. Non-permanent residents did not appear to be disadvantaged in terms of economic performance with respect to other groups. The latter is reflected in their intermediate position between all groups and close proximity to the location of the university degrees indicator.

In summary, an MDS application to the data suggests that groups of different citizenship status were not randomly scattered across the four quadrants of the plot. Visible minority groups were found either in the centre or in the bottom portions, whereas, with the exception of recently arrived European immigrants, most predominantly non-visible minority groups occupy positions in the upper quadrants. Economic performance in the labour markets thus appears to be more closely associated with the visible minority status of the group than with the citizenship status per se. A case in point is that of U.K.- and U.S.-born immigrants: regardless of their citizenship status, they fared much better than other groups.

Conclusions

Visible minority immigrants are becoming Canadian citizens in greater numbers. They are also becoming integrated as labourers at different points of the occupational hierarchy of the major metropolitan areas, such as Toronto, Montreal, and Vancouver. The 1991 census microdata, albeit a rich data source for describing citizenship and visible minority characteristics of labourers, imposed significant data constraints and may have hidden significant inter- and intra-group variations among the citizenship-visible-minority groups examined. Canadian citizens were not disaggregated by visible minority status, and non-permanent residents were not distinguished by their birthplace. The groups examined here require further examination for more conclusive results. However, preliminary analysis of demographic sources such as naturalization statistics and the microdata files of the population census reveals a complex pattern of their integration as workers and as citizens or citizens. It also appears that visible and non-visible minority groups occupy non-homogeneous positions in the Canadian labour force.

Among non-visible minority groups, immigrants who were born in the United States or Britain, naturalized or not, had a greater access to occupational status and earnings power in the Canadian labour force. Naturalized U.K./U.S.-born workers had positions of privilege in the occupational hierarchy. Naturalized and citizenship eligible from Europe constituted a typical "blue collar" segment of workers. "Late" naturalizers are frequently found among those immigrants born in European countries; many, despite being eligible for Canadian citizenship, remained loyal to their country of former allegiance at the time of the 1991 census. This study revealed that these individuals were, on average, older and established workers who originated in European countries that have standards of living comparable to those of Canada.

Among visible minority groups, those who were naturalized and born in Asia or elsewhere appeared to perform in the labour market better than other visible minority groups, such as non-permanent residents and citizenship-ineligible immigrants. Despite their moderate or even high human capital endowments, naturalized Asian born and elsewhere did not fare as well as naturalized immigrants from the United States, United Kingdom, and European countries. The most disadvantaged segments of the working population found in this analysis were citizenship-ineligible recent immigrants. Immigrants from Europe and Third World regions, for the most part Toronto residents, were the most affected by high unemployment and gravitated towards low incomes. Despite their moderate human capital endowments, they were clearly disadvantaged in the labour markets. Non-permanent residents apparently were neither advantaged nor disadvantaged in the labour markets. Their sociodemographic and economic attributes reflected the typical characteristics of a very heterogeneous human aggregate.

In view of these findings, the general conclusion of the analysis undertaken is that both citizenship status and socio-economic characteristics of the labour force of workers of different citizenship and visible minority mix are indirectly mirroring the multidimensionality of the immigrant integration process. The fact that that citizenship eligibility is a function of the length of residence in the country may partly explain some of the economic outcomes examined in this chapter. *It is also apparent, however, that regardless of their citizenship status, groups with larger numbers of visible minorities occupied somewhat secondary positions in the occupational hierarchy.* Five of the seven visible minority groups were located in the quadrants of lower economic performance. Visible minority groups of similar citizenship status, demography, and/or human capital, compared with non-visible minority groups, did not occupy commensurate positions in the Canadian labour force.

Are some segments of visible minority workers in danger of becoming "underclass" members of Canadian society? Bottomore's view on the matter is that if formal citizenship does not allow immigrants to access substantive forms of citizenship while income-wealth disparities remain large, there is a danger of creating a large mass of citizens who are, in fact, "underclass" members of society.[18] This analysis provides no definite answer to Bottomore's question, although there is preliminary evidence that the granting of Canadian citizenship to new immigrant visible minorities appears to have no bearing on their patterns of integration in the labour market. In terms of their economic participation, visible minority workers seem to be more vulnerable than their non-visible counterparts. The situation of recent visible minority immigrants of different citizenship status born in Latin America and the Caribbean is of some concern. Individuals from these countries currently are experiencing the most serious integration problems and risk being confined to the lower strata of Canada's economic hierarchy. These problems may range from difficulties related to the recognition of their educational credentials to plain racial discrimination practised by employers.

A final point to be made here concerns the pressing need to study in more detail the linkages between citizenship acquisition and the legal and substantive status of ethnic and racial minorities in the country. Data quality and availability are essential prerequisites to a movement towards this important research direction goal in Canada. Reliance on census data is limiting in many aspects. Relevant hypotheses can be tested only with sound cross-sectional and/or longitudinal data. Administrative data tracking, which would follow cohorts of immigrants of different ethnic and racial backgrounds over time and collect valuable information on their entry to Canada, immigration histories, socio-economic integration, and subsequent naturalizations, are interesting possibilities.

Notes

1 The opinions expressed in this paper are those of the author and do not necessarily reflect the views of the Department of Canadian Heritage.

2 While formal citizenship may be defined as a legal expression of membership in the state, substantive citizenship refers to an array of civil, political, and social rights, also involving some kind of participation in the business of government.

3 Black, *Design Specifications*; Kymlika, *Multicultural Citizenship*.

4 Akbari, *Ethnicity and Earnings Discrimination*.

5 Castles, "Multicultural Citizenship"; Kymlika, *Multicultural Citizenship*.

6 De Vries, *Becoming Canadian Citizens*.

7 Samuel, *Visible Minorities in Canada*.

8 Hammar, "Propensity to Apply for Naturalization"; Yang, "Ethnicity and Naturalization"; Kitayama, "Obtaining Citizenship in the United States."

9 Neice, *Ethnicity and Canadian Citizenship*.

10 Black, *Design Specificications*.

11 Originally published by the Department of the Secretary of State and Multiculturalism and Citizenship Canada, the Canadian Citizenship Statistics series was discontinued in 1991. It provided basic information about persons granted citizenship by their gender, year of immigration, sections of the Citizenship Act, birthplaces, and countries of former allegiance.

12 Akbari, *Ethnicity and Earnings Discrimination*; Pendakur and Pendakur, *Earning Differentials*.

13 Reitz, "Ethnic Group Control of Groups."

14 Definitions of the original census variables upon which these measures were constructed are found in the manual *User Documentation for Public Use Microdata File of Individuals – 1991 Census* (Statistics Canada Catalogue No. 48-039 E).

15 A more detailed report of this analysis is available in Mata, "Citizenship and Visible Minority Status."

16 Multidimensional scaling (MDS) techniques use proximity matrices among objects as their input. A proximity is a number that indicates how dissimilar or similar two objects are or are perceived to be. The chief output is a spatial representation, consisting of a geometric configuration of points, as on a map. Each point in the configuration corresponds to one of the objects. $R = 2$ solutions are preferred because they are easier to comprehend than other more complex solutions. A more generalized form of factor analysis, multidimensional scaling is implemented in the SPSS ALSCAL algorithm developed by Y. Takane, F.W. Young, and J. Leeuw; see

their article, "Nonmetric Individual Differences Multidimensional Scaling: An Alternating Least Squares Method with Optimal Scaling Features," *Psychometrica* 42 (1977): 7–67. See also F.W. Young and R.M. Hamer, *Multidimensional Scaling: History, Theory and Applications* (Hillsdale, NJ: Erlbaum, 1979).

17 Waganaar and Padmos, "Quantitative Interpretation of Stress."

18 Bottomore, "Citizens, Classes and Equality."

Literacy Policy and the Value of Literacy for Individuals[1]

LINDA M. PHILLIPS and STEPHEN P. NORRIS

The quest for a good life is at the very core of citizenship and citizenship education. How one tries to achieve a good life depends on one's "theory of success," which does vary vastly and may or may not include a high value placed on literacy acquisition. Without nurturing the conditions that support a heightened "theory of success," such as solid economic prospects, then valuing literacy and language facility will remain unchanged. As we shall show, however, there is a positive correlation between educational level and a heightened civic participation that is an essential aspect of active democratic citizenship. Without a reasonable mastery of the symbolic codes of one's society, possibilities for living democracy are seriously limited.[2]

We focus on Newfoundland and Labrador, where the average literacy levels fall below the national average.[3] Frequently encountered explanations for this shortfall posit differential effects on literacy from a variety of demographic factors, such as years of schooling, parents' education, and rurality. Using the data from the Statistics Canada study, however, Norris, Phillips, and Bulcock found such demographic explanations to be implausible.[4] When the differences in literacy between provinces that are due to a number of demographic factors are removed, the average reading literacy in Newfoundland and Labrador remains virtually unchanged when compared with the national average.

This study, which attempted to account for this unexplained discrepancy, was motivated primarily by the work of anthropologist John Ogbu, who has hypothesized that a proportion of school performance can be explained by the value that individuals place on schooling.[5] Those individuals who believe that schooling leads to a good life can be expected to perform better, Ogbu reasoned. We surmise that the same relationships could occur for literacy: those who value literacy because they see it as leading to a better life might acquire more literacy. Maybe, in Newfoundland and Labrador, people place a different value on literacy than they do in the rest of the country. If so, this difference could account for the differences in literacy between Newfoundland and Labrador and the rest of Canada that are as yet unexplained. Since common values are part of citizenship and literacy equips individuals to serve as active citizens, we also explored the relationship between literacy and citizenship engagement, that is, with political, social, and civic participation in institutional and associative life.[6]

Why might it be reasonable to propose that in Newfoundland and Labrador literacy has a different value? Perhaps the unique history of the province may justify such a proposal. Only the briefest summary of some of the social, political, and economic history that may influence contemporary literacy levels in Newfoundland and Labrador is possible in this chapter. Associating literacy with quality of life is a recent phenomenon in Newfoundland and Labrador, where compulsory schooling did not take effect until 1942 and was not enforced until the mid-1950s. Most early settlers were unlettered fisher-folk from England, and Irish immigrants from peasant stock. The British fishing admirals, who ruled the colony in its early years, were interested primarily in their own wealth, not in the security and independence of the settlers. Settlers were forced to exchange their yearly catch of fish for food and supplies, creating a servitude similar to that discussed by Holsoe.[7] Despite attempts by early missionaries to establish schools, it was not until the middle half of the twentieth century that the perceived connection between literacy and quality of life became widespread. Before that time, most employment was fishing. There was no established context for literacy, because the early settlers did not need or perceive a need for it, or they were not permitted to see a need. There were too few schools, and access to education was limited because of a small population in a large number of isolated communities scattered along 17,500 kilometres of coastline. As a consequence, most of the individuals examined in this study belong to only the first or the second generation in the province to experience compulsory schooling. Even so, many did not complete school, and leave to the schools the job of literacy development. It is in such a context that literacy achievement in Newfoundland and Labrador must be understood.[8]

In this study, we sampled only individuals who were living in Newfoundland and Labrador. Therefore, we are not able to determine whether

FIGURE 1   A Model for Literacy Attainment, Outcomes, and Activities

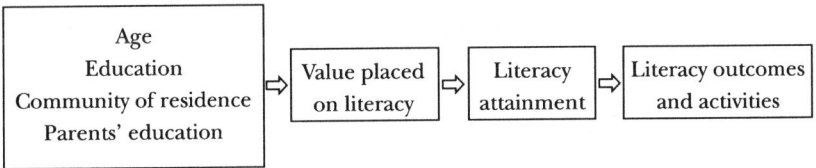

the differences between Canadian and Newfoundland and Labrador levels of literacy are due to differences in the value of literacy held by both groups. Instead, we tried to answer the following questions relevant to an initial exploration of Ogbu's idea:

1 Do demographic factors influence the value that individuals place on literacy?
2 Does the value that individuals place on literacy affect their literacy attainment?
3 Does literacy attainment lead to perception of a higher quality of life and to greater participation in the labour force?
4 Does literacy attainment lead to greater participation in literacy activities?

Questions 2 and 3, in particular, are crucial indicators of the viability of Ogbu's hypothesis. If the value individuals place on literacy is unrelated to their literacy attainment, and if individuals' literacy attainment is not related to how well they perceive their lives to be and to what affects the quality of their lives, then Ogbu's hypothesis is called into question. If, on the other hand, the relationships exist, then it would be worth exploring the hypothesis on a wider, national level, especially to examine links between literacy, citizenship, work, and education.

The general approach to the study was to gather questionnaire and literacy achievement data on a broad cross-section of individuals in the province. The data allowed us to explore a four-part model of literacy (figure 1), with paths of causation that flow from left to right. Demographic factors, such as age, education, parents' education, and community of residence, are assumed to influence the value placed on literacy. Literacy attainment is assumed to be influenced both by the demographic factors and by the value placed on literacy. Literacy outcomes and activities are assumed to be influenced both by demographic factors and by literacy attainment. Thus, in the model, the effect on literacy attainment of the value placed on literacy is over and above the effects of the demographic factors on literacy attainment. Similarly, the effect of literacy attainment on literacy activities and outcomes is over and above the demographic factors.

Motivation and Background

Ogbu's anthropological interpretations of literacy acquisition have received wide endorsement.[9] He has proposed a cultural-ecological model of human competence that "requires that we study the transmission and acquisition of competencies in a given population in the context of the demands of the population's cultural tasks."[10] Ogbu believes that people from different cultural groups essentially want the same things for themselves and their children, namely, wealth, power, social credit, and self-esteem. The means to attaining these goals, however, vary as a response to the ecology, that is, the pressures and resources of the immediate environment.

The means to goal attainment constitute for a given population what Ogbu calls their theory of "making it," or their theory of success.[11] A theory of success comprises a set of beliefs about successful living, that is, about how to reach the sorts of goals mentioned above. These beliefs can define for the belief holder what constitutes a successful life, who can have such a successful life, what restrictions are placed on obtaining the successful life, what role in becoming successful is played by individual effort, whether successful living is beyond the reach of some groups, and so on. In particular, theories of success typically contain a number of beliefs about the meaning of literacy and its value in becoming successful. For instance, one theory might maintain that literacy is the key to success; another might hold that literacy is the key to success only for certain groups; another theory might hold that literacy is a key to partial success, but that the threshold of success is determined ultimately by one's social status. Furthermore, in terms of citizenship engagement, models of civic involvement indicate a positive correlation between participation and several factors, including language ability, educational level, quality of life, and locus of control – that is, with success.[12]

In general, Ogbu maintains, if success in school is perceived by a cultural group over a long enough period of time to be related to successful living, then people will include school success as part of their theory of success. Consequently, they will value schooling, encourage their children to do well in school, expend effort to attain schooling, and so on. More than mere lip service to education is implied here. For success in school to be part of a theory of success, children must be readily able to see evidence of schooling's worth; that is, they must see evidence in their immediate surroundings, such as individuals who have become successful because of schooling, and those who have not succeeded because of lack of schooling.

Ogbu offers this framework as an explanation of low achievement among certain groups. On the basis of large numbers of counter examples, he rejects explanations of low achievement that appeal to language and cultural discontinuities, to genetic deficiencies, or to institutional discrimination. He concludes that none of these theories can explain why some minority groups succeed while others fail.

The connections to Newfoundland and Labrador are clear. In a 1987 Southam News survey, the province showed the highest rates of basic and functional illiteracy in the country, and recent studies have shown that the average literacy levels in Newfoundland and Labrador fall below the national average.[13] Newfoundland and Labrador student achievement in the Canadian Tests of Basic Skills is consistently below the national norm. In some testings in the past, not one school board in the province scored above the national norm. School children in this province thus "experience persistent disproportionate school failure" in a manner similar to that experienced by the minorities that Ogbu has studied.[14] The general question we are addressing is: Is there something in the theory of success held by people of this province that contributes to this failure?

If this question is answered affirmatively, then the policy implications are profound. Theories of success are adaptive reactions to existing conditions. Therefore, they are not modified easily as long as the conditions supporting them continue to exist. Such conditions in Newfoundland and Labrador probably include chronic high unemployment, insufficient opportunity in the province, the traditional availability of jobs in the fishery requiring little schooling, and the substantial barter economy. Such conditions can make the connection between success in school and successful living tenuous. If such is the case, then trying to change theories of success without altering the conditions that support them is likely to be unsuccessful in furthering literacy goals. Correlatively, if chronic unemployment and lack of opportunity were eliminated, then the attractiveness of schooling would likely increase, because the connection between schooling and successful living would be stronger.

The increase could not be expected to occur overnight, however, since cultural values take time to develop.

Methodology

Sample

The sample was chosen using a three-stage procedure that first selected communities, then households within communities, and then individuals within households.

Community Level
Fourteen communities were selected from Newfoundland and Labrador. They represent different regions, economies, and populations. Using Statistics Canada data,[15] all communities in Newfoundland and Labrador were ranked by population and, starting with the largest, divided into five groups, as shown in table 1.

The entire population of the first group was chosen as one sampling base, because the capital city area, which makes up this group, is unique to the province and must be represented in any study that purports to give a valid picture of the province. Additional communities were selected from the remaining four groups to represent each of the following types:

small, isolated, and traditional resource based;
large, isolated, and traditional resource based;
small, traditional resource based;
large, traditional resource based;
small, industrial, or non-traditional resource based;
large, industrial, or non-traditional resource based.

Traditional resource-based communities are those that grew out of the coastal fishery; non-traditional resource-based communities include those that grew around mines, and shipping associated with industries. Three communities were selected from each of the second, third, and fourth groups, and four were taken from the fifth group.

Household Level
A sample of 125 households was allotted to each of the five groups of communities for a total sample of 625 households. The household sam-

TABLE 1
Community groupings and their combined populations

Community size	Number in group	Combined population
≥25,000	1	122,763
≥5,000–<25,000	11	104,927
≥2,000–<5,000	31	96,147
≥600–<2,000	117	110,906
≤599	533	133,555

ple size for a given community was calculated as the proportion of 125 equal to the proportion of that community's size relative to the total population in its group. The resulting calculations were rounded to the nearest five. Households within communities were selected by residential telephone numbers from local directories.

Individual Level
Individuals within households were selected so as to ensure equal numbers of males and females in the entire sample. Interviewers asked in alternate interviews for males and females who also met each of the following criteria: (a) head or one of the heads of household; (b) between 21 and 65 years of age, inclusive; and (c) had not participated in the 1989 Statistics Canada *Survey of Literacy Skills Used in Daily Activities*.

Instrumentation

Two instruments were used: (a) a questionnaire developed especially for the study, and (b) a literacy skills measure selected from a set of possible candidates.

Questionnaire
The questionnaire was used to collect data on the following: (a) individual's age, birthplace, and language; (b) educational history, levels, and plans; (c) work history, workplace literacy requirements, and plans; (d) literacy use at home; (e) children's age, education, and occupations (if appropriate); (f) activities conducted with and plans for children still in school; (g) educational philosophy; and (h) perceptions of quality of life in Newfoundland and Labrador. The questionnaire had fifty-nine items, which were grouped into seven sections, as depicted in table 2. Many items contain thematically related sub-items. The questionnaire

TABLE 2
Numbers of items in each section of the paths to literacy and illiteracy
in Newfoundland and Labrador questionnaire

Section	Types of information collected	No. of items
1	Personal/demographic	4
2	Educational history and aspirations	4
3	Work history, aspirations, and type of literacy and numeracy skills required by current or previous employment	18
4	Use of literacy and numeracy skills around the home	3
5	Educational and employment profile of children, spouse, and parents; educational aspirations for children and role of home in education	14
6	Perceived relationship between formal education, literacy, numeracy, and employment success	7
7	Conceptions of the quality of life in Newfoundland and Labrador; conceptions of the employment opportunity structure in Newfoundland and Labrador, its relationship to formal education, and its effects on mobility; perceived quality of local education	9

employed a branching structure, so that no individual was required to answer all items. A respondent who finished the questionnaire answered between seventy-five and one hundred questions, and spent from thirty to forty-five minutes.

The questionnaire has five types of item. The first type asked for either a "yes" or "no" response. The second type looked for short answers to requests for facts such as age, place of birth, and highest level of education attained. The third type asked how frequently respondents engage in certain characteristically literate practices listed for the respondents by the interviewers. The fourth type asked a question, provided interviewers with a list of precoded responses and space to write other responses; the interviewers did not read the list aloud. The fifth type asked a question and provided space for the interviewer to record the verbatim (or as verbatim as possible) reply to the question.

Three categories of data were compiled from the questionnaire for deriving the results reported here: (a) demographic factors, (b) value placed on literacy, and (c) literacy outcomes and activities.

Demographic factors. Information on respondents' ages and education, the education of their parents, and their communities of residence was taken directly from the questionnaire.

Value placed on literacy. Eighteen items from the questionnaire were selected to represent the value respondents placed on literacy. The items
referred to education rather than directly to literacy. We assumed, however, that for most individuals education would serve as a near-enough
equivalent to literacy and would be comprehended more easily. The
responses to the items were coded such that higher scores were hypothesized to indicate a greater value of literacy. The following is a sample of
the items used and the responses taken to indicate a higher value of
literacy:

Do you hope to get more education in the next few years? ("Yes" re-
  sponse)
How much education do you encourage your children to get? (Any
  response greater than high school)
Do you help your children with homework? ("Yes" response)
What kinds of things do you do with your children? (Literacy-related
  responses)
Do you think a high school education is enough? ("No" response)
What is important for getting a good job? ("Education" response)
Are you happy with the quality of schooling in your area? ("No" re-
  sponse)
Should parents have a greater say in schooling? ("Yes" response)

In an analysis of these eighteen items that will not be reported here, ten
items were selected as suitable measures of the value placed on literacy.
These items were judged by a series of theoretical and statistical considerations to fall into two groups. The first group represented what we
called "action-related value" of literacy and the second "career-related
value." In the first group, individuals expressed a desire to take control
over their education and to continue to advance it. In the second group,
individuals expressed an awareness of the importance of education to
successful work. The statements representing each of these groups are
displayed in table 3.

Literacy outcomes and activities. For the results reported here, only two
literacy outcomes were considered: (a) workforce participation, and
(b) perception of having a good life in Newfoundland and Labrador.
Literacy activities were determined using three lists of activities: (a) a
fifteen-item list of reading activities, (b) a seven-item list of writing
activities, and (c) a nine-item list of activities involving the use of num-

TABLE 3
Items representing value placed on literacy

Action-related value	Career-related value
Parents should have more say in what goes on in schools	The most educated get the top jobs in Newfoundland and Labrador
I am not satisfied with the quality of schooling in my area	One's education is most important for getting a good job
One can't have a good life in Newfoundland Newfoundland and Labrador without a high school diploma	One can't get too much education
I hope to get more education in the next few years	A high school diploma is not enough to build a good career
Education must continue even past one's mid-twenties	
Education is no more important for those who live in cities and large towns	

bers. For each activity, respondents were asked whether they engaged in it often, sometimes, hardly ever, or never.

Literacy Tests
The choice of a literacy test was preceded by an extensive review of existing English-language literacy tests. Preliminary work included a thorough search of major listings of tests. Provincial agencies that offer literacy assessment services were asked about test usage and preference. We preferred a test that was standardized, widely used, reliably able to identify broad gradations of adult literacy, and easy to administer. Few of the tests identified were standardized and fewer were used widely. The most frequently used standardized tests of literacy are the *Test of Adult Basic Education* (TABE) and the *Canadian Adult Achievement Test* (CAAT).[16]

In the end, the *Survey of Literacy Skills Used in Daily Activities* was selected for use in this study.[17] The SLSUDA was preferred over the TABE and CAAT for several reasons. First, it is designed not as a placement test but as a direct measure of literacy attainment. Second, it requires no specialized training to administer. The latter was important for this study, because individuals hired to administer the instrument lacked professional training in reading assessment. Third, because it had already been administered to a sample of 600 adults from Newfoundland and Labrador, the opportunity existed to compare our results with this original sample. Fourth, the instrument was designed with content appropriate for Canadian adults.

Procedures

Interviewer Selection

Seventeen interviewers were hired. Each resided in the community where they would collect data. Three interviewers were used for St John's and two for Corner Brook. One interviewer was used for each of the other twelve communities. Interviewers were responsible for collecting data from twenty to fifty respondents.

In selecting interviewers, preference was given to mature individuals who were known and respected in their communities. Names of potential interviewers were given by such people as community college administrators, school district administrators, and school principals. Ten of the seventeen interviewers were educators – often retired school principals and teachers, and substitute teachers. Two interviewers were school secretaries. Fifteen interviewers had at least some university education. Their ages ranged from thirty to fifty-eight years, with an average age of forty-six. Interviewers were brought to Memorial University of New-foundland's St John's campus for a day of orientation and training prior to data collection.

Interviewing and Testing

The estimated time required to complete the questionnaire and the literacy skills survey was between one and four hours. Because interviewing and testing could take so long, two meetings were arranged with respondents in their homes. During the first meeting, the questionnaire and the screening test of the SLSUDA were administered. A second session for administering the main part of the SLSUDA instrument was arranged only when respondents correctly answered at least three items on the screening test. Otherwise, respondents were told that all the necessary information had been gathered. Interviewing and testing were completed within eight weeks in the majority of communities.

Coding and Scoring

Three senior undergraduate students were hired to score and code the instruments and to perform data input. At an introductory meeting, the students were instructed in the proper coding of the questionnaire. At a second training session, the students were assigned a scoring rehearsal task. The scoring guide for SLSUDA was adapted from Statistics Canada.[18] Scoring instructions were used unchanged. Ten completed SLSUDA booklets were selected randomly (one from each of ten communities), and each student was given copies. Students were instructed to score all ten tests using the SLSUDA scoring guide.

At a third meeting, scoring discrepancies across students were identified and discussed. In each case where one student scored an item differently from the other two, the item was analysed and the appropriate scoring identified.

Each student was assigned to score a different one-third of the SLSUDA booklets for each of the fourteen communities. In addition, in order to estimate inter-rater reliability, a randomly selected sample consisting of 20 per cent of the total sample was scored by all three assistants.

Results

Effects on Value Placed on Literacy

As discussed previously, there were two indicators of the value individuals placed on literacy, action-related value, and career-related value. The results show that age, education, and community of residence affected the value placed on literacy in a variety of ways. First, there was a tendency for the youngest age groups (below 40 years old) to place more value on literacy than the older groups. In the case of those less than 30 years old, they tended to place more action-related value only.

Second, more highly educated individuals placed more action-related value on literacy, but the degree of career-related value placed on literacy did not differ for individuals with different educational levels.

Third, community of residence affected both the action-related and career-related value placed on literacy. Individuals from eight communities placed less action-related value on literacy than individuals from St John's, who were used as the basis of comparison. Individuals from eight communities placed more career-related value on literacy than individuals from St John's. There was an overlap of four communities in these comparisons, so that four communities placed both less action-related value and more career-related value on literacy than St John's.

Effects on Literacy Attainment

The factors with the strongest effects on literacy attainment were age and education. Younger and more educated individuals tended to have higher reading literacy, and more educated individuals also tended to have higher writing literacy and numeracy.

Fathers' education had a positive effect on reading literacy and numeracy, but mothers' education had no effect over and above the effect of fathers' education on any aspect of literacy.

When the individuals' educational attainment was not considered in the calculations, the education of their mothers had a significant effect on both their reading and writing literacy, while the effect of their father's education on reading literacy and numeracy increased somewhat. The implication is that mothers' education contributed more than that of fathers to the literacy of the individuals surveyed.

Five communities had higher reading literacy than St John's, and one had lower. There were few differences among communities in writing literacy and numeracy. When the effects of education on literacy attainment were not considered in the calculations, five communities had lower reading literacy than St John's, and only one had higher reading literacy. This finding suggests that many of the differences in literacy attainment between communities in the province are due to differences in educational attainment.

Action-related value placed on literacy had a positive effect on writing literacy and no effect on the other aspects of literacy. Career-related value placed on literacy had a negative effect on reading literacy but no effect on the other aspects of literacy. When the effects of education on literacy attainment were not considered in the calculations, then action-related value had a positive effect on both reading and writing literacy, and career-related value had a negative effect on reading literacy, as before.

Effects on Literacy Outcomes

Labour Force
Each younger age group had higher representation in the labour force than the oldest group. More educated individuals had a greater tendency than less educated to be in the labour force, but literacy attainment had only a slight influence. Only writing literacy affected presence

in the labour force, and then weakly and negatively. When educational attainment is not considered, the effect of age on presence in the labour force increased, and there was no effect of literacy attainment.

Good Life
More educated individuals tended more often to think that they lead a good life in Newfoundland and Labrador, and the youngest age group (less than 30 years old) that they do not. Literacy attainment had no effect on the perception of the good life, whether or not educational attainment was considered in the equation.

Effects on Literacy Activities

All of the younger age groups engaged more often in all three forms of literacy activities (reading, writing, and numeracy) than the oldest group (more than 60 years old). More educated individuals also engaged in more literacy activities of all sorts. Mothers' education positively affected reading and writing activities, but when the educational attainment of the individuals was not considered, then mothers' education positively affected all three sorts of activities. Community of residence had considerable effect on writing activities, with nine communities engaging in more writing activities than St John's. Only reading literacy attainment affected literacy activities, with greater attainment leading to more activity of all three sorts.

Discussion of the Results

In the following, we discuss only the results that bear directly on the four questions raised at the beginning, dealing with one at a time.

1. Do demographic factors influence the value that individuals place on literacy?

Yes, in a variety of ways. It is easy enough to explain the result that more educated individuals placed more action-related value on literacy. It is this very value that helped them to obtain their education. Perhaps more important for literacy development in the long run is that younger individuals tended to place more action-related value on literacy. Since action-related value on literacy had a positive influence on literacy attainment, this finding is encouraging.

Although more study is needed to be sure of the meaning of the latter result, it perhaps suggests a changing attitude towards literacy attainment in the province. Certainly, those younger than 30 years would have been exposed more that any other group in the history of the province to the need for literacy. Although for older individuals the connection between literacy and employment may have been tenuous, the connection would have been much more obvious to the younger group. Reder and Green studied an Alaskan fishing village that had experienced colonialization patterns very similar to those of Newfoundland and Labrador, including early indebtedness to the company store.[19] Individuals found security of income through indentured labour. The result was that opportunity for economic success was available regardless of educational attainment. Indentureship, however, may not be positively related to active civic participation, as described by Sears and Hughes, who present a continuum of conceptual types of citizenship, ranging from the passive elistist model, in which citizens are informed voters, to an active model, in which citizens value participation as equals and engage in association to resolve issues and problems of oppression and inequalities.[20] Moreover, competencies in literacy, that is, reading and writing, are fundamental to a more recent dimension of citizenship: the cultural component, which requires knowledge of one's own cultural heritage, of history, and an awareness of a multicultural heritage.[21] Without a reasonable mastery of the symbolic codes of one's society, possibilities for participation in political, civic and social life are seriously limited. Furthermore, as Ogbu argues, when individuals do not have clear evidence that the quality of their lives is connected to schooling, then they will not value it. The connection between literacy and quality of life is tighter in the province than ever before. Ogbu's theory leads to the prediction that there should be a corresponding increase in the value placed on literacy, whereas the Sears and Hughes model of active and passive citizenship suggests that the link may be tenuous, given the historical passivity inherent in indentureship. Perhaps our results indicate that such a change is occurring among the youngest adults of the province.

On the other hand, eight communities placed less action-related value on literacy than St John's did. In five of these communities, their reading literacy scores were lower than those of St John's. In all eight cases, the communities were small and isolated. This finding suggests that there is something about the culture of these communities that inhibits taking positive action towards affecting education, for example, by demanding that parents have more say. Since this tendency is also related to lower literacy levels, there appears to be room for a politicization of smaller communities regarding education. The career-related value of literacy that many of these communities hold is, in fact, related to lower literacy levels.

It is just such career-related value, however, that is often promoted by governments in an effort to encourage citizens to acquire more literacy. Discussing inner-city youngsters, Scribner argues that "appeals to individuals to enhance their functional skills might founder on the different subjective utilities communities and groups attach to reading and writing activities."[22] According to Ogbu, only if some connection can be seen between increased literacy and employment will the prospect of employment opportunity entice individuals to increase their literacy levels. Since this connection is rather weak in many communities in the province, the findings were to be expected. The policy implication is that the approach to increasing employment through increasing literacy works in the wrong direction. First, individuals need to see a demand for workers with higher literacy levels. Those individuals will then do what is necessary to acquire the requisite literacy.

2. *Does the value that individuals place on literacy affect their literacy attainment?*

As mentioned in the discussion of the first question, it does. The effect is subtle, however, and perhaps surprising. If the value placed on literacy is such that it motivates individuals to action – to want to get more education, to be dissatisfied with the educational system in their community, and to want to have more say in education and political life – then this is related to increased literacy levels. If, on the other hand, the value placed on literacy is based on seeing literacy as a route to employment, then this is related to decreased literacy levels. These findings would seem to have profound implications for many current government policies regarding the promotion of literacy as a precursor to citizenship engagement.

Furthermore, the results may be difficult to interpret in the light of Ogbu's theory. If we assume, on the basis of evidence amassed by Ogbu, that his theory is correct, how might they be explained? The theory would lead us to expect that, if individuals possessed career-related value for literacy, then their literacy levels should be higher than those who do not hold such a value. Why were they lower in this study? One speculation is that, in fact, individuals in Newfoundland and Labrador do not see a close connection between career opportunity and literacy (except, perhaps, for the youngest adults); the connection is weaker than it is just about anywhere else in the country. A further speculation is that the individuals *say* that they value literacy because of its connection to career opportunity, even though they do not believe in their hearts that there is such a connection. Regarding their literacy the individuals act on the basis of what they believe, rather than on what they say, and thus we witness the lower literacy levels for those who possess higher career-related value for literacy. We acknowledge that this explanation is speculative and needs further study.

3. Does literacy attainment lead to perception of a higher quality of life and to greater participation in the labour force?

Perhaps surprisingly, no. If education is the factor, then the answer is positive for both outcomes. For literacy, however, the answers are negative. Again, these findings have fairly serious implications for government literacy policy. Literacy is being advocated largely because of the beneficial outcomes that accrue from it, but these outcomes do not seem related directly to literacy.

Scribner has argued that there is no universal value in particular literacy competencies. Different communities and settings foster different ranges of literacy activities. Perhaps, she surmises, in seeing "the great variety of beliefs and aspirations that various people have developed toward literacy in their particular historical and current life circumstances,"[23] we will develop a scepticism towards finding the one best answer to the improvement of literacy. Although we are likely never to be satisfied with the inequality of cultural, educational, and economic opportunity that derives from inequalities in literacy, we are likely to be unable to reduce such inequalities without attending to the different values individuals attach to literacy and the reasons they have for so doing.

4. Does literacy attainment lead to greater participation in literacy activities?

It does, but little more than other factors, such as age and community of residence. This finding suggests that literacy activities result largely from situations that demand them. Again, the evidence suggests that no universal value of literacy and no universal approach to literacy improvement that will work in all situations are likely to be found.

Concluding Comments

This study confirms some and disconfirms other widely held views on literacy. It confirms the work of Scribner with the Vai people of West Africa in at least two ways: that there is no "one best answer" approach to literacy improvement; and that the particular historical and current life circumstances of peoples influence their beliefs and aspirations.[24] School children in Newfoundland and Labrador "experience persistent disproportionate school failure"[25] in a manner similar to some ethnic minorities in the United States and Canada. Given that most individuals of Newfoundland and Labrador do not belong to an ethnic minority in Canada, however, finding explanations of their school failure forces us to look beyond the visible features of ethnic and cultural minorities to the underlying beliefs, attitudes, and expectations that people of the province hold about literacy.

Our research confirms the view that literacy develops better when it is valued, but not just any kind of valuing will do. If the value seen in literacy is its role in gaining employment, this, in fact, detracts from literacy. Furthermore, greater literacy does not seem to lead to a perception of a higher quality of life, an outcome that is often touted by its advocates. It seems that public policies would be more effective if they promoted literacy for its own sake: not for job acquisition, but for greater involvement in social, civic, and political life.

The research also confirms the view that literacy is related to politicization; that is, it is related to individuals' becoming a part of an active literate citizenry that makes its own demands on institutions, including schools. Those who take action to increase their literacy will have it increased. Taking such action involves breaking with everyday experience to envisage the extraordinary options for living and thinking and to see the current world as only one of a number of possibilities.[26] The effect is that the knowledge, skills, and attitudes of literate citizens not only assist them in making informed decisions and exercising rights and responsibilities in a democratic society,[27] but also allow them to see how language can be used by others to persuade or even to manipulate them in forms of oppression and inequalities. Thus, the relationship between literacy and citizenship appears reciprocal: citizens who actively value literacy and place demands upon educational institutions for quality literacy instruction, attain the highest literacy levels; those with the highest literacy levels have much to contribute to society.

Notes

1 This research was supported by a grant from the National Literacy Secretariat, Department of Secretary of State of Canada.
2 Freire, *Pedagogy of the Oppressed* and *Pedagogy of Freedom.*
3 Southam Newspaper Group, 1987; Statistics Canada, *Reading the Future* and *International Adult Literacy Survey.*
4 Norris, Phillips, and Bulcock, *Demographic Causes of Reading Literacy Levels.*
5 Ogbu, "Diversity and Equity in Public Education."
6 Munro, "Literacy."
7 Holsoe, "Slavery and Economic Response."
8 Phillips et al., "Effect of Early Literacy Intervention."
9 Smith, "Anthropology of Literacy Acquisition."
10 See Ogbu, "Origins of Human Competence," 423.
11 Ogbu and Matute-Bianchi, *Understanding Socio-Cultural Factors,* 84.
12 See, for example, Frideres, "Civic Participation, Awareness, Knowledge and Skills."
13 Southam Newspaper Group, 1987; Statistics Canada, *Reading the Future* and *International Adult Literacy Survey.*
14 Ogbu and Matute-Bianchi, *Understanding Socio-Cultural Factors,* 73.
15 Statistics Canada, *Census Subdivision,* table 3, 3-1-3-8; *Census Subdivisions,* table 2, 2-1-2-17.
16 *Test of Adult Basic Education* and *Canadian Adult Achievement Test.*
17 Statistics Canada, *Survey of Literacy Skills.*
18 Statistics Canada, *Survey of Literacy Skills ... Scoring Guide.*
19 Reder and Green, "Contrasting Patterns of Literacy."
20 Sears and Hughes, "Citizenship Education and Current Educational Reform."
21 Veedhuis, « La citoyenneté démocratique »; Hébert and Wilkinson, "The Citizenship Debate" in this volume.
22 See Scribner, "Literacy in Three Metaphors," 11.
23 Ibid., 17.
24 Ibid.
25 To use the phrase of Ogbu and Matute-Bianchi, *Understanding Socio-Cultural Factors,* 73.
26 Buchmann and Floden, *Detachment and Concern.*
27 Edwards and Fogelman, *Developing Citizenship in the Curriculum*; Lynch, *Education for Citizenship.*

Citizenship Education:
What Research for the Future?

YVONNE M. HÉBERT and MICHEL PAGÉ

Introduction

Citizenship education in Canada, including Québec, reflects and centres the major debate confronting citizenship. Simply, the objectives, content and pedagogy of citizenship education have not been determined in cognizance of the indeterminable citizenship debate. This raises a basic educational question: *What kind of education is necessary to uphold our pluralistic democratic country?* To respond adequately requires a body of systematic and comprehensive research as well as a renewed working model of citizenship which allows for contemporary realities.

What is most remarkable, in this field as in most research fields, is a lack of coordination and of networking among researchers until very recently with respect to the establishment and implementation of a pan-Canadian research agenda. Without research coordination, there is little likelihood of a sound basis with which to even begin to answer the key question and to develop appropriate and adequate citizenship educational programs and pedagogies. To confront the current dispersion of energies and to attain the necessary educational goals, coordination of the research becomes necessary. Let us reflect then on the matter and consider the new and exciting initiatives which have been undertaken in this regard.

Research Program in Citizenship Education

The development of educational policy and practice of citizenship education, however, cannot continue to follow personal preferences, interests, affinities, and whims or be subject to continuous ideological winds.

It must be based preferably upon a systematic and comprehensive corpus of educational research that allows educators and students to understand the interrelationships of citizenship education and its relevance to their lives and to Canadian society. In order to fill this important gap, a group of interested researchers, decision makers and practitioners met in 1998 and developed consensus around a pan-Canadian research agenda in citizenship education, a historic and unique event in the social sciences and humanities in Canada.[1] To carry out this research program, the group identified itself as the Citizenship Education Research Network. It meets at least twice a year and is open to all interested persons.[2]

Four major themes organize the pan-Canadian research agenda:

- Models of Citizenship, Typologies of Citizens, and Contexts in Citizenship Education
- Values of Citizens and in Citizenship Education
- Behaviours, Attitudes, Skills, and Knowledge in Citizenship Education
- Teaching Practices in Citizenship Education.

For each of the four themes, major research questions, specific objectives, and a series of research projects are outlined below, some of which are already under way. We present here a brief overview of each of these four themes, as they are currently articulated, and some of the recently completed research.

Models of Citizenship, Typologies of Citizens, and Contexts in Citizenship Education

The overarching research question for this theme is: *How has democratic citizenship been conceptualized over time, in different contexts, and by different actors?* Three sets of research objectives and projects are foreseen: one set concerned with historical, social, and philosophical contexts, another with citizens' conceptions of citizenship, and a third with the educational relevance of these conceptions. For the first sub-theme – historical, social and philosophical contexts – the specific objectives are to develop a conceptual framework that would inform all four research themes; to examine the implications of this framework for citizenship education; to elaborate the historical and philosophical background of citizenship education; and to weigh the implications, for school and state, of multiple and transnational citizenship. Taking into account current and past models of citizenship, the principal research tasks are to synthesize the work which has been completed, identify gaps in the knowledge base, and carry out work to address those gaps.

The specific objectives of the next sub-theme – citizens' conceptions of citizenship – are to determine and compare the conceptions of democratic citizenship held by citizens themselves, including those of students, educators, teacher educators, and adults; to determine the impact, if any, of key variables, such as age, gender, ethnicity, race, language, nationality, collective identity, immigration status, and class; and to identify types of citizens and their relevance. The first phase develops a national database of citizens' conceptions of citizenship and of citizen types with respect to key variables. A second phase extends, on a pan-Canadian basis, a typological study of citizens' conceptions to its influences on decisions and actions.

The third sub-theme deals with the educational relevance of these conceptions. The specific objectives are to determine how these conceptions are represented in citizenship educational materials and policy; to examine the relationships between these conceptions and educators' conceptual, attitudinal, and pedagogical understandings of citizenship education; and to examine teacher education programs in order to identify and assess the relationship between conceptions and pedagogical preparation regarding citizenship education. A first study seeks to explore conceptions of citizenship and of citizenship education in existing curricular and policy documents in both official languages. In another study some baseline data would be established on teachers' conceptions and their influence on attitudes and pedagogical stances, whereas another will study citizenship conceptions in teacher education programs.

Values of Citizens and in Citizenship Education

The primary research questions for this theme are *What are Canadians' basic citizenship values and principles? How are they lived and learned?* Examples of values and democratic principles include respect for others and for diversity, interpersonal trust, fairness in play, and for all, belief in democracy and in democratic institutions, social justice, and equal participation in school and in society. The first research phase consists of a thorough review of the literature on citizenship values, examining the academic literature, the policy context, and polling studies. The goal of Phase Two is to determine the citizenship values that Canadians share by surveying children, adolescents, and adults. Phase Three seeks to determine Canadians' perceptions of the values held by particular groups, whereas Phase Four will determine what Canadians do when confronted with situations in which their values apply and with those in which their values conflict. Phrase Five will then determine whether available citizenship materials reflect the values to which Canadians subscribe.

Behaviours, Attitudes, Skills, and Knowledge in Citizenship Education

The central questions for this theme are *What are the behaviours, attitudes, skills, and knowledge that Canadians hold with respect to citizenship? How are they lived and learned? How confident are citizens, including students, that they can contribute to the evolution of society?* In a first research study, indicators of citizenship behaviours, attitudes, skills, and knowledge are defined, and the relationships between them, in terms of pedagogy, outcomes, and citizen efficacy are addressed, that is, their perceived influence on public decision-making. In a second study, the democratic concepts, behaviours, attitudes and skills held by children, adolescents and adults on a pan-Canadian basis are examined and then linked to international studies. In the next study, situational and contextual factors that influence the development of individuals notable for their considerable civic participation are determined. In a final study, citizenship engagement and efficacy as characterizing the "good citizen" from the perceptions of students, teachers, and adults are researched.

Teaching Practices in Citizenship Education

The research questions central to this theme are *What are the current teaching practices in citizenship education? How are they played out in educational institutions as social spaces? How do these patterns contribute to the understanding, development and dissemination of exemplary practices?* The specific objectives of this theme are to identify the current state of citizenship education; to determine the impact of implicit and explicit practices and norms of institutions on citizenship education and notions such as equality/equity, individual/group, minority/majority; to examine the roles of schools and other institutions as contested spaces for citizenship conceptions and practices; to determine what exemplary practices means for citizenship, the criteria and identification, in different sectors. To meet the first objective, practices are examined in each of three settings: in initial and continuing teacher development, in adult immigrant citizenship preparation, and in teachers' implementation of existing materials and curriculum. To meet the second objective, citizen-ship practices are examined in classrooms and schools as contested sites in which different conceptions and practices of citizenship meet. In a final study exemplary practices of citizenship education are documented and examined.

Although the Citizenship Education Research Network (CERN) is re-spectful of the autonomy of researchers, its primary task is the coordina-tion of the research efforts of the founding members as well as of all others who wish to participate in the process. Researchers, while respecting the need for networking, collaboration, coordination, and accountability to the group, take up specific parts of the CERN research agenda, as deter-mined at the founding Think Tank held in Kananaskis, Alberta, in March 1998 and followed up in June in Ottawa. A first subsequent development was the establishment of a web page within the Metropolis web site[3] and other developments are currently under way. One is to expand and main-tain the network, that is, to introduce more researchers, practitioners, and decision makers, since this initiative offers hope for the future in difficult uncertain times. Another is to meet the most immediate research needs, fundamental to the research agenda, which means the development of a general conceptual framework for citizenship education research, of state-of-the-art papers and reports on citizenship values, practices, as well as behaviours, attitudes, skills, and knowledge.

The appeal of this effort at coordination lies in its uniqueness, its nature, its respect for researchers, and its timely relevance. Never before have researchers in education and the other social sciences come to-gether to agree on what research should be done on a national basis. The development is based upon a profound respect for the benefits of educational research towards the betterment of schools and society. Since the cohesiveness of societies is influenced by globalization, techno-logical and demographic pressures, greater social differentiation, and shifting social values, as part of the worldwide transformation from industrial to knowledge-based societies, the preparation of future citi-zens takes on primary importance, as does the need for research as basis for policy, programs, and pedagogies. Hence the timeliness of the Citi-zenship Education Research Network initiative.

Conceptual Framework for the Analysis of Citizenship

The first step in the implementation of a research agenda is the develop-ment of a conceptual framework which presents all the macro and secondary concepts necessary to grasp the overall meaning of citizenship, based on a large variety of discourses dealing with different conceptions of citizenship. Such an endeavour must succeed in defining concepts and explicating terminology for the adoption of interested parties, so as to foster a common vocabulary for citizenship and research, going beyond particularistic understandings and usages. Such a conceptual framework must also succeed in including complexity, that is, the dimensions of the citizenship debate, the cultural diversity which characterizes Canadian society, as well as the keen need for belonging at local, national, and international levels.

Criteria for Developing a Conceptual Framework

To be useful in this way, a conceptual framework is not a normative theory but is intended to serve as a descriptive tool of the range of possible citizenships in different liberal democratic societies. The following criteria were respected in the recent elaboration of this framework:[4]

- The inclusion of all aspects of citizenship present in the essential writings that characterize a liberal society, in a cognitive schema;
- The description of the possible patterns of interrelations between different aspects which characterize citizenship in a given society;
- The definition of the concepts without tying them to a particular conception of citizenship, yet capturing the particular meanings; and
- The naming of the concepts in language which is generally employed to refer to the realities included.

Developing progressively in an interactive way, a conceptual framework is modified and enriched as necessary to enclose all unforeseen aspects of citizenship. Its full development is achieved when saturation is reached. This occurs when the consideration of additional writings on the topic brings no new insight and, thus, when there is no further necessity of modifying the conceptual framework.

Citizenship: Four Interrelated Macro-Concepts

Developed by two colleagues in Montréal, the conceptual framework incorporates four macro-concepts which are defined by a network of second- and third-level concepts.[5] Although citizenship is frequently defined only in terms of legal and political status, this macro-conceptual framework makes us acutely aware that a citizen is also defined in terms of his/her shared identity with others.

National identity includes a set of characteristics that all citizens in a society share more or less consciously and voluntarily; these characteristics refer to the collective identity of their society. Many liberal societies like Canada are actually engaged in a debate on their national identity, a debate which is a product of their internal diversity, on the one hand, but also the product of current reflections – both theoretical and political – on the nation state and nationality that originate in the process of globalization.

The second- and third-order concepts defining national identity serve to clarify what constitutes a society's identity and its unique character. In this respect, four second-order concepts are necessary to characterize national identity. Civic culture is defined essentially by the legal and political principles embodied in a tradition peculiar to each society (for example, the Canadian constitution and its Charter of Rights and Freedoms). Societal culture refers to everything that characterizes the public lifestyle of individuals in this society, such as institutional standards, official language(s), and media. Heritage is the third sub-concept of national identity and is composed of several elements related to nature (natural resources, national parks, etc.), history (including symbols and founding myths), cultures, heritage languages and cultural products (works of art, architecture). Finally, allegiance and patriotism also constitute sub-components of national identity.

Social, cultural, and supranational belonging constitutes a second macro-concept of citizenship, of considerable importance in a society, since its citizens may define themselves in terms of one or several subgroups. In Canada there are many minority components whose origins carry a specific cultural identity, as well as other types of minority. Cultural and religious diversity, however, must not be associated only with immigration; it is also the result of citizens' exercising their freedom, in liberal democracies, of religion, conscience, and association. Although many different poles of belongings are included in this second macro-concept, they can only be enumerated here: national minorities, cultural and linguistic minorities, religious minorities, sociological minorities, regional belongings, and, finally, supranational and plurinational belonging. Relative importance is another second-order concept which is necessary to characterize diversity in a society. On the one hand, it subdivides into demographic size and weight and, on the other hand, into geographic concentrations of the different poles of belonging already enumerated.

The *effective system of rights* is the third macro-concept. It refers to public norms which define the citizen's political and legal status: charters of rights and freedoms, laws, constitutions, and so on. An effective system of rights in a liberal democratic society like Canada is designed to ensure the equality of citizens in a liberal democracy, and it comprises four different types of rights: fundamental, political, social, and cultural. This component also includes programs and measures implemented to counter socio-economic inequalities and to promote equitable access to societal and institutional resources. They include anti-discrimination measures and equity measures as well as identity recognition measures.

Political and civil participation brings together the competencies, actions, and steps expected of a citizen, which serve to display commitment to the governance of the society. In a democratic context, participation in political life and civil society represents both a right and a responsibility for citizens. In its broadest sense, citizenship is intrinsically linked to the conditions of participation by citizens in the life of their political and civil community. This view of citizenship, which has been riding a wave of popularity for some years, forms the basis of studies on the duties, responsibilities, and qualities of the model citizen and is also advanced to encourage the social cohesion of a political community.[6] This fourth macro-concept includes three sub-components: areas of participation (political life and civil society), the citizenship skills required for participation and, finally, the duties and responsibilities tied to participation.

Application of the Conceptual Framework

As a working model, the conceptual framework was tested by applying it to the analysis of citizenship in several societies: Canada and Québec, the United States, Australia, Great-Britain, and France.[7] The principal questions which guided this analysis were: What are the principal minorities of the country? To what extent do they enjoy an effective recognition of their respective identities and their specific needs? What progress has been made with respect to the recognition of rights of minorities, their identities, and their collective needs? What are the most marked conflicts between majority and minority which involved identities? What body of human rights benefits its citizens and to what extent do these rights take into account particular identities? What means of participation on the political and civil levels are of benefit to the citizens and how do these structures allow for the participation of minorities?

During the analysis, it became apparent that issues and conflicts around citizenship have a direct relationship to tensions and difficulties between particular identities and a national identity. This finding is in keeping with the citizenship debates of the last decade, whose primary analytic focus is the interrelationship of identities, linking particular belongings, with the national identity, the system of rights, as well as the civic and civil participation. Reflected in the conceptual framework, the analysis of the social dynamics which underlie and maintain a diversity of identities remains a priority. However, a fine question is thus raised: On what basis may a priority upon identities be established in liberal democratic societies in question?

The conceptual framework helps to describe the national identity with which the ordinary citizen is incited to identify, the part of his/her distinct identity that can be preserved in his/her life, the system of rights by which he/she can benefit, as well as the structures of political and civil involvement that are thereby opened. Its application to six liberal democracies, however, did not examine significant issues unrelated to identity which assume primacy in citizenship debates on an international scene. How far the description applies to the ordinary citizen can be determined only by empirical studies, such as those on the CERN agenda, advantageously guided by the conceptual framework. One of these studies is ongoing; anglophone and francophone college-level students in Québec and New Brunswick are examined. The subjects' conceptions of themselves as citizens are compared: the way they describe their own social identity, their representation of national identity, their acceptance of diversity, their agreement with the norms of equality that prevail in their society, and their dispositions towards political and civil participation.[8]

Towards an Analytic Framework for Citizenship Values

Another analytic framework, based on a state-of-the-art review of literature on the topic, has been developed as a fundamental for research on citizenship values.[9] Undertaken by two colleagues linked in a Prairie-wide research centre, it seek answers to four questions:

- What are citizenship values, virtues, principles, dispositions, and concepts?
- How are they linked to or situated within basic dimensions/conceptions of citizenship?

- How does current work on values shift and, within the citizenship debate, inform the analysis of citizenship values?
- What future directions seem promising in terms of research, policy development, and citizenship education?

The Terminology Question

The terms "values, virtues, principles, dispositions and concepts" are used variably, almost interchangeably, by different authors. Epistemologically,[10] the terms "values" and "virtues" have aesthetic, moral, religious, and sociological understandings which have evolved over time; the term "virtues" originally was associated with republican conceptions of citizenship. These terms refer to a constellation of ideals relating to democratic citizenship which may be manifested as acquired principles, dispositions, concepts, attitudes, and abilities. Some examples include loyalty, sincerity, openness, civic-mindedness, respect for self and others, solidarity, self-reliance, and a sense of belonging. "Principles" refers to a set of basic moral rules of conduct, whereas "dispositions" refers to acquired inclinations to engage altruistically with others, rather than to ideals, as do "values" and "virtues." "Concepts" has come to refer to dynamic schemata of thought, rather than static configurations of notions, as illustrated by democratic concepts such as majority rule, constitutional practice, the public good, freedom, liberty, justice, and equality. With no attempt to be definitive or exhaustive, the links between citizenship values, principles, dispositions, and concepts are set in four orders of logical relations so as to form an analytic framework.

Relevant to this framework, four domains of citizenship represent the evolution of different kinds of rights: civil, political, socio-economic,[11] and cultural[12] rights, all viewed as being in dynamic interaction. Central to the *civil domain*, such rights include freedom of speech and expression, equality before the law, as well as freedom of association and access to information. Rights within the *political domain* involve the right to vote and to political participation. Referring to the relationship between individuals in a societal context and requiring relational loyalty and sincerity, the *socio-economic domain* of citizenship refers to rights of participation, in political spaces and to social and economic rights, for example, the right to social security, to work and to minimum means of subsistence. The fourth fundamental component of citizenship is the *cultural domain*, which refers to the manner in which countries take into account the increasing cultural diversity in societies, diversity due to a greater openness to other cultures, to global migration, and to increased mobility.

Four Domains of Citizenship Values

In the analytic framework, the values of loyalty, sincerity, openness, and civic-mindedness cluster together in the *civil-civic domain of citizenship*. The value of loyalty is illustrated by a principled sharing of responsibility for group dynamics, which is then linked to dispositions to support others and to be able to estimate the scope of group activities. These dispositions are, in turn, linked to concepts, such as group cohesion, networks of associations, and majority rule, which are essential to civil/ civic life. In another example, the value of sincerity is exemplified by the principles of speaking honestly and truthfully as well as of respecting others' accomplishments and excellence. These principles dispose one to act without intention to deceive and to be capable of evaluating public officials. Linked to key democratic concepts such as truth and constitutional practice, they are also part of civil/civic life. Similarly, the value of openness is exemplified by a principled search to understand society, which then feeds a willingness to listen to others' perspectives. This disposition is linked to the concept of multiple perspectives, key to the democratic realization of civic/civil life. Civic-mindedness entails a principled sharing of responsibility for the public good which is linked to dispositions to participate and to engage in common public projects. They are linked to the philosophical idea of the "public good" and to interdependence, both key concepts for the civil-civic domain.

In a second quadrant of the analytic framework, valuing freedom and equality as well as respecting oneself and others cluster as first-order values in the *political domain of democratic life*. For example, valuing freedom is linked to a principled preference for democracy and for respect for human life and for the rights of others. The application of this principle disposes persons to obey the law without harassing or imposing unduly upon others. These dispositions are linked to the democratic concepts of freedom and liberty, all part of political life. Another example deals with valuing equality. As a value, it is linked to the principle of generosity, actualized as treating others fairly. In turn, this disposition is based on concepts of equality and of egalitarian relationships between individuals, for example, between spouses, between parents and offspring and among offspring. Respecting oneself and others is a value linked to the democratic principle of justice as reasonableness, which disposes people to treat others with mutual respect and reciprocity, and to a willingness to engage in public discourse. The democratic concepts linked to these dispositions are justice, deliberation, and rationality, all central to political life.

In the third quadrant of the values clock, solidarity, self-reliance, and valuing the earth exemplify values which are situated in the *socio-economic domain*. The value of solidarity gives way to a principled consideration of children as an investment in the future, which disposes one to collaborate and cooperate with others, to trust others, and to share duties and benefits. Linked to the democratic concepts of the right to unionize and to assembly, these dispositions are essential to socio-economic life. Another example in this domain, self-reliance as a first-order value, is linked to fiscal prudence and constraint as principles, which are actualized as a willingness to work hard. Linked to the democratic concept of the dual rights to work and to leisure, these dispositions are a central part of socio-economic life. A more recent value, that of valuing the earth, is linked to a principled openness to planetary perspectives. Dispositions to act with others to achieve democratic goals are linked to the citizens' rights to quality of life and to a safe environment, all part of the socio-economic domain.

In the final quadrant of the clock are situated values relative to the *cultural/collective domain of citizenship*. The culture-state relationship is based upon human rights which recognize an anthropological dimension of the person and imply a certain conception of human beings, their dignity, and the affirmation of legal equality against all forms of discrimination on the basis of membership in a particular group or category. Two examples of values are a sense of belonging and human dignity. The first is realized as a principle responsibility for the collective, leading to a willingness to compromise for the good of the group as a disposition. This disposition is linked to the concept of group identification, set within the most recent domain dealing with cultural and collective life. The second value is linked to the recognition of the dignity of others and to the recognition of one's own self-esteem as fundamental principles. They are then linked to dispositions to respect for diversity, to mutual respect, to compassion, and to a commitment to pluralism. The democratic concepts underlying these logical relationships are multiculturalism and acceptance of others, all central to the cultural or collective domain. In dealing with the relationship between culture and the state, the cultural domain is contentious and is hotly debated in Europe and North America, as is the social domain of citizenship.

Values Shift and the Citizenship Debate

How does the current debate inform values held by Canadian students and adults, their understandings of plurality, activism, and understandings of citizenship? Two different hypotheses inform the debate on values shift. One is that cultural traits like values persist over long periods of time and have an important impact on the economic and political performances of the societies in question.[13] The contrary hypothesis holds that economic development is accompanied by an erosion of traditional values and by a process of secularization, bringing about a decline of religion. Although the World Values Survey (1990–95) is limited by its sample size, two dimensions illustrate the positions of national societies: the passage of traditional values linked to religion towards rational-legal and secular values, and the passage of values linked to survival and necessity towards values of self-realization, self-expression, and well-being.[14] By crossing these dimensions against four types of societies within broad cultural/religious areas, it is possible to show that values are changing slowly towards greater tolerance of cultural diversity.[15]

Canadian life presumes a minimum of shared values, principles, and dispositions, including a commitment to pluralism. The slow shift towards a post-materialist society[16] entails a profound consideration of the need for the individual to belong to collectivity and community; for the development of self-esteem in the face of major social upheavals; and for quality of life defined in terms of economic, political, work, ethical, moral, and familial considerations. Current research on values shift tends to focus upon single, value-laden notions related to democracy, including satisfaction with democracy, citizen information base, representation, interpersonal trust, respect for others, and social harmony. Leading to greater insights into the relationships between society and citizenship values, this ensemble of work is set within three domains of citizenship: the civic,[17] political,[18] and social.[19] The emphasis on citizen information and representation is situated within public forms of citizenship[20] and towards the passive/elitist end of a continuum of citizenship conceptions.[21] The fourth and most recent domain, focused upon the cultural or collective, has begun to receive much attention, since social cohesion seems to be critical to Canadian society at this time.[22] Research on the impact of notions of multiple, postmodern citizenship upon values, on the expansion of the cultural domain of citizenship, and on reasonable limits to pluralism is greatly needed so as insightfully to inform policy development and citizenship education.[23]

Research on Learning Behaviours, Attitudes, Skills, and Knowledge

What research has been completed or undertaken to date on the CERN agenda concerning behaviours, skills, attitudes, and knowledge? In the comparative research undertaken by the Groupe de recherche sur l'ethnicité et l'adaptation au pluralisme en éducation, au Centre d'études ethniques de l'Université de Montréal the content and practices of citizenship education were examined, in different countries[24] and in different Canadian provinces, notably Ontario and Québec.[25] This work is now being extended to two other provinces, New Brunswick and Alberta, with the assistance of CERN colleagues at the University of New Brunswick and the University of Calgary. In addition to presenting a comparison of major tendencies of citizenship education in both provinces,[26] this research group produced six monographs featuring lighthouse pedagogical activities of three schools in each of two major cities, Toronto and Montréal.

Research done by the Citizenship Education team of the University of New Brunswick is important for its theoretical and practical implications. It bears specifically on youth's understanding of key democratic concepts, such as the concept of freedom and dissent. A precise assessment of the understanding of such concepts by children of primary and secondary school age provides some precious benchmarks for the teaching of democratic citizenship.[27] To date, three masters theses based on this work have been successfully completed and defended.[28] The research team is currently refining its analysis of the process of concept mapping of the ideas expressed by the learners. Work has begun to develop stimuli for generating students' thinking aloud about the concepts of justice and due process; data collection is currently under way. Two other projects are now beginning. Funded by CIDA to strengthen democracy in Russia, a three-year project, called "The Spirit of Democracy," will develop case studies to be used in Russian schools to stimulate discussion and debate and to explore the meaning of ideas such as citizenship, privacy, and equality. In association with the Russian Association for Civic Education, this project will also make use of the Internet to disseminate educational material and as a forum of exchange for young people and teachers. The other project involves curriculum development with educators in Bhutan.

Since citizenship education is typically assumed to be part of social studies within the anglophone tradition, a critical assessment of students' performance by a team of researchers at Simon Fraser University is relevant to the research to be done on citizenship behaviours, skills, attitudes, and knowledge base. A 1996 study of 135,000 British Columbia students in grades 4, 7, and 10, in both French and English, measured key attitudinal outcomes of the B.C. social studies curriculum, in terms of their tolerance/appreciation of others and their willingness to participate in citizenship activities, including community-based ones.[29] In general, students at all three grade levels exhibited very positive attitudes towards multiculturalism in Canadian society, towards creating a sustainable environment, and towards equity for women. There was a small but perceptible core of boys who exhibited much less positive attitudes, and the proportion of boys with negative attitudes grew as students moved through the grades. Across all grades, however, more boys than girls wished they could vote – a public aspect of citizenship involvement. As they advanced through the grades, students reported an increasing level of discussion about political and international issues with friends, parents, teachers, and other students.

Overall, students had very little opportunity to participate in citizenship activities. Despite the goal of encouraging discussion about and participation in citizenship activities, efforts at cultivating important citizenship attitudes and practices were sporadic and inconsistent, and a core group of boys appeared largely unaffected by what little was done in classrooms. There was a large gap between vision and reality, since students did not demonstrate many of the citizenship attitudes and practices envisioned by social studies education. Recommendations were made to reduce the amount of information expected to be covered in eleven years and return to an emphasis on the founding vision of social studies education, giving greater priority to attitudinal and citizenship participation goals.

Research on Teaching Practices of Citizenship Education

The development of curriculum materials is designed to enhance teaching practices and student learning. Reflecting the current state of knowledge,[30] a team of researchers at the Université du Québec à Rimouski produced a CD-ROM on children's rights according to the United Nations Convention.[31] Basic concepts of citizenship education and cultural diversity were introduced in a manual,[32] and four principles of citizenship education[33] informed the development of a teachers' guide with objectives and examples of pedagogical practice, organized around concepts of citizenship education in order to live together more harmoniously.[34] Focusing on the preparation of teachers, two researchers at Queen's University initiated a study of citizenship practices in a faculty of education.[35]

From a global perspective, two recent books enrich the field of citizenship education in Canada and the Middle East.[36] An on-going research project at the University of Prince Edward Island is focused on the preparation of teachers for international teaching posts, while another project on an exchange of practice-teaching students in a country other than their own is proposed as part of a Canada-European Community program for cooperation in higher education and training, involving seven universities (three in Canada, four in Europe) and including a program of activities around citizenship education to be delivered at the host institution.[37] Starting in September 2001, a fifteen-month Education for Global Citizenship Research project at the Ontario Institute for Studies in Education involves case study research to explore initiatives in the related fields of citizenship education, education for democracy and human rights, and global education in seven countries: Brazil, Czech Republic, Japan, Jordan, South Africa, United Kingdom (England and Wales), United States.[38] The genesis of initiatives in global citizenship education is being explored, as is the rationale and proposals for curriculum change put forward by originators of each initiative. The research also examines how each rationale and its attendant proposals have been received by key stakeholders in the education system and how they have been acted upon by teachers in schools and by teacher educators in teacher training institutions. Some attention is also being given to the adjacent development of global citizenship education in non-formal and community education settings. The principal project outcome will be a book documenting the research.

Future Directions

In order to assure the implementation of the CERN research agenda in a systematic and timely fashion, a national team of researchers was formed in autumn 1999 to work collaboratively. This team is responsible for securing funding as well as the overall implementation of the pan-Canadian research agenda. They work in conjunction with Canadian and international scholars of relevant disciplinary perspectives in education, philosophy, sociology, anthropology, psychology, and political science. Despite the scarcity of funding for educational research and for schools in a Canadian context, negotiations nonetheless have begun to assure sufficient funding. In the light of the importance of this research agenda, the team hopes to succeed in securing collaboration across Canada and internationally.

The CERN research agenda is clearly germane to crucial questions regarding the relationships between common values and the unity and stability of society, the impact of participation upon social cohesion, and the relationship between citizenship education and national identity. These questions are inherent in current debates and relevant to all Canadian citizens. Although we do not presume to answer all possible questions, it is useful, nonetheless, to signal those that are relevant to current multiple realities and which deal with the potential outcomes of citizenship education in terms of the impact of values education, the preparation for participation in society, and contentious curriculum choices.

How much can we reasonably expect the values and political principles of liberal democracy to ensure unity and stability of a society like Canada? Hotly debated, this question raises at least two positions. As far as unity of the citizenry is concerned, Kymlicka writes that shared political values are a "mirage," which consists of believing that, because some values are shared across national and linguistic lines, they provide a basis for a common solidarity and a common national identity.[39] Yet in a postmodern world, European educators consider values education to be essential; for young people need values and concomitant democratic principles upon which to base their actions and decisions in an uncertain world.[40]

Another question addresses active participation in civil society, which is important to citizenship education. Many educators are partisans of what is termed the "civil society argument": "The hope is that in so doing, [citizens] will develop all-purpose 'associative virtues,' such as the spirit of compromise, a sense of justice in interpersonal dealings, tolerance, and civility, and that an indirect consequence of their development of these virtues will be to facilitate their relations with their fellow citizens at large."[41] How much impact do they have on an emerging sense of social cohesion? These questions cannot be answered only by philosophical and political thought or by individual subjective convictions. They deserve to be examined in all their complexity by research which deals with issues on the empirical ground of the school and the classroom.

A third crucial question flows from research on the realities of citizenship education, which reveals that the issue of Canadian national identity receives little attention.[42] Osborne observes that, starting in the 1980s, there is a substantial timidity about making any claims about national identity in school curricula.[43] Citizenship education has not yet developed the artful ability of composing with a national identity as complex as the Canadian one.

The orientation of the teaching of history is closely related to national identity in that this discipline traditionally narrates the historic path along which the identity of a nation is constructed. Across Canada, the teaching of history is controversial as soon as it touches upon the face of national identity, which is still under construction. It is inevitable that our national identifications expressed throughout history will be complex. Should it not be the school's proposed task to hoist itself above the traditional historical divisions and to situate the question of how best to live together now within a social and political community with a complex identity? Doubtless what is needed is an education designed to understand contemporary society more clearly. Such an education would permit the diverse components of society to truly know each other and all young citizens to more deeply understand both the complementarities which link components of contemporary Canada as well as the common challenges and issues which concern all Canadians. Citizenship education researchers have an essential contribution to bring to the answers which should be given to those crucial questions, among many others.

Notes

1 The Kananaskis Think Tank was held with the financial support of the federal Department of Canadian Heritage and with the kind support of the University of Calgary.

2 For additional information, including reports on the initial Think Tank and subsequent meetings, see the website of the Citizenship Education Research Network (http://canada.metropolis.net/research-policy/cern-pub/index.html). At the time of writing, CERN meets at the annual national conferences of the Metropolis project and of the Canadian and International Education Society of Canada (CIESC), within the Canadian Society for the Study of Education (CSSE).

3 See the current web page address http://www.metropolis.net/ and watch for developments!

4 Gagnon and Pagé, *Conceptual Framework*, 2 vols.

5 See ibid., vol. 1, for a fuller discussion as well as the five diagrams representing the three levels of concepts.

6 See, for example, Canada, *Social Cohesion Research Workplan*; Jenson, *Les contours de la cohésion sociale*; Bernard, « La cohésion sociale ».

7 See Gagnon and Pagé, *Conceptual Framework*, vol. 2.

8 Michel Pagé, Alan Sears, et al., « Conceptions de la citoyenneté des anglophones et francophones canadiens: comparaison Québec/Nouveau-Brunswick ». Recherche subventionnée par Multiculturalisme Canada, CRSH et FCAR, 1999–2001.

9 Wilkinson and Hébert, "Citizenship Values."

10 Alain Rey (ed.), *Dictionnaire historique de la langue française*, 2nd ed. (Paris: Le Robert).

11 As first identified by Marshall, "Citizenship and Social Class."

12 Audigier, « Points de repères pour l'éducation ».

13 Huntington, *Le choc des civilisations.*

14 Ruano-Borbalan, « Valeurs et cultures ».

15 Inglehart, *Modernization and Postmodernization.*

16 For a discussion of post-materialist values, see Nevitte, *Decline of Deference*; and for a different view, see Peters, *Exploring Canadian Values.*

17 Nadeau, "Satisfaction with Democracy"; Young, "Civic Engagement, Trust and Democracy."

18 Kanji, "Information, Cognitive Mobilization"; and Dougherty, "Citizens and Legislators."

19 Schneider, "Women, Violent Sport and Citizenship"; and Roese, "Are Canadians Becoming Less Trusting of Government?"

20 For examples of multiple forms of public/private discourse, see Rosenau, *Postmodernism and the Social Sciences*; Macpherson, *Political Theory of Possessive Individualism*; Foucault, *Power/Knowledge.*

21 Sears, "Something Different to Everyone"; Sears and Hughes, "Citizenship Education."

22 Jenson, « Les contours de la cohésion sociale »; Bernard, « La cohésion sociale ».

23 Wilkinson and Hébert, "Citizenship Values."

24 McAndrew, Tessier, et Bourgeault, « L'éducation à la citoyenneté en milieu scolaire au Canada ».

25 McAndrew, Bourgeault, et Pagé, « L'éducation à la citoyenneté dans une société pluraliste ».

26 McAndrew and Tessier, « L'éducation à la citoyenneté en milieu scolaire québécois ».

27 Sears, "Freedom and Dissent"; Hughes and Sears, "How Do Children and Young People Learn Citizenship?"

28 Corbett, "Children's Understanding"; Hillman, "Grade Eight Students' Understanding"; and Bourgeois, "Colouring Outside the Lines."

29 Bognar, Cassidy, and Clarke, *Social Studies in British Columbia.*

30 Côté and Kabano, *Recueil bibliographique.*

31 Côté and Kabano, *Éducation aux droits.*

32 Marzouk, Côté, and Kabano, *École, éducation à la citoyenneté.*

33 Hébert, "Citizenship Education."

34 Marzouk, Kabano, and Côté, *Éducation à la citoyenneté à l'école.*

35 Lee and Krugly-Smolska, "Role of Faculties of Education in Citizenship Education."

36 Pike and Selby, *In the Global Classroom* and *Global Education.*

37 Graham Pike (University of Prince Edward Island) is currently working on the teacher preparation project and has coordinated the Canada-European Community exchange project.

38 The project is led by David Selby, professor of curriculum, teaching and learning, and director of IIGE, Ontario Institute for Studies in Education at the University of Toronto. As principal investigator, he works with a team of six IIGE-based and/or country-based country-specific researchers. Funding has been provided by the Ford Foundation.

39 Kymlicka, *Finding Our Way*, 150–1.

40 Pouwels, "Values Education in a Postmodern World."

41 Weinstock, "Citizenship and Social Unity." Calls for "civility" have been used to refer to rudeness, profanity, and excesses of various sorts, thus missing the point between politeness and civility. The notion of "civility" is defined as a willingness on the part of citizens to tolerate imperfect solutions and is the enabling condition of a larger debate about the world we want, a world in which there may be real justice; see Kingwell, *The World We Want*, 8–10, 93–5. See also Franklyn Griffiths, who argues for a culture of civility in his paper, "Culture of Change," as essential to human security and as synonymous with the practice of cultural diversity.

42 Sears, Clarke, and Hughes, "Canadian Citizenship Education."

43 Osborne, "Education is the Best National Insurance."

Appendix
Analysis of Models of
Democratic Citizenship

Analysis of Models of Democratic Citizenship

Model	Key concepts	Locus of power	Role of government	Role of citizen	Implications for	
					Educational policy*	Federal policy*
Athenian conception	Participatory Ideal.	Public Assemblies.	Execution of decisions of assemblies: Formalization of myth of egalitarianism of civic participation, despite disparities of wealth and inequality of participation.	For free men only, active and regular participation in governance, in assemblies and government.	Home responsibility for the development of civic virtues: public speaking; decision-making skills; practical judgment.	Devolution of government to local public civic or municipal assemblies; Promotion of myth of common descent; Promotion of pursuit of happiness, securing the good life through collective associations such as households, villages and city states.
Roman republican model	Legal Status; Citizenship as a force for assimilation; Cosmopolitan character of citizenship.	Emperor plus Senate, as well as city magistrates, and other officials; Populace exercised influence by public demonstrations, by agitation, and riots.	Holding of elective office became hereditary in practice.	Individuals as subject of Republic, i.e., a legal being subject to a uniform body of law; Upon age of maturity, Roman citizens had the right to vote in assemblies, stand for office, contract civil law marriage, own property, enter commercial contracts, having standing in court, and execute wills. Free men were barred from holding office and serving in the legions	Cultivation of respect for authority and pride in republic; Emphasize participation in parallel or alternative forms of civic life, which include funeral ceremonies, military triumph rites, demonstrations, games, festivals and theaters.	To craft flexible citizenship policies to integrate a rapidly growing and increasingly diverse population; To bestow citizenship broadly, according to a hierarchy of personal legal statuses, i.e., universalization of citizenship.

Analysis of Models of Democratic Citizenship—(continued)

Model	Key concepts	Locus of power	Role of government	Role of citizen	Implications for Educational policy*	Federal policy*
				but enjoyed most other rights. At the bottom of the hierarchy of citizens were the slaves who had no rights of any kind.		
Machiavellian model for Florence	Virtue defined as free civic participation and self-rule; Corruption defined as private preoccupation with self-interest.	Balance of power between aristocracy and populace, in sharing governance.	Civic republican tradition à la Aristotle; War gives citizens an outlet for aggression, target for ambitions and a cure for idleness; Victory in battle brings glory and reinforces allegiance to political community; Assumes need for coercion to complete preservation of liberties and republican life.	Dependent upon citizens who support themselves through their work and who are capable of independent political judgment, staunch patriotism, respect of fellow citizens, discipline and inspired by love of honour and glory.	Military service best school for citizen; Inculcation of necessity of work and of virtues of discipline, endurance, courage and self-sacrifice.	To assure necessary conditions to foster virtue and maintain civic spirit: rough equality between aristocracy and populace; work for citizens and military service as lieu of inculcation; To assure strong laws and institutions.
Enlightenment Liberal Theorists: John Locke and Adam Smith	Unity; Membership based on either social contract (Locke) or instrumental self-interest (Smith).	Authority and laws of the sovereign; Fundamental criterion was naturally free man's consent to make him subject to the laws of the government.	A minimalist model of a polity to maintain peace and security, preserve property rights, and defend against foreign invaders.	Citizen as a juridical subject, i.e. a bearer of legal rights and duties; subject of monarchical states and collective members of a people; Belonging to an artifical political construct; no adequate account of civic membership.	Cultivation of obligations, obedience, and allegiance.	Development of justification for political authority and laws with mechanisms for consent and regulations for contract.

Analysis of Models of Democratic Citizenship—(*continued*)

Model	Key concepts	Locus of power	Role of government	Role of citizen	Implications for Educational policy*	Implications for Federal policy*
The Jacobin Model for 17th-Century France	Universal suffrage, revolution, central-ized government, secular, anti-monarchist, inde-pendent nation-state.	Power resides in the ruling minority. Rules would no longer be part of the "masses" but were a group of informed individuals who make decisions based on their own judgment – hence the distinction be-tween rulers and constituents.	To prevent external in-vasion and to maintain peace and harmony within the nation-state; Historical laws over-turned because they do not allow for equality of all men; A republican government without hereditary rulers or nobility.	Universal manhood suf-frage regardless of property ownership; Citizens instructed to work hard and to observe law and order; Must carefully monitor the state and its institu-tions for any abuse of power; State representatives can be recalled by citi-zens for misconduct; Conformity to standards of middle-class decency.	Compulsory public edu-cation for all children re-gardless of class; Education is used to teach the habits of good citizens including disci-pline, thrift, hard work, respect for authority; Equality of opportunity, all careers open to talented individuals.	Renounce historical laws to ensure equality; Basis of the state is a sovereign people; Government is highly centralized to prevent external attack and maintain internal cohesion; Highly nationalistic; National unity based on common ethnicity, language and culture.
Edmund Burke Model for 17th-Century England	Natural aristo-cracy; Tradition; History; Continuity; anti-revolutionary.	Power remains with aristocracy. They have access to edu-cation, business and capital. They have the lei-sure time necessary to pursue the edu-cation required for effective rule.	To maintain stability of society in emphasizing tradition and history; Radical change is dis-couraged and would re-sult in tyranny because the stabilizing forces of traditional rules and insti-tutions would be de-stroyed; the highest pri-ority is to preserve politi-cal institutions so that customs and beliefs would provide certainty and guidance to citizens.	Voting rights for property owners as only these individuals have access to education and political power; Elected officials should act on their own knowl-edge and not on those of the constituents; The rights of the nation supersede individual rights.	History and tradition are paramount in ensuring the stability of society; without them, society would be thrown into chaos and revolution. Emphasis on education of the natural aristocracy so that they may ensure traditional practices in government are main-tained.	Maintenance of tradi-tional rules and laws; Superiority of national concerns over indi-vidual concerns; Limiting citizenship rights to all male landowners; Allowance for reli-gious freedom for all people regardless of citizenship status.

Analysis of Models of Democratic Citizenship—(continued)

Model	Key concepts	Locus of power	Role of government	Role of citizen	Implications for	
					Educational policy*	Federal policy*
American Revolutionary Republican Ideal	Principles of consent and universalism; independence from subjugation; Understanding of citizenship as volitional allegiance and as a formal legal status with certain rights and duties.	Sovereignty vested in the people who could overthrow rulers who abused their authority; Developed a system of representative democracy in which citizens transferred actual governance to elected representatives who ruled in their name.	Restoration of political rights; exclusion of many groups without their consent; inadequate attention to practical substantive conditions that make full participation in public life possible; overthrow of monarchical govt.	Right to decide to be a citizen or an alien; right of dissent; Citizenship from birth became law in 1868 and equal rights of political participation were guaranteed a century later; An instrumental understanding of politics as the pursuit and arbitration of private interests.	Development of independence, knowledge of and respect for formal rights; skills in claiming rights and retribution. Later on, broad-based system of public education and mass conscription; Civic education including knowledge of rights.	Development of means for equalizing formal rights; Development of instructional programs for civic education, including knowledge of rights for adult citizens and newcomers.
French Revolutionary Republican Model	Modern conception of citizenship by forging union of people, nation and a state; no common language at the time of the Revolution.	Constitution; distinction between active and passive citizens according to age, gender and property; with gradation of rights according to wealth; distinction removed in 1793; Popular sovereignty.	Ideal of an activist, virtuous citizen as a member of a democratically governed political community, united by common will and equal under the law; Nation as sovereign political community.	Participatory citizenship incorporated into representative democratic government; Conception of 'nationality' as a volitional choice and of 'people' largely in republican terms; Link between rights of citizen and productive work; a powerful weapon to attack nobility; race of legal or moral significance to citizenship; slavery abolished in colonies because of bloody rebellions.	Preparation for work and active participation as citizen; Inculcation of knowledge of rights of man.	Cultivation of writers and intellectuals as having higher status, in practice, within a sovereign political community; Development of citizenship programs that support participation in representational democracy and full employment.

Analysis of Models of Democratic Citizenship—(continued)

Model	Key concepts	Locus of power	Role of government	Role of citizen	Implications for	
					Educational policy*	Federal policy*
Marxian Critique of French Revolutionary Republican Model	Socialist citizenship; deterministic view of history.	Integration of polarized dualism between abstract political community without substantive content of its own and material civil society devoid of political character.	Focus on modes of production, thus Marx ignored cities as sites of activist participatory citizenship and democratic self-government.	Workers participate in political life, being liberated for this role by modern industry and technology; Rejection of consensual relationship in modern liberal society; Universally shared material abundance as enabling humans to discover their fundamental unity.	Valuing of the communal, the collective; preparation for revolution.	Preservation of material structures, of domination within civil society; Establishment of gestapo as thought police; Fiction of equality; dominant and subordinate groups; exploitation and suppression of subordinate groups.
Rousseau's Vision	Conception of a common good with a civic obligation to promote that good; Notion of civic solidarity.	Sovereign has absolute authority over citizen as it is constituted through citizenry as collective body; sovereignty vested in ill-defined 'general will'.	Preference for a smaller polity; the larger the polity, the greater the coercive powers that a govt. needs to rule and the greater the distance from the citizens; No naturalization or colonies.	Republican citizenship as equal sharing in the exercice of sovereignty; Collective association means entering into a compact with the transfer of rights to whole community; Citizens as a homogeneous body; Invested notion of 'people' with a national character but independent of ethnicity and kinship.	Importance attached to inculcation of young; Broad program of public education through which the young could learn civic virtues and duties.	Responsibility for moulding moral character of citizens; Morality learned and practised in community, with private property seen as the greatest source of corruption; Stern coercive measures to discipline character and enforce solidarity.

Analysis of Models of Democratic Citizenship—(continued)

Model	Key concepts	Locus of power	Role of government	Role of citizen	Implications for	
					Educational policy*	Federal policy*
Liberal Nationalism: John Stuart Mill	Nationality as basis for membership in state; Commitment to principle of utilitarianism; Abandonment of universalism of rights.	People as 'nation' as a particular, historically descended, cultural community as new basis for popular allegiance; Sovereignty vested in people of shared background in a common political community.	Imperial colonialism justifiable; Democratic representative govt.; Promotion of rightful actions which promote the greater collective happiness.	Rejection of idea of universal natural rights as grounds for revolution; Membership in nation with common sympathies such as shared race, descent, language, religion, geography, and national history; Obligations of loyalty and obedience derived from benefits of protection provided by govt.; Active involvement in monitoring and participating in conduct of public affairs.	Expansion of schools and print media; Teaching of obedience as first step in civilizing process.	To advance the level of development of people; To focus on nationality and to cultivate common traits, to the exclusion of others. To promote the virtue and intelligence of the people themselves; To understand the evolutionary nature of human progress.
Hannah Arendt's Meditation on Dark Times	Deeply rooted paradox in Western liberal thought between principle of universal human rights and role of exclusive national state as primary enforcer of rights.	People as sovereign, source of all law and author of government; Only power can check power.	Independent statehood; Government as authority to protect rights and as institution to enforce them; Willingness and ability to uphold extensive rights; Issues of agency and context.	Citizens vested with universal rights, with natural rights inherent in every person by virtue of common humanity; and yet human rights can only be asserted by sovereign peoples through instrument of statehood; Basis for statelessness and exclusion results from an ethnicized nationhood which gives political content to ethnic and racial differences.	Stress importance of political virtues such as courage, love of glory, public-spiritedness to motivate political participation; non-violence; human speech so enabling free agents to act in a public realm created for themselves.	To effectively guarantee human rights of citizens on a collective basis, i.e., within political community; Participation in international guarantees of human rights which set norms, frame discourses, engineer legal categories and legitimate models, and thus enjoin obligations of nationstates.

Analysis of Models of Democratic Citizenship—(continued)

Model	Key concepts	Locus of power	Role of government	Role of citizen	Implications for	
					Educational policy*	Federal policy*
Social Democratic Model: T.H. Marshall	Social democratic citizenship, with civic, political, and social rights.	Democratically elected government, 20th-century views.	Guarantee minimal levels of income, education, and health care so that citizens can fully utilize their rights.	Juridical subject, i.e., a legal status based on equality, with a common civilization; Passive consumers of goods and service within a welfare states; Ignores states' increasing demands upon citizens (e.g., conscription, more taxes), subsequent popular pressure for more rights, for explicit guarantees of specific liberties, for immunities and entitlements, for a voice in political decision making, and for greater accountability of government; did not anticipate issues of cultural pluralism.	Introduction of national system; Assure knowledge of civic, political and social rights, including duty to work.	To establish minimal fees for courts, introduce inexpensive pleading procedures, provide free legal services and other measures; To provide for the welfare of citizens by measures such as national insurance, children's allowances, and pensions.
Communitarian Understanding of Liberal Citizenship	Preservation and enhancement of cultural identities; Commitment to welfare state, democratic-representative government.	Democratic populism.	Need to protect bounded nature of cultural communities; Questions of identity as preliminary to definition of citizenship; Principles of justice derived from shared mean-	Civic membership, understood from the specific cultural context that gives nation its distinctive character and national belonging its substantive meaning; Universal egalitarianism	Inclusion of community languages in school curricula and programs; as well as cultural studies; Study and promotion of ethnocultural groups; Emphasis on need and belonging to ethno-	Collaboration between school and ethnocultural community groups; Emphasis on collective Identity; Clarification of multiple forms of citizen-

Analysis of Models of Democratic Citizenship—(concluded)

Model	Key concepts	Locus of power	Role of government	Role of citizen	Implications for	
					Educational policy*	Federal policy*
			ings, defined within specific, concrete contexts; principle of 'deep diversity' legitimizes different ways of belonging to a common polity.	of modern western democratic understanding leads to ever-widening demands for equal recognition of particular characteristics of personal identity; Notion of 'shared collective goods' focusses on needs of people as expressivist cultural beings rather than as participants in a range of civic projects.	cultural groups; identify communities' fundamental characteristics; preservation as essential of those elements which define personal identity such as language, gender, ethnicity, religion, race.	ship, i.e., how terms for political belonging, i.e., citizenship, should be drawn and how different forms of cultural belonging should be recognized; Definition of 'community' without creating powerful basis for exclusion of those without set of essential attributes; Clarification of how kinship can be a defining element in democracies which developed as a framework for inclusion in ruling on a non-kinship basis.

The chart was conceptualized and prepared by Yvonne M. Hébert with the collaboration of Lori Wilkinson.

*Shaded areas indicate that the proponents of a particular model of citizenship did not spell out the educational or policy implications, although their critics may have done so by raising issues and questions which may be seen as the appropriate purview of schools and federal departments/agencies. Statements made within the shaded areas indicate my understanding of implications for educational and federal policy and should not be taken as explicitly stated in any of the references utilized.

Sources: Clarence Crane Brinton, *The Jacobins: An Essay in the New History* (New York: Russell and Russell, 1961); Michael Freeman, *Edmund Burke and the Critique of Political Radicalism* (Oxford: Basil Blackwell, 1980); Iain Hampsher-Monk, *The Political Philosophy of Edmund Burke* (New York: Longman, 1987); Douglas B. Klusmeyer, *Between Consent and Descent: Conceptions of Democratic Citizenship* (Washington, D.C.: International Migration Policy Program, Carnegie Endowment for International Peace, 1996); John MacCunn, *The Political Philosophy of Burke* (London: Edward Arnold, 1913); Anne Sa'adah, *The Shaping of Liberal Politics in Revolutionary France: A Comparative Perspective* (Princeton, N.J.: Princeton University Press, 1990); Charles Taylor, *Reconciling the Solitudes: Essays on Canadian Federalism and Nationalism*, ed. Guy Laforest (Montréal and Kingston: McGill-Queen's University Press, 1993).

Selected Bibliography:
Citizenship and Citizenship Education

Abdallah-Pretceille, M. 1992. *Quelle école pour quelle intégration?* Paris: Éditions Hachette.

Abella, Rosalie Silberman. 1984. *Report of the Commission on Equality in Employment.* Ottawa: Ministry of Supply and Services.

Ackerman, B. 1980. *Social Justice in the Liberal State.* New Haven, Conn.: Yale University Press.

Adler, Mortimer J. 1990. *Reforming Education: The Opening of the American Mind.* New York: Macmillan.

Ajzenstat, J., and P. Smith, 1995. Liberal-Republicanism: The Revisionist Picture of Canada's Founding. In J. Ajzenstat and P. Smith (eds.), *Canada's Origins: Liberal, Tory, or Republican?* Ottawa: Carleton University Press.

Akbari, A. 1994. *Ethnicity and Earnings Discrimination in Canadian Labour Markets.* Report presented for the Multiculturalism Directorate, Multiculturalism and Citizenship Canada, Ottawa.

Akins, T.B. 1869. *Selections from the Public Documents of the Province of Nova Scotia.* Halifax: Annand.

Apple, M. 1982. *Education and Power.* Boston: Routledge and Kegan Paul.

Archibald, Jo-ann, and Celia Haig-Brown. 1995. Kisti Notin. Background paper. Exemplary Schools Project. Toronto: Canadian Education Association.

Arendt, Hannah. 1959. *The Human Condition.* Garden City, N.Y.: Doubleday Anchor Books.

– 1977. *The Origins of Totalitarianism.* New York: Harcourt Brace.

– 1990. *On Revolution.* London: Penguin.

Ashcroft, Bill, Gareth Griffiths, and Helen Tiffin. 1989. *The Empire Writes Back: Theory and Practice in Post-Colonial Literatures.* London and New York: Routledge.

Audigier, François. 1996. Valeurs et enseignement de l'histoire et de la géographie. Manuscrit. Paris: Institut Nationale de Recherche Pédagogique.

- 1998. Citoyen, civique, citoyenneté. *Éducations : Revue de diffusion des savoirs en éducation* 16: 2–3.
- 1998. Points de repères pour l'éducation. *Éducations : Revue de diffusion des savoirs en éducation* 16: 4–9.
Audigier, François, et Guy Lagelée. 1996. *Éducation civique et initiation juridique dans les collèges.* Postface de Jacqueline Costa-Lascoux. Paris: Institut National de Recherche Pédagogique.
Audinet, Jacques. 1998. Vous avez dit « métis »? *Sociétés, cultures, communautés.* Un numéro thématique de la revue *Projet* 255 : 63–70.
Avery, Donald H. 1995. *Reluctant Host: Canada's Response to Immigrant Workers, 1896–1994.* Toronto: McClelland & Stewart.
Axelrod, Paul. 1997. *The Promise of Schooling: Education in Canada, 1800–1914.* Toronto: University of Toronto Press.
Babcock, Robert H. 1974. *Gompers in Canada: A Study in American Continentialism before the First World War.* Toronto: University of Toronto Press.
Bacchi, Carol. 1983. *Liberation Deferred? The Ideas of the English-Canadian Suffragists, 1877–1918.* Toronto: University of Toronto Press.
Bancroft, D. et al. 1990. *Framework and Issues for Research and Analysis.* Ottawa: Secretary of State.
Bannerji, Himani. 2000. *The Dark Side of the Nation: Essays on Multiculturalism, Nationalism and Gender.* Toronto: Canadian Scholars' Press.
Barman, Jean, Yvonne Hébert, and Don McCaskill (eds). *Indian Education in Canada.* Vol. 1: *The Legacy.* Vol. 2: *The Challenge.* Vancouver: UBC Press, 1986, 1987.
Barsh, R. 1986. The Nature and Spirit of the North American Political System. *American Indian Quarterly* 110: 181–98.
Battye, John. 1979. The Nine Hour Pioneers: Genesis of the Canadian Labour Movement. *Labour / Le Travailleur* 4: 25–56.
Baxter, J. 1916. *Documentary History of the State of Maine.* Vol. 23. Portland, M.: Fred L. Tower and Maine Historical Society.
Bear-Nichols, Andrea. 1996. Citizenship Education and Aboriginal People. *Canadian and International Education* 25, 2: 59–107.
Beiner, R. 1992. *What's the Matter with Liberalism?* Berkeley: University of California Press.
- 1995. *Theorizing Citizenship.* Albany: State University of New York Press.
- 1997. *Philosophy in a Time of Lost Spirit.* Toronto: University of Toronto Press.
Bellah, R., et al. 1985. *Habits of the Heart.* New York: Harper and Row.
- 1991. *The Good Society.* New York: Vintage Books.
Bernard, Paul. 1999. La cohésion sociale : Critique dialectique d'un quasi-concept. *Lien social et politique* 41 (automne); 47–59. Published in English

as Social Cohesion: A Critique. CPRN Discussion Paper No. F.09. Ottawa. htpp://www.cprn.ca.

Berthelot, Jocelyn. 1991. *Apprendre à Vivre Ensemble : Immigration, société et éducation.* Québec: Centrale de l'enseignement au Québec et Montréal, Éditions coopératives Albert Saint-Martin.

Berthoff, R. 1997. *Republic of the Dispossessed: The Exceptional Old-European Consensus in America.* Columbia: University of Missouri Press.

Black, Jerome. 1995. *Design Specifications for the Survey of Naturalization Decisions.* Report presented to Citizenship and Immigration Canada. Ottawa.

Bliss, J. Michael. 1974. *Living Profit: Studies in the Social History of Canadian Business, 1883–1911.* Toronto: McClelland & Stewart.

Blitzer, C. 1980. Democracy. *Encyclopedia International.* New York: Lexicon.

Bognar, Carl, Wanda Cassidy, and Pat Clarke. 1998. *Social Studies in British Columbia: Results of the 1996 Social Studies Assessment.* Victoria: Ministry of Education.

Bottomore, Tom. 1991. Citizens, Classes and Equality. In T.H. Marshall and T. Bottomore (eds), *Citizenship and Social Class.* London: Pluto Press.

Bourgeois, Michael K. 1998. Colouring outside the Lines: Grade 12 Students' Prior Knowledge of the Concept of Dissent. Unpublished MEd thesis, University of New Brunswick.

Bradbury, Bettina. 1993. *Working Families: Age, Gender and Daily Survival in Industrializing Montreal.* Toronto: McClelland & Stewart.

Brewer, M. 1993. The Role of Distinctiveness in Social Identity and Group Behavior. In M.A. Hogg, and Abrams, D. (eds), *Group Motivation.* London: Harvester/Wheatsheaf.

Brinton, Clarence Crane. 1961. *The Jacobins: An Essay in the New History.* New York: Russell and Russell.

Brownlie, I. 1990. *Principles of Public International Law.* 4th ed. Oxford: Clarendon Press.

Bruno-Jofré, Rosa, and Gonzalo Jover (eds). 2000. *Building Common Spaces: Citizenship and Education in Canada and Spain. Construyendo espacios comunes: Ciudadanía y Educacion en Canadá y España. Construisant des espaces communs: L'éducation et la citoyenneté au Canada et en Espagne.* Thematic number of a monograph series, *Encounters on Education / Encuentros sobre Educación / Rencontres sur l'Éducation.* Vol. 1 (Fall). Queen's University and Universidad de Madrid.

Bruno-Jofré, Rosa, and Colleen Ross. 1993. Decoding the Subjective Image of Women Teachers in Rural Towns and Surrounding Areas in Southern Manitoba. In R. Bruno-Jofré (ed.), *Issues in the History of Education in Manitoba: From the Construction of the Common School to the Politics of Voices.* Lewiston: Edwin Mellen Press.

Buchmann, M., and R.E. Floden (eds). 1993. *Detachment and Concern*. London: Cassell.

Butts, R. Freeman. 1980. *The Revival of Civic Learning*. New York: Phi Delta Kappa Educational Foundation.

Cairns, Alan. 1995. *Reconfigurations: Canadian Citizenship and Constitutional Change*. Toronto: McClelland & Stewart.

– 2000. *Citizens Plus: Aboriginal Peoples and the Canadian State*. Vancouver: UBC Press.

Cairns, Alan, and Cynthia Williams. 1985. *Constitutionalism, Citizenship and Society in Canada: Report of the Royal Commission on the Economic Union and Development Prospects for Canada*. Toronto: University of Toronto Press.

– (eds). 1986. *The Politics of Gender, Ethnicity and Language in Canada*. Toronto: University of Toronto Press.

Cairns, Alan C., John C. Courtney, Peter MacKinnon, Hans J. Michelmann, and David E. Smith (eds). 1999. *Citizenship, Diversity and Pluralism: Canadian and Comparative Perspectives*. Montréal: McGill-Queen's University Press.

Calhoun, C. 1995. *Critical Social Theory*. Cambridge, Mass.: Blackwell.

Callan, Eamonn. 1997. *Creating Citizens: Political Education and Liberal Democracy*. Oxford: Clarendon Press.

– 2000. Discrimination and Religious Schooling. In W. Kymlicka and W. Norman (eds), *Citizenship in Diverse Societies*. Toronto: Oxford University Press.

Calliste, Agnes, and George J. Sefa Dei (eds). 2000. *Anti-Racist Feminism: Critical Race and Gender Studies*. With the assistance of Margarida Aguiar. Halifax: Fernwood Books.

Cameron, D. 1996. *Canadian Studies in the Nineties*. Montréal: Association for Canadian Studies.

Cameron, Linda, and Manju Varma. 1997. Citizens for a New Century. *Canadian Ethnic Studies* 29, 2: 121–35.

Camilleri, Carmel. 1990. Identité et gestion de la disparité culturelle : essai d'une typologie. In C. Camilleri, Joseph Kasterstein, Edmond Marc Lipiansky, Hanna Malewska-Peyre, Isabelle Taboada-Leonetti, et Ana Vasquez (eds), *Stratégies identitaires*. Presses Universitaires de France.

Campbell, Gail G. 1991. Disfranchised but Not Quiescent: Women Petitioners in New Brunswick in the Mid-Nineteenth Century. In V. Strong-Boag and A.C. Fellman, eds, *Rethinking Canada: The Promise of Women's History*. 2nd ed. Toronto: Copp Clark Pittman.

Canada. 1960. Canada Elections Act, S.C. 1960. c.39.

– 1984. House of Commons, Second Session of the Thirty-Second Parliament, 1983–84. *Equality Now: Report of the Special Committee on Visible Minorities in Canadian Society*. Ottawa: Minister of Supply and Services.

– 1985. 1994. *The Canadian Citizen*. Ottawa: Citizenship and Immigration / Minister of Supply and Services.

– Department of the Secretary of State. 1987. *Citizenship '87: Proud to Be Canadian – A Discussion Paper.* Ottawa: Minister of Supply and Services.
– 1988. Bill C-93, An Act for the Preservation and Enhancement of Multiculturalism in Canada (known as the Multiculturalism Act). Passed by the House of Commons 12 July 1988.
– 1991. *Symbols of Nationhood.* Ottawa: Minister of Supply and Services.
– 1996. *Outlook on Program Expenditures and Priorities, 1996–1997 to 1998–1999.* Ottawa: Supply and Services Canada.
– 1996. *People to People, Nation to Nation: Highlights from the Report of the Royal Commission on Aboriginal Peoples.* Ottawa: Minister of Supply and Services.
– 1997. *A Newcomer's Introduction to Canada.* Ottawa: Citizenship and Immigration / Minister of Public Works and Government Services.
– 1997. *Social Cohesion Research Workplan:* Department of Canadian Heritage, Reference SRA-266. Ottawa: Policy Research Sub-committee on Social Cohesion, March.
Canadian Youth Commission. 1947. *Youth Speaks Out on Citizenship.* Toronto: Ryerson Press.
Cancelli, Noel A. 1993. *Canadian Citizenship: Sharing the Responsibility.* Standing Senate Committee on Social Affairs, Science and Technology. Ottawa: Minister of Supply and Services.
Carens, J.H. 1990. Difference and Domination: Reflections on the Relation between Pluralism and Equality. 226–50. In J., Chapman and A. Wertheimer (eds), *Majorities and Minorities.* Nomos 32. New York: New York University Press.
Carter, Sarah. 1990. *Lost Harvest: Prairie Indian Reserve Farmers and Government Policy.* Montréal and Kingston: McGill-Queen's University Press.
Castles, Stephen. Multicultural Citizenship. Unpublished research paper. Canberra: Parliamentary Research Service, ISR.
Chaiton, Alf. 1974. The History of the National Council of Education. MA thesis, University of Toronto.
– 1977. "Attempts to Establish a National Bureau of Education, 1892–1936." In A. Chaiton and N. MacDonald (eds), *Canadian Schools and Canadian Identity.* Toronto: Gage Educational.
Chambers, S. 1995. Discourse and Democratic Practices. In S.K. White (ed.), *The Cambridge Companion to Habermas.* Cambridge: Cambridge University Press.
Charlot, B. 1989. L'intégration scolaire des jeunes d'origine immigrée : Éléments de synthèse. Dans B. Lorreyte (ed.), *Les politiques d'intégration des jeunes issus de l'immigration.* Paris: CIEMI/L'Harmattan.
Citizenship Studies. An international journal on contemporary issues in citizenship, human rights, and democratic processes from an interdisciplinary perspective; available in print and on line at: http://www.tandf.co.uk

Clifton, Rodney A., and Lance W. Roberts. 1993. *Authority in Classrooms.* Scarborough, Ont.: Prentice-Hall.

Colombo, J.R. 1976. Franchise. *Colombo's Canadian References.* Toronto: Oxford University Press.

Conrad, Margaret, Alvin Finkel, with Veronica Strong-Boag. 1993. *History of the Canadian Peoples.* Vol. 2. Toronto: Copp Clark Pitman.

Conseil Supérieur de l'Education. 1987. *Les défis éducatifs du pluralisme.* Ville de Québec : Avis au Ministre de l'Education, octobre.

Conway, D. 1996. Capitalism and Community. In E. Paul, F. Miller, and J. Paul (eds), *The Communitarian Challenge to Liberalism.* Cambridge: Cambridge University Press.

Conway, M.W. 1993. The Theory and Practice of Political Education in Canada. In M.W. Conway and C.A. Torres (eds), *Political Education: North American Perspectives.* Hamburg, Germany: Kramer.

Conway, M.W., and K. Osborne. 1988. Civics, Citizenship, State Power and Political Education: The Canadian Experience. In B. Claussen and S. Kili (eds), *Changing Structures of Political Power, Socialization and Political Education.* Frankfurt, Germany: Verlag Peter Lang.

Cook, Ramsay. 1994. Nation, Identity, Rights: Reflections on W.L. Morton's Canadian Identity. *Journal of Canadian Studies* 29, 2: 5–19.

Cook, Ramsay, and Wendy Mitchinson (eds). 1976. *The Proper Sphere: Woman's Place in Canadian Society.* Toronto: Oxford University Press.

Cope, B., et al. 1995. *Immigration, Ethnic Conflicts and Social Cohesion.* Sidney, Australia: NLLIA Centre for Workplace Communication and Culture.

Corbett, Barbara. 1997. Children's Understanding of the Concept of Dissent. Unpublished MEd thesis, University of New Brunswick.

Côté, Pauline et John Kabano. 1995. *Éducation aux droits : Didactitiel pour l'éducation aux droits de l'enfant selon la Convention des Nations Unies relative aux droits de l'enfant.* Rimouski: Les éditions du GREME, Université du Québec à Rimouski.

Côté, Pauline et John Kabano. 1993. *Recueil bibliographique sur les droits de l'enfant.* Rimouski: Les éditions du GREME, Université du Québec à Rimouski.

Council of Ministers of Education, Canada. 1988. *Agreed Memorandum on a Council of Ministers of Education, Canada.* Toronto: CMEC.

– 1993. *Joint Declaration; Future Directions for the Council of Ministers of Education, Canada.* Toronto: CMEC.

– 1994. *SAIP School Achievement Indicators Program, Report on Reading and Writing Assessment.* Toronto: CMEC.

– 1995. *Pan-Canadian Education Indicators Program (PCEIP).* Brochure. Toronto: CMEC.

Crispo, J. 1992. *Making Canada Work.* Toronto: Random House.

Daniels, Roger. 1977. The Japanese Experience in North America: An Essay in Comparative Racism. *Canadian Ethnic Studies* 9: 91–100.

Day, Richard J.F. 2000. *Multiculturalism and the History of Canadian Diversity.* Toronto: University of Toronto Press.

Deem, Rosemary, Kevin Brehony, and Sue Heath. 1995. *Active Citizenship and the Governing of Schools.* Buckingham (U.K.) and Philadelphia: Open University Press.

Delors, Jacques, et al. 1996. *L'éducation : Un trésor est caché dedans.* Rapport à l'UNESCO de la Commission internationale sur l'éducation pour le vingt-et-unième siècle. Avec *Sommaire exécutif.* Available in English as *Education: A Hidden Treasure Within.* Paris: Éditions Odile Jacob et UNESCO.

DePass, Cecille. 1992. Centring on Changing Communities: The Colours of the South in the Canadian Vertical Mosaic. *Canadian Ethnic Studies* 24, 3, 99–112.

Derkatz, Marcella. 1993. Ukrainian Language Education in Manitoba Public Schools: Reflections on a Centenary. In R. Bruno-Jofré (ed.), *Issues in the History of Education in Manitoba: From the Construction of the Common School to the Politics of Voices.* Lewiston: Edwin Mellen Press.

Derwing, Tracey M. 1992. Instilling a Passive Voice: Citizenship Instruction in Canada. In B. Burnaby and A. Cumming (eds), *Sociopolitical Aspects of ESL.* Toronto: OISE Press, 1992.

Derwing, Tracey M., and Murray J. Munro. 1987. *Citizenship Instruction for Adult ESL learners: An Assessment of Programmes and Services.* Ottawa: Secretary of State.

DeVries, John. 1992. *Becoming Canadian Citizens: An Analysis of Trends among Immigrants from Twenty-Six Countries.* Report prepared for the Social Trends Analysis Directorate. Ottawa: Multiculturalism and Citizenship Canada.

Dewitte, Philippe (dir.). 1999. *Immigration et intégration : L'état des savoirs.* Paris: Éditions La Découverte.

Dickason, Olive Patricia. 1992. *Canada's First Nations. A History of Founding Peoples from Earliest Times.* Toronto: McClelland & Stewart.

Dougherty, David C. 2002. Citizens and Legislators: Different Views on Representation. In Neil Nevitte (ed.), *Value Change and Goverance in Canada.* Toronto: University of Toronto Press; Montréal: Les Presses de l'Université de Montréal.

Driedger, Leo. 1996. *Multi-Ethnic Canada: Identities and Inequalities.* Toronto: Oxford University Press.

Drucker, Peter E. 1993. *Post-Capitalist Society.* New York: Harper Collins.

Dubinsky, Karen. 1993. *Improper Advances: Rape and Heterosexual Conflict in Ontario, 1880–1929.* Chicago: University of Chicago Press.

Du Bois, W.E.B. 1969. *The Souls of Black Folk.* New York: New American Library. Original work published in 1903.

Dworkin, R. 1977. *Taking Rights Seriously.* Cambridge, Mass.: Harvard University Press.

Edwards, J., and K. Fogelman (eds), 1993. *Developing Citizenship in the Curriculum.* London: David Fulton.

Etzioni, A. 1993. *The Spirit of Community: Rights, Responsibilities, and the Communitarian Agenda.* New York: Crown.

– 1995. *New Communitarian Thinking.* Charlottesville: University of Virginia Press.

Falk, Richard A. 2000. *Human Rights Horizon: The Pursuit of Justice in a Globalizing World.* New York and London: Routledge.

Ferrer, Catalina (ed.). *L'éducation dans une perspective planétaire.* Numéro thématique. *Revue des sciences de l'éducation* 23, 1–232.

Fitzpatrick, Alfred J. 1919. *Handbook for New Canadians.* Toronto: Ryerson Press.

Fleras, A., and J. Leonard Elliot. 1999. *Unequal Relations.* Scarborough, Ont.: Prentice-Hall Allyn Bacon Canada.

Foster, V. 1995. Schooling for Citizenship: A Site of Desire and Threat for Girls. Paper Presented at the Annual Meeting of the American Educational Research Association, San Francisco, April.

Foucault, Michel. 1980. *Power/Knowledge: Selected Interviews and Other Writings, 1972–1977.* New York: Pantheon Books.

Francis, Leslie J. 1999. *The Values Debate: A Voice from the Pupils.* London and Portland, Oreg.: Woburn Press.

Francoeur, Jean Paul. 1998. Former des bons citoyens : Est-ce l'affaire de l'école? *Vie pédagogique* 109 (nov.-déc.) : 12–15.

Freire, P. 1978. *Education for Critical Consciousness.* New York: Seabury Press.

– 1983. *Pedagogy of the Oppressed.* New York: Continuum.

– 1998. *Pedagogy of Freedom: Ethics, Democracy and Civic Courage.* Lanham, Md.: Rowman & Littlefield.

Frideres, Jim. 1997. Civic Participation, Awareness, Knowledge and Skills. Paper presented at the Second National Metropolis Conference, for a session on Civic Participation of Immigrants: Policy and Research Issues, Montréal, 23 November.

Gagnon, France, and Michel Pagé. 1999. *Conceptual Framework for an Analysis of Citizenship in Liberal Democracies.* Vol. 1: *Conceptual Framework and Analysis.* Vol. 2: *Approaches to Citizenship in Six Liberal Democracies. Cadre conceptuel d'analyse de la citoyenneté dans les démocraties libérales.* Vol. 1: *Cadre conceptuel et analyse.* Vol. 2: *Les approches de la citoyennité dans six democraties libérales*. Ottawa: Department of Canadian Heritage / Patrimonie Canada. Available at http: //canada.metropolis.net/research-policy/cern-pub/index.html.

Gagnon, France, Marie McAndrew, et Michel Pagé (dir.). 1996. *Pluralisme, citoyenneté et éducation*. Collection Èthikè. Paris et Montréal: Harmattan.

Galston, W.A. 1991. *Liberal Purposes: Goods, Virtues and Diversity in the Liberal State*. Cambridge: Cambridge University Press.

Gaskell, Jane. 1995. *Secondary Schools in Canada: The National Report of the Exemplary Schools Project*. Toronto: Canadian Education Association.

Germain, Annick. 1997. L'étranger et la ville. *Canadian Journal of Regional Science / Revue canadienne des sciences régionales* 20, 1/2: 237–54.

Giroux, H. 1983. *Theory and Resistance in Education*. South Hadley, Mass.: Bergin & Garvey Press.

– 1988a. *Schooling and the Struggle for Public Life*. Minneapolis: University of Minnesota Press.

– 1988b. *Teachers as Intellectuals*. New York: Bergin & Garvey.

– 1992. *Border Crossings: Cultural Workers and the Politics of Education*. New York: Routledge, Chapman, and Hall.

Goodlad, John I. 1984. *A Place Called School: Prospects for the Future*. New York: McGraw-Hill.

Greene, M. 1989. Educate the "Fortunate Few" to Care. Paper presented at the conference, Curriculum at the Centre: A National Conference on Curriculum, Instruction, and Leadership, Montréal, 30 April–3 May.

Griffiths, Franklyn. 1999. The Culture of Change. Paper for the Cultural Parameters Overview, Project on Trends, a joint initiative of the SSHRC and the Policy Research Secretariat, Ottawa.

Grinter, R. 1992. Multicultural or Antiracist Education? The Need to Choose. In J. Lynch, C. Modgil, and S. Modgil (eds), *Cultural Diversity and the Schools*. Vol. 1, *Education for Diversity: Convergence and Divergence*. London and Washington, DC: Falmer Press.

Gutmann, Amy. 1987. *Democratic Education*. Princeton: N.J.: Princeton University Press.

Gutmann, Amy, and D. Thompson. 1990. Moral Conflict and Political Consensus. In R.B. Douglass, G.M. Mara, and H.S. Richardson (eds), *Liberalism and the Good*. New York: Routledge.

Habermas, J. 1991. *Morale et communication*. Paris : Éditions du Cerf.

Haig-Brown, Roderick.1950. *Measure of the Year*. Toronto: Collins.

Hamilton, Robert M., (ed.) 1952. *Canadian Quotations and Phrases Literary and Historical*. Toronto: McClelland & Stewart.

Hammar, Tomas. 1990. Propensity to Apply for Naturalization in Democracy and the Nation State. In Tomas Hammar (ed.), *Aliens, Denizens and Citizens in a World of International Migration*. Sydney: Avebury.

Hansen, Marcus J., and John Barlett Brebner. 1940. *The Mingling of the Canadian and American Peoples*. New Haven, Conn.: Yale University Press.

Harding, Sandra. 1991. Rethinking Standpoint Epistemology: What Is "Strong Objectivity"? In *Feminist Epistemologies*. New York: Routledge.

Harney, Robert F., and Harold Troper. 1975. *Immigrants: A Portrait of the Urban Experience, 1890–1930*. Toronto: Van Nostrand Reinhold.

Harvey, D.C. 1928. National Sovereignty and the League of Nations. *Western School Journal* 23 (March): 99–100.

Harvey, L.-G. 1995. The First Distinct Society: French Canada, America, and the Constitution of 1791. In J. Ajzenstat and P. Smith eds, *Canada's Origins: Liberal, Tory, or Republican?* Ottawa: Carleton University Press.

Hawthorn, H.B. (ed.). 1966. *A Survey of the Contemporary Indians of Canada*. 2 vols. Ottawa: Indian Affairs Branch.

Hébert, Yvonne. 1997. Citizenship Education: Towards a Pedagogy of Social Participation and Identity Formation. *Canadian Ethnic Studies / Études ethniques au Canada* 29, 2: 82–96.

– 1998. A Research-Based Focus on Literacy and Citizenship Education Issues. Paper presented as part of the Netherlands-Canada Panel, at the 3rd International Metropolis Conference in Israel. Available at http://www.canada.metropolis.net/policy&research/.

– 2001. Collectivized Identity among Shi'a Imami Isma'ili Muslims of Calgary: Implications for Pluralism and Policy. With Rani Murji. In Yngve G. Lithman and Mette Andersson (eds), *Youth in the Plural City: Individualized and Collectivized Identities*. Oxford: Berg.

Hébert, Yvonne, Daniel Buteau, et Renée Delorme. 1999. *Rapports entre apprentissage, identité, communauté, citoyenneté et l'enseignement des sciences humaines favorisant un public scolaire francophone en milieu minoritaire*. Avec la collaboration de Christine Racicot. Edmonton: Ministère de l'éducation en Alberta.

Henderson, J.Y. 1994. Empowering Treaty Federalism. *Saskatchewan Law Review* 58: 241–329.

– 1994. Implementing the treaty order. In R. Gosse, J.Y. Henderson, and R. Carter (eds), *Continuing Poundmaker and Riel's Quest*. Saskatoon: Purich. Reprinted 1996. In *Final Report of the Royal Commission of Aboriginal Peoples*. Vol. 2(1): 248–50. Ottawa: Canada Communications Group-Publishing.

– 1996. First Nations Legal Inheritance in Canada: The Mi'kmaq Model. In D. Guth and W.W. Pue (eds), *Canada's Legal Inheritance*. Winnipeg: Canadian Legal History Project, Faculty of Law, University of Manitoba.

Henry, Frances, Carol Tator, William Mattis, and Tim Rees. 1995. *The Colour of Democracy: Racism in Canadian Society*. Toronto: Harcourt Brace.

Hillman, Barbara. 1997. Grade Eight Students' Understanding of the Concept of Dissent. Unpublished MEd thesis, University of New Brunswick.

Hirsch, E.D., Jr. 1988. *Cultural Literacy: What Every American Needs to Know*. New York: Random House.

Holsoe, S.E. 1977. Slavery and Economic Response among the Vai. In S. Miers and I. Kopytoff (eds), *Slavery in Africa: Historical and Anthropological Perspectives*. Madison: University of Wisconsin Press.

Hrimech, Mohammed, et France Jutras (dir.) 1997. *Défis et enjeux de l'éducation dans une perspective planétaire*. Sherbrooke, Qué: Éditions du CRP.

Hughes, Andrew W., and Alan M. Sears. 1998. How Do Children and Young People Learn Citizenship? Address to the Executive Meeting of the Russian Association for Civic Education, Moscow, 16 August.

Huntington, Samuel P. 1993. The Clash of Civilizations. *Foreign Affairs* 72, 32: 22–49.

– 1996. *The Clash of Civilization and the Remaking of World Order*. New York: Simon and Schuster. Published in French as *Le choc des civilisations*. Paris: Odile Jacob, 1997.

Huntington, Samuel, and Lawrence Harrison. 2000. *Culture Matters*. New York: Basic Books.

Hutchinson, A.C. 1989. *Waiting for Coraf: A Critique of Law and Rights*. Toronto: University of Toronto Press.

Hutchinson, A., and L. Green. 1989. *Law and Community: The End of Individualism?* Toronto: Carswell.

Ichilov, Orit (ed.). 1998. *Citizenship and Citizenship Education in a Changing World*. London and Portland, Oreg.: Woburn Press.

Inglehart, Ronald. 1997. *Modernization and Postmodernization: Cultural, Economic and Political Change in 43 Societies*. Princeton, N.J.: Princeton University Press.

– 1999. Choc des civilisations ou modernisation culturelle du monde? *Le Débat* 105: 23–54.

Jackel, S. Women's Suffrage. 1988. *Canadian Encyclopedia*. 2nd ed. Edmonton: Hurtig.

Jaenen, C. 1981. *Canada as Diversity. Our Many Selves: Multiculturalism and Educational Policy*. Ottawa: Canadian Teachers' Federation.

Jenson, Jane. 1998. *Les contours de la cohésion sociale : L'état de la recherche au Canada*. Ottawa: Réseaux canadiens de recherche en politiques publiques.

Johnston, Darlene. 1993. First Nations and Canadian Citizenship. In W. Kaplan (ed.), *Belonging*.

Johnston, Ingrid. 1997. Dilemmas of Identity and Ideology in Cross-Cultural Literacy Engagements. *Canadian Ethnic Studies* 29, 2: 97–107.

Juteau-Lee, Danielle. 1979. *Frontières ethniques en devenir*. Ottawa: Éditions de l'Université d'Ottawa.

Kallen, Evelyn. 1995. *Ethnicity and Human Rights in Canada*. 2nd ed. Toronto: Oxford University Press.

Kaltsounis, T. 1990. Letter to the editor. Citizenship Education. *Social Education* 54, 2: 65.

Kanji, Mebs. 2000. Information, Cognitive Mobilization and Representative Governance. In Neil Nevitte (ed.), *Value Change and Governance in Canada*. Toronto: University of Toronto Press; Montréal: Les Presses de l'Université de Montréal.

Kaplan, William. 1993. Who Belongs? Changing Concepts of Citizenship and Nationality. In Kaplan, *Belonging*.

Kaplan, William (ed.) *Belonging: The Meaning and Future of Canadian Citizenship*. Montréal and Kingston: McGill-Queen's University Press.

Karlson, B., and E.F. Gardner. 1986. *Adult Basic Learning Examination*. 2nd ed. New York: Psychological Corporation and Harcourt Brace Jovanovich.

Kealey, Gregory S. 1984. 1919: The Canadian Labour Revolt. *Labour / Le Travail* 13 (Spring): 11–44.

Kealey, Gregory, and Bryan Palmer. 1982. *Dreaming of What Might Be: The Knights of Labor in Ontario*. New York: Cambridge University Press.

Keith, N.Z. 1995. Relationship Building as the New Citizenship: Tales from a School Community Service Program. Paper presented at the annual meeting of the American Educational Research Association, San Francisco, April.

Keller, Betty. 1981. *Pauline: A Biography of Pauline Johnson*. Vancouver and Toronto: Douglas and McIntyre.

Kingwell, Mark. 2000. *The World We Want: Virtue, Vice, and the Good Citizen*. Toronto: Viking, Penguin.

Kitayama, Kathy. 1994. Obtaining Citizenship in the United States: Determinants of Immigrant Naturalization. MA thesis, Department of Demography, Georgetown University.

Klein, Juan-Luis, et Suzanne Laurin. 1998. *L'éducation géographique : Formation du citoyen et conscience territoriale*. Québec: Presses de l'Université du Québec.

Klusmeyer, Douglas B. 1996. *Between Consent and Descent: Conceptions of Democratic Citizenship*. Washington, D.C.: International Migration Policy Program, Carnegie Endowment for International Peace.

Kymlicka, Will. 1989. *Liberalism, Community and Culture*. Oxford: Clarendon Press.

– 1992. *Recent Work in Citizenship Theory / Théories récentes sur la citoyenneté*. Ottawa: Multiculturalism and Citizenship / Multiculturalisme et Citoyenneté Canada.

– 1994. Return of the Citizen: Survey of Recent Work on Citizenship Theory. *Ethics* 104: 352–81.

– 1995. *Multicultural Citizenship: A Liberal Theory of Minority Rights*. Toronto: Oxford University Press.

– 1998. *Finding Our Way: Rethinking Ethnocultural Relations in Canada*. Toronto: Oxford University Press.

Kymlicka, Will (ed.) 1995–present. *Citizenship, Democracy and Ethnocultural Diversity Newsletter*. Back issues posted at http://qsilver.queensu.ca/~philform/news.html

Kymlicka, Will, and W. Norman (eds) 2000. *Citizenship in Diverse Societies*. Toronto: Oxford University Press.

Lapeyronnie, Didier. 1999. De l'altérité à la différence : L'identité, facteur d'intégration ou de repli? In Philippe Dewitte (dir), *Immigration et intégration : L'état des savoirs*. Paris : Éditions La Découverte.

Larmore, Charles. 1987. *Patterns of Moral Complexity*. Cambridge: Cambridge University Press.

Larochelle, Gilbert, Suzie Robichaud, et Joseph Tremblay. 1997. Le développement de l'employabilité au Canada : De la morale au contrôle social. *Revue de l'Université de Moncton* 30, 2: 95–114.

Lasch, Christopher. 1995. *The Revolt of the Elites and the Betrayal of Democracy*. New York: W.W. Norton.

Laurin, Suzanne, et Juan-Luis Klein.1998. *L'éducation géographique : Formation du citoyen et conscience territoriale*. Sainte-Foy: Les Presses de l'Université du Québec.

Laville, Christian. 1996. History Taught in Québec Is Not Really That Different from the History Taught Elsewhere in Canada. *Canadian Social Studies* 31, 1: 22–4.

Laville, Christian, et Jean Dionne. 1996. *La construction des savoirs*. Montréal et Toronto: Chenelière et McGraw-Hill.

Laycock, David. 1990. *Populism and Democratic Thought in the Canadian Prairies, 1910–1945*. Toronto: University of Toronto Press.

Lee, Mark, and Eva Krugly-Smolska. 1999. The Role of Faculties of Education in Citizenship Education: An Initial Inquiry of One Faculty. Paper presented at the First National Citizenship Education Research Forum, held on 8 June at the University of Sherbrooke, with the program of the Comparative and International Education Society of Canada, at the annual conference of the Canadian Society for the Study of Education.

Le Gal, Jean. 1999. *Coopérer pour développer la citoyenneté : La classe coopérative*. Paris: Hatier.

Létourneau, Jocelyn. 1997. L'affirmationisme québécois à l'ère de la mondialisation. *Revue de l'Université de Moncton* 30, 2: 19–36.

Levin, Benjamin. 1993. The Struggle over Modernization in Manitoba Education, 1924–1960. In R. Bruno-Jofré (ed.), *Issues in the History of Education in Manitoba: From the Construction of the Common School to the Politics of Voices.* Lewiston: Edwin Mellen Press.

Lewe, G. 1984. *The Department of the Secretary of State: An Historical Overview.* Ottawa: Office of the Under Secretary of State, 1984.

Leydet, D. 1995. Théorie démocratique de la citoyenneté, libéralisme et souveraineté. Document polycopié. Département de philosophie, Université du Québec à Montréal.

Lister, Ruth. 1993. Tracing the Contours of Women's Citizenship. *Policy and Politics* 21, 1, 3–16.

Littlebear, Leroy. 1993. The Criminal Justice System and Aboriginal Men: Foundational Roots of the Problems. Unpublished manuscript prepared for the Royal Commission on Aboriginal Peoples.

Lorber, Judith. 1994. *Paradoxes of Gender.* New Haven, Conn.: Yale University Press.

Lovelace v. Canada. 1985. United Nations, Human Rights Committee – Selected Decision under the Optional Protocol, 1:83. UN.DOC.CCRP/C/DR/[XII]R6/24 (31 July 1983).

Lynch, J. 1993. *Education for Citizenship.* London: Cassell.

Lynch, J., C. Modgil, et S. Modgil. 1992. *Cultural Diversity and the Schools,* Vol. 1: *Education for Cultural Diversity: Convergence and Divergence.* London and Washington, D.C.: Falmer Press.

Macedo, S. 1990. *Liberal Virtues: Citizenship, Virtue, and Community.* Oxford: Oxford University Press.

– 1992. Charting Liberal Virtues. In J.W. Chapman and W. Galston (eds), *Virtue.* Nomos 34. New York: New York University Press.

MacIntyre, A. 1981. *After Virtue: A Study in Moral Theory.* London: Duckworth.

Macpherson, C.B. 1962. *The Political Theory of Possessive Individualism: Hobbes to Locke.* Oxford: Clarendon Press.

Marshall, T.H. 1963. 1998. Citizenship and Social Class. In T.H. Marshall (ed.), *Class, Citizenship and Social Class.* New York: Doubleday, Bantam. Repr. in Shafir Gershon, (ed.), *The Citizenship Debates: A Reader.* Minneapolis: University of Minnesota Press.

Marshall, T.H., and T.B. Bottomore. 1991. *Citizenship and Social Class.* London: Pluto Press.

Martel, Marcel. 1998. *French Canada: An Account of its Creation and Break-up, 1850–1967.* Canada's Ethnic Group Series, Booklet No. 24. Ottawa: Canadian Historical Association.

Martin, Paul. 1983. *A Very Public Life: Far from Home.* Ottawa: Deneau.

Martineau, Robert, et Christian Laville. 1998. L'histoire : Voie royale vers la citoyenneté? *Éducations : Revue de diffusion des savoirs en éducation* 16 (sept.) : 33–7. Ré-imprimé dans *Vie pédagogique* 109 (nov.-déc.) : 35–7.

Marzouk, Abdellah, Pauline Côté, et John Kabano. 1997. *École, éducation à la citoyenneté et diversité culturelle.* Rimouski: Les éditions du GREME, Université du Québec à Rimouski.

Marzouk, Abdellah, John Kabano, et Pauline Côté. 2000. *Éducation à la citoyenneté à l'école : Guide pédagogique.* Montréal: Les Éditions Logiques.

Masemann, Vandra. 1987. The Current Status of Teaching about Citizenship in Canadian Elementary and Secondary Schools. In Keith A. McLeod ed., *Canada and Citizenship Education.* Toronto: Canadian Education Association.

Masny, Diana. 1996. Meta-Knowledge, Critical Literacy and Minority Language Education: The Case of Franco-Ontarian Student Teachers. *Language, Culture and Curriculum* 9, 3: 260–78.

Mata, Fernando. 1998. Citizenship and Visible Minority Status: A Snapshot of the Canadian Labour Force. *Multiculturalism/Interculturalisme* 17, 2: 36–43.

Maxwell, Judith. 1996. *Social Dimensions of Economic Growth.* Eric John Hanson Commemorative Conferences, Vol. 8. Edmonton: University of Alberta.

McAndrew, Marie, et Caroline Tessier. 1998. L'éducation à la citoyenneté en milieu scolaire québécois : Situation actuelle et perspectives comparatives. *Études ethniques au Canada / Canadian Ethnic Studies* 29, 2 : 58–81.

McAndrew, Marie, Guy Bourgeault, et Michel Pagé. 1996–98. L'éducation à la citoyenneté dans une société pluraliste : étude comparative d'expériences novatrices dans les écoles secondaires en milieu pluriethnique à Montréal et à Toronto. Ottawa: Programme d'études ethniques, Multiculturalism Directorate, Dép. de Patrimoine Canada.

McAndrew, Marie, Caroline Tessier, et Guy Bourgeault. 1997. L'éducation à la citoyenneté en milieu scolaire au Canada, aux États-Unis et en France : Des orientations aux réalisations. *Revue française de pédagogie* 121 : 57–77

McIntosh, P. 1983. *Interactive Phases of Curricular Re-vision: A Feminist Perspective.* Wellesley, Mass.: Center for Research on Women, Wellesley College.

McKay, Ian. 1986. By Wisdom, Wile òr War: The Provincial Workmen's Association and the Struggle for Working-Class Independence in Nova Scotia, 1897–97. *Labour / Le Travail* 18: 13–62.

McKenzie, H. 1993. *Citizenship Education in Canada.* Ottawa: Research Branch, Library of Parliament.

McLaren, P. 1989. *Life in Schools.* Toronto: Irwin.

McLaughlin, T.H. 1992. Citizenship, Diversity and Education: A Philosophical Perspective. *Journal of Moral Education* 21, 3: 235–50.

McLeod, K. 1989. Exploring Citizenship Education: Education for Citizenship.

In K. McLeod (ed.), *Canada and Citizenship Education*. Toronto: Canadian Education Association.

Menzies, Heather. 1996. *Whose Brave New World? The Information Highway and the New Economy*. Toronto: Between the Lines.

Michelman, Frank I. 1988. Law's Republic. *Yale Law Journal* 97, 8: 1493–537.

Milan, R.W. 1980. Education and the Reproduction of Capitalist Ideology: Manitoba 1945–1960. MEd thesis. University of Manitoba.

Milen, R.A. (ed.). 1991. *Aboriginal Peoples and Electoral Reform in Canada*. Vol. 9. Toronto: Dundurn Press.

Mitchell, T. 1996–97. The Manufacture of Souls of Good Quality: Winnipeg's 1919 National Conference on Canadian Citizenship, English-Canadian Nationalism, and the New Order after the Great War. *Journal of Canadian Studies* 31, 4 (Winter): 5–28.

Mill, John Stuart. 1969. *Autobiography*. Jack Stillinger (ed.). Houghton Mifflin.

– 1993. *Utilitarianism, On Liberty, Considerations on Representative Government*. Geraint Williams (ed.). London: Dent.

Monkman, Leslie. 1981. *A Native Heritage: Images of the Indian in English Canadian Literature*. Toronto: University of Toronto Press.

Moore, Clarence. 1939. The Social Studies. *Manitoba School Journal* 2, 4: 6.

Morrison, R.B., and C.R. Wilson (eds). 1995. *Native Peoples. The Canadian Experience*. Toronto: McClelland & Stewart.

Morton, W.L. 1968. *The Canadian Identity*. Toronto: University of Toronto Press.

Mouffe, C.E. (ed.). 1992. *Dimensions of Radical Democracy: Pluralism, Citizenship, Community*. London: Verso.

Munro, B. 1989. Literacy: A Citizenship Participation Issue. *TESL Talk* 19, 1: 80–5.

Nadeau, Richard. 2000. Satisfaction with Democracy: The Canadian Paradox. In Neil Nevitte (ed.), *Value Change and Governance in Canada*. Toronto: University of Toronto Press; Montréal: Les Presses de l'Université de Montréal.

Nagel, T. 1994. *Égalité et partialité*. C. Beauvillard (trans.). Paris: Presses Universitaires de France.

Neice, David. 1978. *Ethnicity and Canadian Citizenship: A Metropolitan Study*. Ottawa: Department of the Secretary of State, Citizenship Registration Branch.

Nevitte, Neil. 1996. *Decline of Deference: Canadian Value Change in Cross-National Perspective*. Peterborough, Ont.: Broadview Press.

Newton, Janice. 1995. *The Feminist Challenge to the Canadian Left, 1990–1918*. Montréal and Kingston: McGill-Queen's University Press.

Nieto, S. 1992. *Affirming Diversity: The Sociopolitical Context of Multicultural Education*. White Plains, N.Y.: Longman.

Noddings, N. 1992. The Gender Issue. *Educational Leadership* 49, 4: 65–70.

Norris, Pippa (ed.). 1999. *Critical Citizens: Global Support for Democratic Government.* Oxford and New York: Oxford University Press.

Norris, S.P., L.M. Phillips, and J.W. Bulcock. 1992. *Demographic Causes of Reading Literacy Levels in Newfoundland and Labrador.* Report Number 2, Summary Reports of Paths to Literacy and Illiteracy in Newfoundland and Labrador. St John's: Memorial University of Newfoundland, Faculty of Education.

Norton, Ann. 1992. Ruling Memory. *Political Theory* 21, 3: 453–63.

Nozick, R. 1974. *Anarchy, State and Utopia.* New York: Basic Books.

Ogbu, J.U. 1988. Diversity and Equity in Public Education: Community Forces and Minority School Adjustment and Performance. In R. Haskins and D. Macrae (eds), *Policies for America's Public Schools: Teachers, Equity, and Indicators.* Norwood, N.J.: Ablex.

– 1981. Origins of Human Competence: A Cultural-Ecological Perspective. *Child Development* 52: 413–29.

Ogbu, J.U., and M.E. Matute-Bianchi. 1987. *Understanding Socio-Cultural Factors: Knowledge, Identity, and School Adjustment.* Los Angeles: California State University, Evaluation, Dissemination and Assessment Center.

Okin, Susan Millar. 1992. Women, equality, and citizenship. *Queen's Quarterly* 99, 1: 56–71.

Oriol, M. 1991. Les communautés culturelles et la recherche. In E. Tarrab, G. Plessis-Belair, and Y. Girault (eds), *Les communautés culturelles au Québec et la recherche en éducation.* Montréal: Publications de la Faculté des sciences de l'éducation, Université de Montréal.

Orr, Jeff, and Roberta McKay. 1997. Living Citizenship through Classroom Community. *Canadian Social Studies* 31, 3: 131–4.

Osborne, K.W. 1988. *Educating Citizens: A Democratic Socialist Agenda for Canadian Education.* Toronto: Our Schools / Our Selves Education Foundation.

– 1993. Political Education and Participant Citizenship: Implications for School, Curricula and Pedagogy. In M.W. Conway and C.A. Torres (eds), *Political Education: North American Perspectives.* Hamburg, Germany: Kramer.

– 1994. *Citizenship Education in Canada.* Report to the Citizenship Education Policy Study, under the direction of John Cogan. Minneapolis: University of Minnesota Press.

– 1994. Education and Citizenship. *Manitoba Social Science Teacher* 21, 1: 13–24.

– 1994. I'm Not Going to Think about How Cabot Discovered Newfoundland When I'm Doing My Job: The Status of History in Canadian High Schools. Paper presented to the Annual Meeting of the Canadian Historical Association, Calgary, June.

- 1996. Education is the Best National Insurance: Citizenship Education in Canadian Schools, Past and Present. *Comparative and International Education* 25, 2: 31–58.
- 1997. Citizenship Education and Social Studies. In Ian Wright and Alan Sears (eds), *Trends and Issues in Canadian Social Studies.* Vancouver: Pacific Educational Press.
- 1998–99. One Hundred Years of History Teaching in Manitoba Schools. Part 1: 1897–1927. *Manitoba History* 36 (Autumn/Winter): 3–25.

Ouellet, Fernand, Lucie Benoît, Louise Bernard, Irène Drolet, Carole Morelli, Monika Thoma-Petit, Martine Sabourin, et Louise Sarrasin. 1998. *L'éducation à la citoyenneté dans une perspective mondiale : Cadre conceptuel.* Québec: Centre d'éducation interculturelle et de compréhension internationale (CEICI).

Owen, Diana, and Linda M.G. Zerilli. 1991. Gender and Citizenship. *Society* 28, 5: 27–34.

Pagé, Michel. 1997. Citoyenneté et pluralisme des valeurs. Dans F. Gagnon, M. McAndrew, et M. Pagé (dir.), *Pluralisme, citoyenneté et éducation.* Paris et Montréal: Harmattan.

- 1992. Pluralistic Citizenship: A Reference for Citizenship Education. *Canadian Ethnic Studies* 29, 2: 22–31.

Pagé, Michel, Fernand Ouellet, et Luiza Cortesão (réds). 2001. *L'éducation à la citoyenneté.* Sherbrooke, Qué.: Éditions du CRP, Université de Sherbrooke.

Pal, L.A. 1989. Identity, Citizenship, and Mobilization: The Nationals Branch and World War Two. *Canadian Public Administration* 32, 3: 407–26.

- 1983. *Working-Class Experience: The Rise and Reconstitution of Canadian Labour, 1800–1900.* Toronto: Butterworth.

Palmer, Bryan D. 1979. *A Culture in Conflict: Skilled Workers and Industrial Capitalism in Hamilton, Ontario, 1860–1914.* Montréal: McGill-Queen's University Press.

Pang, V.O. 1995. Intentional Silence and Communication in a Democratic Society: The Viewpoint of One Asian American. Paper presented at the annual meeting of the American Educational Research Association, San Francisco, April.

Parker, P. 1978. *Movement in Black.* Ithaca, N.Y.: Firebrand Books.

Patterson, Robert. 1986. The Implementation of Progressive Education in Canada, 1930–1945. In N. Kach, K. Mazurek, R.S. Patterson, and I. DeFavery, (eds), *Essays in Canadian Education.* Calgary: Detselig Enterprises.

Paul, E., F. Miller, and J. Paul. 1996. *The Communitarian Challenge to Liberalism.* Cambridge: Cambridge University Press.

Pendakur, K., and R. Pandakur. 1996. *Earning Differentials among Ethnic Groups in Canada.* Strategic Research and Analysis Monograph SRA-34b. Ottawa: Department of Canadian Heritage.

Pentney, William. 1988. The Rights of Aboriginal Peoples of Canada in the

Constitution Act, 1982, Part II – Section 35, the Substantive Guarantee. *UBC Law Review* 22, 2: 207–78.

Pestieau, Joseph. 1999. *Les citoyens au bazar : Mondialisation, nations et minorités.* Collection prisme. Sainte-Foy, Qué: Les Presses de l'Université Laval.

Peters, Suzanne. 1995. *Exploring Canadian Values: Foundations for Well-Being.* Study No. F-01. Ottawa: Canadian Policy Research Network.

Petrone, Penny. 1990. *Native Literature in Canada. From the Oral Tradition to the Present.* Toronto: Oxford University Press.

Pettit, P. 1993. *The Common Mind.* New York: Oxford University Press.

Phillips, L.M., S.P. Norris, J.M. Mason, and B.M. Kerr. 1990. Effect of Early Literacy Intervention on Kindergarten Achievement. In J. Zutell and S. McCormick (eds), *Literacy Theory and Research: Analyses from Multiple Paradigms.* Chicago: National Reading Conference.

Pike, Graham, and David Selby. 2000. *Global Education: Meeting Basic Learning Needs.* Amman, Jordan: UNICEF Middle East and North Africa.

Pike, Graham, and David Selby. 1999. *In the Global Classroom.* Toronto: Pippin.

Plato. 1942. *Republic.* Roslyn, N.Y.: Walter J. Black.

Pocock, J.G.A. 1975. *The Machiavellian Moment.* Princeton, N.J.: Princeton University Press.

– 1995. The Ideal of Citizenship since Classical Times. In R. Beiner (ed.), *Theorizing Citizenship.* Albany: State University of New York Press.

Portelli, John P., and Patrick Solomon (eds). 2001. *The Erosion of Democracy in Education.* Calgary: Detselig Enterprises.

Pourtois, H. 1993. La démocratie délibérative. *Lekton* 3, 2: 105–34.

Pouwels, Jan. 1997. Values Education in a Postmodern World. In Dave Evans, Harald Grässler, and Jan Pouwels (eds), *Human Rights and Values Education in Europe: Research in Educational Law, Curricula and Textbooks.* Freiburg: Fillibach Verlag.

Prentice, Allison, et al. 1988. *Canadian Women: A History.* Toronto: Harcourt Brace Jovanovich.

Putnam, R.D. 1995. Bowling Alone: America's Declining Social Capital. *Journal of Democracy* 6, 1: 65–78. Out of print. Available at http://www.press.jhu.edu/demo/journal_of_democracy/v006/putnam.html.

– 2000. *Bowling Alone: Collapse and Revival of American Community.* New York: Simon and Schuster.

R.V. Sparrow, [1990] 1 S.C.R. 1075; 3 C.N.L.R. 178.

Ravitch, J. 1990. Multiculturalism. *American Scholar* (Summer): 337–54.

Rawls, J. 1971. *A Theory of Justice.* London: Oxford University Press.

– 1993. *Political Liberalism.* New York: Columbia University Press.

Reder, S., and K. Reed Green. 1983. Contrasting Patterns of Literacy in an Alaska Fishing Village. *International Journal of Sociology of Language* 42: 9–39.

Reeve, G.J. 1926. *Canada: Its History and Progress, 1000–1925.* Toronto: Oxford University Press.

Reiter, Ester. 1991. *Making Fast Food: From the Frying Pan into the Fryer.* Montréal: McGill-Queen's University.

Reitz, J.G. 1982. Ethnic Group Control of Groups. Research Paper No 133. University of Toronto, Centre for Urban and Community Studies.

Report of the Committee on the Review of the Programme of Studies. 1926. Winnipeg: Department of Education.

Resnick, P. 1997. *Twenty-First Century Democracy.* Montreal and Kingston: McGill-Queen's University Press.

Riesenberg, P. 1992. *Citizenship in the Western Tradition.* Chapel Hill: University of North Carolina Press.

Roese, Neal J. 2000. Are Canadians Becoming Less Trusting of Government? In Neil Nevitte (ed.), *Value Change and Governance in Canada.* Toronto: University of Toronto Press; Montréal: Les Presses de l'Université de Montréal.

Rosenau, Pauline. 1992. *Postmodernism and the Social Sciences: Insights, Inroads and Intrusions.* Princeton, N.J.: Princeton University Press.

Ross, Colleen Mary. 1997. Franco-Manitobans and the Struggle for the Preservation of Religion and Language: Public Schools and the Township of Ste Anne, 1946–1955. MEd thesis, University of Manitoba.

Royal Commission on Electoral Reform and Party Financing and the Committee for Aboriginal Electoral Reform. 1991. *The Path to Electoral Equality.* Ottawa: Ministry of Supply and Services.

Ruano-Borbalan, Jean-Claude. 2000. Valeurs et cultures : Allons-nous devenir postmoderne? *Sciences humaines* 3 (mars): 16–20.

Russell, Dan. 2000. *A People's Dream: Aboriginal Self-Government in Canada.* Vancouver: UBC Press.

Russell, R.J. 1984. Multiculturalizing the Social Studies in Canada. Paper presented at the annual conference of the National Council for Social Studies, Washington, D.C.

Samad, Yumas. 1997. The Plural Guises of Multiculturalism: Conceptualising a Fragmented Paradigm. In Tariq Modood and Pnina Werbner (eds), *The Politics of Multiculturalism in the New Europe: Racism, Identity and Community.* London: ZED Books.

Samuel, J.T. 1992. *Visible Minorities in Canada: A Projection.* Toronto: Canadian Advertising Foundation.

Sandel, M. 1982. *Liberalism and the Limits of Justice.* Cambridge: Cambridge University Press.

– 1992. The Procedural Republic and the Unencumbered Self. In S. Avineri and A. de-Shalit (eds), *Communitarianism and Individualism.* Oxford: Oxford University Press.

– 1996. *Democracy's Discontent: America in Search of a Public Philosophy.* Cambridge, Mass.: Harvard University Press.

Saul, John Ralston. 1997. *Reflections of a Siamese Twin: Canada at the End of the Twentieth Century.* Toronto: Viking Books.

Schermerhorn, R.A. 1970. *Comparative Ethnic Relations: A Framework for Theory and Research.* New York: Random House.

Schmuck, P. (ed.). 1987. *Women Educators: Employees of Schools in Western Countries.* Albany: State University of New York Press.

Schneider, Angela J. 1999. Women, Violent Sport and Citizenship: An Ethical Analysis. Paper presented at the National Seminar of Value Change and Governance. Toronto, 11 June.

Schutz, A. 1967. Common-Sense and Scientific Interpretation of Human Action. In *Collected Papers I: The Problem of Social Reality.* The Hague: Martin Njhoff.

Scott, W.J. Gordon. 1920. Democracy in the Classroom. *Western School Journal* 15, 6: 231.

Scribner, S. 1984. Literacy in Three Metaphors. *American Journal of Education* 93, 1: 6–21.

Sears, Alan. 1994. Social Studies as Citizenship Education in English Canada: A Review of Research. *Theory and Research Social Education* 22, 1: 6–43.

– 1996. "Something Different to Everyone": Conceptions of Citizenship and Citizenship Education. *Canadian and International Education* 25, 2: 1–16.

– 1997. Social Studies in Canada. In Ian Wright and Alan Sears (eds), *Trends and Issues in Canadian Social Studies.* Vancouver: Pacific Educational Press.

– 1998. Freedom and Dissent: What Do Students Know about Democratic Citizenship? Presentation to Citizenship Education for Democracy in the 21st Century, a public education conference of the British Columbia Teachers' Federation, Vancouver, 21 February.

Sears, A.M., and A.S. Hughes. 1996. Citizenship Education and Current Educational Reform. *Canadian Journal of Education* 21, 2: 123–42.

Sears, Alan, Gerald Clarke, and Andrew S. Hughes. 1999. Canadian Citizenship Education: The Pluralist Ideal and Citizenship Education for a Multinational State. In J. Torney-Purta, J. Schwille, and J.-A. Amadeo (eds), *Civic Education across Countries: Twenty-Four National Case Studies from the IEA Civic Education Project.* Amsterdam: IEA Secretariat.

– 2000. Learning Democracy in a Pluralist Society: Building a Research Base for Citizenship Education in Canada. In Y. Lenoir, W. Hunter, D. Hodgkinson, P. de Broucker, and A. Dolbec (eds), *A Pan-Canadian Education Research Agenda. Un programme pan-canadien de recherche en éducation.* Ottawa: Canadian Society for the Study of Education.

Selznick, P. 1992. *The Moral Commonwealth.* Berkeley: University of California Press.

Senate of Canada. See Cancelli, Noel A.

Shack, Sybil. 1993. The Making of a Teacher, 1917–1935: One Woman's Perspective. In R. Bruno-Jofré (ed.), *Issues in the History of Education in Manitoba: From the Construction of the Common School to the Politics of Voices.* Lewiston: Edwin Mellen Press.

Shafir, Gershon (ed.). 1998. *The Citizenship Debates: A Reader.* Minneapolis: University of Minnesota Press.

Shapiro, Ian, and Casiano Hacker-Cordón (eds). 1999. *Democracy's Edges.* Cambridge and New York: Cambridge University Press.

– 1999. *Democracy's Value.* Cambridge and New York: Cambridge University Press.

Siemiatycki, Myer, and Engin Isin. 1998. Immigration, Diversity and Urban Citizenship in Toronto. *Canadian Journal of Regional Science* 20, 1/2: 73–102.

Sigurdson, Richard A. 1996. First Peoples, New Peoples and Citizenship in Canada. *International Journal of Canadian Studies, Special Issue on Citizenship and Rights* 14: 53–76.

Simms, Glenda. 1993. Racism as a Barrier to Canadian Citizenship. In William Kaplan (ed.), *Belonging.*

Smith, D.M. 1986. The Anthropology of Literacy Acquisition. In B.B. Schieffelin and P. Gilmore (eds), *The Acquisition of Literacy: Ethnographic Perspectives.* Norwood, N.J.: Ablex.

Smith, P. 1995. Civic Humanism versus Liberalism: Fitting the Loyalists in. In J. Ajzenstat and P. Smith (eds), *Canada's Origins: Liberal, Tory, or Republican?* Ottawa: Carleton University Press.

– 1995. The Ideological Origins of Canadian Confederation. In J. Ajzenstat and P. Smith (eds), *Canada's Origins: Liberal, Tory, or Republican?* Ottawa: Carleton University Press.

Smits, Hans. 1997. Citizenship Education in Postmodern Times: Some Questions for Reflection. *Canadian Social Studies* 31, 3: 126–30.

Spinner, J. 1994. *The Boundaries of Citizenship.* Baltimore: Johns Hopkins University Press.

Statistics Canada. 1986. *Census Subdivision in Decreasing Population Order* Catalogue No. 92-109. Ottawa: Statistics Canada.

– 1986. *Census Subdivisions and Unincorporated Places by Census Division and Census Consolidated Subdivision.* Catalogue No. 92-121. Ottawa: Statistics Canada.

– 1989. *Survey of Literacy Skills Used in Daily Activities.* Catalogue Nos. 8-5103-225.1 and 8-5103-226.1. Ottawa: Statistics Canada.

– 1989. *Survey of Literacy Skills Used in Daily Activities: Scoring Guide.* Catalogue No. 7-5030-1215. Ottawa: Statistics Canada.

– 1995. *International Adult Literacy Survey.* Ottawa: Statistics Canada.

– 1996. *Reading the Future: A Portrait of Literacy in Canada.* Ottawa, Ontario: Statistics Canada.

Stevenson, Garth. 1992. The Decline of Consociational Democracy in Canada. In *Canadian Politics: Past, Present and Future.* St Catharines, Ont.: Department of Political Science, Brock University.

Strong-Boag, Veronica. 1987. Peace-Making Women: Canada, 1919–1939. In Ruth Roach Pierson (ed.), *Women and Peace: Theoretical, Historical, and Practical Perspectives.* London: Croom-Helm.

– 1996. Independent Women and Problematic Men: Canadian Anti-feminism from Goldwin Smith to Betty Steele. *Histoire sociale / Social History* 29, 57: 1–22.

– et al. 1998. *Painting the Maple: Issues of Race, Gender and the Construction of Canada.* Vancouver: UBC Press.

Strong-Boag, Veronica, and Anita Clair Fellman (eds.). 1991. *Rethinking Canada: The Promise of Women's History.* 2nd ed. Toronto: Copp Clarke Pitman.

Sunstein, C. 1988. Beyond the Republican Revival. *Yale Law Journal* 97, 8: 1539–58.

Sweeney, Thomas T. 1998. La pédagogie du service. *Éducation: Revue de diffusion des savoirs en éducation* 16: 69–71.

Taillefer, Jean-Marie. 1988. Les Franco-Manitobains et l'éducation, 1870–1980 : Une étude quantitative. PhD thesis, University of Manitoba.

Tarrow, Sydney. 1992. *Power in Movement: Social Movements, Collective Action, and Politics.* Cambridge: Cambridge University Press.

Taylor, Charles. 1989. Cross-Purposes: The Liberal-Communautarian Debate. In N. Rosenblum (ed.), *Liberalism and the Moral Life.* Princeton, N.J.: Princeton University Press.

– 1992. *Multiculturalism and the "Politics of Recognition."* An Essay with commentary by Amy Gutmann (ed.), Steven C. Rockefeller, Michael Walzer, and Susan Wolf. Princeton, NJ: Princeton University Press.

– 1993. *Reconciling the Solitudes: Essays on Canadian Federalism and Nationalism.* Guy Laforest (ed.). Montréal and Kingston: McGill-Queen's University Press.

– 1994. The Politics of Recognition." In David Theo Goldberg (ed.), *Multiculturalism: A Critical Reader.* Cambridge. Mass.: Blackwell, 1994.

ten Dam, G., and M. Volman. 1995. "Care" for Feminist Citizenship. Paper presented at the annual meeting of the American Educational Research Association, San Francisco, April.

Thompson, John Herd. 1981. *The Harvests of War: The Prairie West, 1914–1918.* Toronto: McClelland & Stewart.

Tilly, Charles. 1995. Citizenship, Identity and Social Identity. *International Review of Social History* 40, supplement 3: 1–17. Reprinted in Charles Tilly (ed.),

Citizenship, Identity and Social Identity. Cambridge: Cambridge University Press, 1996.

Titley, Brian E. *A Narrow Vision: Duncan Campbell Scott and the Administration of Indian Affairs in Canada*. Vancouver: University of British Columbia Press, 1986.

Tomkins, George S. 1986. *A Common Countenance: Stability and Change in the Canadian Curriculum*. Scarborough, Ont.: Prentice-Hall.

Torney-Purta, Judith. 1994. The Monitoring of Affective Outcomes. In Albert C. Tujnmann and T. Neville Postlethwaite (eds), *Monitoring the Standards of Education*. New York: Elsevier.

– 1996. The Second IEA Civic Education Project: Development of Content Guidelines and Items for a Cross-National Test and Survey. *Canadian and International Education* 25, 2: 199–214.

Torney-Purta, Judith, John Schwille, and Jo-Ann Amadeo (eds) 1999. *Civic Education across Countries: Twenty-four National Case Studies from the IEA Civic Education Project*. Amsterdam: IEA Secretariat.

Troper, Harold. 1972. *Only Farmers Need Apply*. Toronto: Griffin House.

– 1987. Jews and Canadian Immigration Policy: 1900–1950. In Moses Rischin (ed.), *The Jews of North America*. Detroit: Wayne State University Press.

– 1993. Canadian Immigration Policy since 1945. *International Journal* 48: 255–81.

– 1993. Immigration and Multiculturalism. In Mel Watkins (ed.), *Canada*. New York: Facts on File.

Troper, Harold, and Morton Weinfeld. 1999. *Ethnicity, Politics and Public Policy in Canada: Case Studies in Canadian Diversity*. Toronto: University of Toronto Press.

U'mista Cultural Centre. 1988. *Potlatch: A Strict Law Bids Us Dance*. Videotape. Alert Bay, B.C.

Unger, R.M. 1986. *The Critical Legal Studies Movement*. Cambridge, Mass.: Harvard University Press.

Van Steen, Marcus. 1965. *Pauline Johnson: Her Life and Work*. Toronto: Musson.

Veldhuis, Ruud. 1998. La citoyenneté démocratique dans le curriculum néerlandais. *Éducation : Revue de diffusion des savoirs en éducation* 16: 30–2.

Waganaar, W.A., and P. Padmos.1971. Quantitative Interpretation of Stress in Kruskal's Multidimensional Scaling Technique. *British Journal of Mathematical and Statistical Psychology* 24: 101–10.

Waldron, J. 1993. *Liberal Rights*. Cambridge: Cambridge University Press.

Walzer, M. 1983. *Spheres of Justice: A Defense of Pluralism*. New York: Basic Books.

– 1993. Comment. In C. Taylor, *Multiculturalism and "The Politics of Recognition."* Princeton, N.J.: Princeton University Press.

– 1995. The Civil Society Argument. In C. Mouffe (ed.). *Dimensions of Radical Democracy: Pluralism, Citizenship and Community.* London: Routledge.

Warren, Mark E. (ed.). 1999. *Democracy and Trust.* Cambridge and New York: Cambridge University Press.

Watson, Patrick, and Benjamin R. Barber. 2000. *The Struggle for Democracy.* Toronto: Key Porter Books.

Weaver, S. 1981. *Making Canadian Indian Policy: The Hidden Agenda, 1968–1970.* Toronto: University of Toronto Press.

Weber, Max. 1947. *The Theory of Social and Economic Organizations.* Transl. A.R. Henderson and Talcott Parsons. New York: Free Press.

Weinstock, Daniel. 1996. Citizenship and Social Unity. Paper presented at the Canada-Spain Workshop on Citizenship and Nationality. Madrid, May.

Wildsmith, B. 1992. Treaty Responsibilities: A Co-Relational model. *University of British Columbia Law Review* 324: 330–1.

Wilkinson, Lori. 1997. Academic Views of Immigration and Citizenship: Policy Significance. In Y.M. Hébert (ed.), *Citizenship and Social Participation Bulletin* 8: 6–15. Available at: http://www.canada.metropolis.net/policy&research/.

– 1997. The Government View on Immigration and Citizenship Issues. In Y.M. Hébert (ed.), *Citizenship and Social Participation Bulletin* 3: 13–15. Available at http://www.canada.metropolis.net/policy&research/.

Wilkinson, Lori and Yvonne Hébert. Citizenship Values: Towards an Analytic Framework. In Anne Laperrière and Yvonne Hébert (eds), *Identity and Citizenship: Canadian and International Perspecives.* In preparation.

Williams, B. 1990. *L'éthique et les limites de la philosophie.* Paris: Gallimard.

Williams, R. 1989. *Resources of Hope: Culture, Democracy, Socialism.* London: Verso.

Wright, Ian, and Alan Sears (eds). 1997. *Trends and Issues in Canadian Social Studies.* Vancouver: Pacific Educational Press.

Wright, Ronald. 1993. *Stolen Continents: The New World through Indian Eyes.* Toronto: Penguin Books.

Yang, Philippe Q. 1993. Ethnicity and Naturalization. *Ethnic and Racial Studies* 17, 4: 593–618.

Yon, Daniel. 2000. *Elusive Culture.* Albany: State University of New York Press.

Young, Iris Marion. 1989. Polity and Group Difference: A Critique of the Ideal of Universal Citizenship. *Ethics: A Journal of Moral, Political and Legal Philosophy* 99, 2: 117–42.

– 1990. *Justice and the Politics of Difference.* Princeton, N.J.: Princeton University Press.

– 2000. *Inclusion and Democracy.* Oxford and New York: Oxford University Press.

Young, Lisa. 2000. Civic Engagement, Trust and Democracy: Evidence from

Alberta. In Neil Nevitte (ed.), *Value Change and Governance in Canada.* Toronto: University of Toronto Press; Montréal: Les Presses de l'Université de Montréal.

Zuckert, M. 1992. *Natural Rights and the New Republicanism.* Princeton, N.J.: Princeton University Press.

Contributors

Marie Battiste (EdD, Stanford University; EdM, Harvard University) is a Mi'kmaq educator from Potlo'tek First Nations in Nova Scotia and full professor in the Indian and Northern Education Program at the University of Saskatchewan, co-editor of *First Nations Education in Canada: The Circle Unfolds*, and co-author, with J.Y. Henderson, of *Protecting Indigenous Knowledge*. She has been awarded two honorary degrees, from St Mary's University and University of Maine at Farmington.

Guy Bourgeault is a full professor in the Department of Educational Studies and Educational Administration as well as an affiliated researcher of the Centre for Ethnic Studies at the University of Montréal. He has participated with Janine Hohl, Marie McAndrew, and Michel Pagé in several research projects on education in a pluri-ethnic context.

Rosa Bruno-Jofré (PhD, University Calgary) is professor and dean of the Faculty of Education at Queen's University. A historian, she is the author of numerous books, chapters, and articles dealing with Methodist education in Peru, the history of religious and civic education in Manitoba, issues of voice and of inclusivity, as well as institutional planning in higher education. She serves as editor of a monograph series that is a co-project between Spanish and Canadian universities.

Cecille DePass, originally a Commonwealth scholar from Jamaica, has completed a number of collaborative corporate and community development projects, dealing with violence in schools (1996–98), multiculturalism, employment and educational equity, and a review of diversity in curriculum in Prairie schools. An associate professor at the

University of Calgary, she fosters active citizenship within communities of learners.

France Gagnon (PhD, University of Montréal) is a program officer with Ministère des Relations avec les citoyens et de l'Immigration, au Québec. Québec. Affiliated with the Centre for Ethnic Studies at the University of Montréal, she specializes in legal issues, ethnicity, immigration studies, and citizenship. With Michel Pagé, she has co-authored the two-volume *Conceptual Framework for an Analysis of Citizenship in Liberal Democracies* (1999) for the Department of Canadian Heritage.

Celia Haig-Brown (PhD, University of British Columbia) teaches in the Faculty of Education at York University. Her current research interests focus on the possibilities of (de)colonizing research methodologies and teaching, in particular, coalition work between Aboriginal peoples and peoples of European ancestry. Among her publications are "Moving into Difference (with Echo)," a chapter in Carl James's recent edited collection, *Experiencing Difference* (2000), *Taking Control: Power and Contradiction in First Nations Adult Education* (1995), and *Resistance and Renewal: Surviving the Indian Residential Schools* (1988). A former president of the Canadian Association for Curriculum Studies, she teaches courses in adult and community education and research methodologies.

Yvonne M. Hébert (PhD, University of British Columbia), is a professor at the University of Calgary and carries out research in the areas of immigration, democratic values, citizenship education, identity formation, and youth. Recipient of Killam pre-doctoral bursaries and an SSHRC post-doctoral fellowship, she co-edited *Indian Education in Canada*, Vol. 1: *The Legacy*, and Vol. 2: *The Challenge* (1986, 1987). She developed the General Language Education Syllabus within the National Core French National Study. Having published extensively, Dr Hébert is leader of the Education Domain of the Prairie Centre of Excellence for Research on Immigration and Integration, within the Metropolis project (1996–2002). A former president of the Canadian Society for the Study of Education, she serves as coordinator of the Citizenship Education Research Network.

Romulo F. Magsino, former dean of education at the University of Manitoba, specializes in educational policy studies. He has written and edited several books and monographs, and his numerous articles have been included in Canadian and American books and journals. Past president of the Canadian Philosophy of Education Society, he received his education in the Philippines, Australia, and the United States.

Fernando Mata (MA, University of Western Ontario; PhD, York University) is a senior researcher with the Department of Justice Canada, formerly with Multiculturalism Program of the federal Department of Canadian Heritage. For the past twenty years, he has conducted studies on ethnic and immigrant minorities in Canada and social aspects of their integration, such as their philanthropic behaviour, volunteering, and civic participation. Currently, he is counsellor for the Canadian Population Society and sessional lecturer at Carleton University in Ottawa.

Marie McAndrew (PhD in comparative education and foundations) was the founding director (1996–2002) of Immigration et Métropoles, the Montréal centre of excellence for research on immigration, integration and urban dynamics, part of the national and international Metropolis project. An associate professor in the Faculty of Education, she is responsible for the research group on ethnicity and adaptation to pluralism in education.

Stephen P. Norris holds a PhD in philosophy of education from the University of Illinois at Urbana-Champaign. He currently is professor and chair of the Department of Educational Policy Studies, University of Alberta. He has published extensively in the areas of critical thinking, philosophy of science education, philosophy of educational research, and literacy.

Michel Pagé (PhD, Université de Montréal) is a full professor in the Department of Psychology at the University of Montréal, where he is a specialist in social psychology and epistemology. Social and cognitive learning processes, pluralism, and citizenship constitute his principal research interests. Member of the Groupe de recherche sur l'adaptation au pluralisme en éducation (GREAPE), he is one of the founding researchers of the Centre d'études ethniques de l'Université de Montréal (CEETUM). He has also served as leader of the Education Domain of the centre Immigration et Métropoles, the centre of excellence in Montréal, part of the national and international Métropolis project. Within the Citizenship Education Research Network, Michel is responsible for the theme Citizenship Models, Types of Citizens, and Contexts of Citizenship Education.

Linda M. Phillips is a professor and director of the Centre for Research on Literacy, University of Alberta. Her research includes an exploration of the foundations of literacy, an integration of legal and educational research, an examination of the theoretical and pedagogical considerations of assessment within the language arts, and the development of philosophical perspectives within science and reading.

Shazia Qureshi has studied and worked in Calgary most of her life. She was granted two degrees from the University of Calgary, in commerce and the natural sciences, and has taken leadership roles in the workplace and the community. She currently lives in the Netherlands, where she is forging a career and life in the new millennium.

Roberta J. Russell (PhD, University of Ottawa) worked as a secondary school teacher, an educational planner, and an adult educator for school systems in Québec and Ontario prior to joining the federal government. Her doctoral research examined the relationship between organizational socialization, gender, and power in organizations. She has held in a number of positions with the federal government as a program manager, policy analyst, special adviser on policy issues, and evaluator; she is currently director of the Research and Statistics Division, Department of Justice.

Helen Semaganis (BA, BLaws, University of Saskatchewan) is a Cree woman from the Poundmaker First Nation in Saskatchewan. A member of the Law Society of Saskatchewan since 1996, she practises with the law firm Semaganis Worme and Missens, in Saskatoon. She was on leave from the firm in order to accept a special appointment with the Federation of Saskatchewan Indian Nations. As lead official, she negotiated with the federal government and served as liaison with the Office of the Treaty Commissioner with respect to several issues related to treaty rights and/or jurisdictions.

Veronica Strong-Boag is a professor of educational studies and Women's Studies at the University of British Columbia. A former president of the Canadian Historical Assocation, she has published extensively on the history of Canada, including *The New Day Recalled: Lives of Girls and*

Women in English Canada (1988); *Rethinking Canada: The Promise of Women's History*, edited with Anita Clair Fellman (3rd ed., 1997); *Painting the Maple: Essays on Race, Gender and the Construction of Canada* (1998) as co-editor; and with Carole Gerson, *Paddling Her Own Canoe: The Times and Texts of E. Pauline Johnson (Tekahionwake)* (2000).

Harold Troper, PhD, is a professor of theory and policy studies at the Ontario Institute for Studies in Education at the University of Toronto. His special interests include the history of North American immigration, ethnicity, and culture. He is widely published, with ten books and numerous articles to his credit.

Lori Wilkinson (PhD, University Alberta) is an assistant professor of sociology at the University of Manitoba. An affiliated researcher with the Prairie Centre of Excellence for Research on Immigration and Integration, her doctoral research focused on refugee youth and their integration into Canadian society. She specializes in citizenship values, refugee settlement, immigration studies, ethnicity, and research methodologies. She is co-author of "Undereducated and Underemployed: The Experiences of Refugees in the Canadian Labour Market," which appeared in the first issue of the *Journal of International Migration and Integration* (2000).